Black Tom

Dr Thomas Arnold, engraved by Henry Cousins in 1840.

Black Tom

Arnold of Rugby:
The Myth and the Man

Terence Copley

continuum
LONDON • NEW YORK

Continuum

The Tower Building
11 York Road
London SE1 7NX

370 Lexington Avenue
New York NY 10017–6503

© 2002 Terence Copley

British Library Cataloguing-in-Publication Data
A catalogue record for this book is available from the British Library.

ISBN: 0–8264–5723–1

Typeset by RefineCatch Limited, Bungay, Suffolk
Printed and bound in Great Britain by Biddles Ltd, Guildford

Contents

For Dawn and Bryan, with thanks and much love

Preface

Why are biographies written? Is it because the writers are admirers and disciples of their chosen subject, or are biographies born out of the desire sometimes to expose or even to demolish? Do they meet a need within the writer or the reader to have access to the secret lives of others? The history of biographies of Thomas Arnold sees them in the main sharply divided between friends, admirers, even hero-worshippers, and hyper-sceptical critics – usually from a later time – who can find no real, measurable, lasting good in what he did. Those subjects of biography who are called upon to exercise public piety, like members of the clergy or headteachers (Arnold was both) can easily be criticized for hypocrisy, especially by those who have been conscripted into their congregations and school assemblies. Moreover, it is a modern tabloid trend to suggest that the closer one goes into the study of a human life, the more faults will be found. I wish neither to present Arnold as a saint nor to expose him as a villain. He was a multi-talented human being with a phenomenal capacity for work, who made some very serious mistakes.

Arnold marks the junction of three lines of my own professional activities. One is research into the history of religious education and spiritual development in the British school system. Arnold is a dominating figure, among others, in this long and distinguished tradition. He survived as a role model into late

Victorian times and well into the twentieth century where others did not, or not to the same extent. He is also a landmark in Victorian religion, another of my professional concerns, which is neither as distant nor as stuffy as those who know nothing about it might suppose. Arnold was a major figure in Victorian religion, although he was only a Victorian for five years. His vision of a national church has never been attained or significantly bettered; it leaves much of the later tortuous ecumenical movement gasping as it roars past. As a 'broad church' man he was ready to see that the Bible can be studied through the eyes of modern scholarship without destroying faith. As a controversialist opposing 'Newmanism', i.e. the Oxford Movement, Arnold was a doughty fighter for what he believed the essence of the church to be, in the face of a group which was, in his view, taking Christianity backwards.

The other strand in Arnold's life which resonates for me is that he remained a classroom teacher from his arrival at Rugby until his death. Arnold dealt with pupil misbehaviour and misdemeanour on a daily basis. His views about childhood and education were based on daily contact with children. He was never a remote theorist. I, too, was a schoolteacher for many years and the deputy head of a 1200-pupil school for seven of them, like Arnold writing books in the evenings after the completion of the day's other tasks. Like Arnold (letter, 25.1.1841), I found that writing could be a diversion from school work and school work from writing, so that being occupied with both did not increase but rather decreased stress. As a result of these different interests in my own professional life, I had been aware of Arnold for a long time without knowing very much about him. I also had memories of my time as a sixth former studying English Literature at GCE Advanced Level, in which Matthew Arnold's poetry was a 'set book'. Here I first encountered 'Rugby Chapel', that moving elegiac poem, written after Thomas Arnold's death, in which the undoubted father–son tensions are suspended, to be replaced by a tribute to what was good in a giant father. It was to be more than 30 years before I saw Rugby Chapel for real.

The result of all this was that I decided to draw together these different aspects of Arnold and write something about him for the twenty-first century. The way was already paved with lives, written from as early as two years after his death, but their tendency was to make Arnold a clear-cut saint or a sinner, or with Strachey to present Arnold as a hyper-active prig, or in some cases to restrict his significance to his role at Rugby, which was often misrepresented in the process. This means that an attempt to search for a more balanced picture, and one which is relevant to our time, is still needed. But biographical studies, like all historical study, have to be selective. We cannot take a lifetime to tell the story of a life. What we select for our time will reflect our own interests and preoccupations just as much as it reveals those of the subject being written about.

For Christians, Arnold has become an almost unknown figure. For educationalists, his contribution to what is now called 'whole school ethos', as a founder of 'spiritual, moral, social and cultural development' and his contribution to the values debate in education are largely forgotten. For theology, he provides a window into the heats and passions surrounding the Oxford Movement, into changing attitudes towards the Bible and into early Victorian Christian social ideals. For schoolteachers, his enormous energy in running a school, preaching weekly in the chapel, teaching the sixth form personally, preparing students for university entrance, dealing with parents, heading School House with all the duties of a boarding house master (he was petitioned by the pupils to stay on when he sought to relinquish this role), in conducting a voluminous correspondence with former pupils and continuing to coach some former pupils by distance learning, latterly adding work as a part-time professor of modern history – all these activities and more illustrate that the massive overload faced by so many schoolteachers in the twenty-first century UK is not new. For students of Victorian times, Arnold has added interest because he lived out the work ethic that later Victorians so much admired and he provided a role model for family life (and a Victorian role model for a righteous death). The time to re-evaluate Arnold has come. For a new century, a new appraisal.

The question, then, arose how best to tackle this. I considered the traditional biographical approach, chapter by life chapter, from birth through childhood, young adulthood and, in Arnold's case, into early middle age and death. I discounted this in favour of what I hope will be found to be a sharper approach. So after an introduction which discusses the source problems on Arnold, a detailed overview of his life appears as a base for what follows, followed by a consideration of Arnold the educator and his work at Laleham and Rugby. Arnold the theologian and churchman is then addressed. His work in history and classics is considered alongside this, as it has not survived the passage of time as well as his other monuments and his modern audience is less equipped with Latin and Greek to handle it. Finally, an attempt is made to assess what the Arnold legacy is for the twenty-first century. I hope that this approach makes key aspects of Arnold more immediately available for students than if they are dissolved into the detail of a chronological life, while at the same time providing the general reader with a more focused account.

Neutral and objective writing about people is never possible. With so vigorous a controversialist as Arnold, whose vehemence and forcefulness could and frequently did prove divisive, costing him a bishopric and almost the headship of Rugby, there is the vexed question of his 'real' identity. For some commentators he is a prophet, for others almost a roaring and unstable monster. These divergent approaches existed in his own lifetime. One must not be tempted to state in the face of this that the facts that follow will speak for themselves. That would be simplistic. 'Facts' never 'speak'; they are interpreted. Some 'facts' are open to question and all the 'facts' that follow have been selected by the writer, with the corollary that others have been omitted. Arnold is very much a person of 'obstinacity'. That is, he exhibits two-sided characteristics. For example, what his friends would call tenacity, his critics might call obstinacy. The idea of 'obstinacity' means that the human quality is the same; it is merely perceived differently according to whose side one is on. What I have tried to do is to let both 'sides' speak about Arnold as they understand him, so as to induct the reader into the debate. Arnold himself has been quoted extensively so that he can be heard in his own words. But whatever 'side' one takes in the end, the story of Arnold remains a gripping one.

Terence Copley
School of Education,
University of Exeter
December 2001

Acknowledgements

Part of the research and writing of this book was undertaken during a period of study leave provided by my University and School in the first part of 2000 and for that I am very grateful to the University of Exeter and in particular the School of Education.

To the staff at Continuum International, in particular Robin Baird-Smith, Daniel Bouquet and Alan Worth, real thanks for their enthusiastic, professional work with the MS towards publication, and to Gill Copley for valiant support – again! – in the indexing of the book.

Thomas Arnold is primarily associated in the public mind with Rugby and I am extremely grateful for the assistance provided by Rugby School in the person of its archivist, Rusty MacLean. He made archive material available to me in the Temple Reading Room, a pleasant facility to work in, with cups of coffee provided. Rusty also gave real help in research conducted on site and supplementary questions by email.

Jacky and John Gray provided detailed information and photographs of the Penrose family home at Fledborough. Clare Matson, from her Ryde base, Isle of Wight, generously undertook research into Arnold's Island background and family homes, and her findings have been fed into the text. R. C. Shorrock of Waterhead Tourist Information Centre, Ambleside, provided

Acknowledgements

information about the Arnold house at Fox How. The Reverend Doreen Harrison provided photographs and background history on the house at Fox How. Professor Peter Wiseman of Exeter University provided comment on Arnold's historical writings and on the 'Triste lupus' incident in *Tom Brown*. To all these people, my sincere thanks.

Finally, my thanks to two very special people in Richmond, Virginia, to whom this book is dedicated. Their friendship is irreplaceable.

List of Illustrations

Frontispiece: Dr Thomas Arnold, engraved by Henry Cousins in 1840 from the portrait by Thomas Phillips (reproduced on the cover).

1. Title page of *Tom Brown's School Days* by Thomas Hughes (1857).
2. The house at Laleham, in a photograph taken soon after Arnold's death.
3. Fledborough Parsonage, *circa* 1811, where Mary Penrose met Thomas Arnold for the first time.
4. A drawing by Mary Penrose's sister Lydia showing Arnold and Mary at a picnic shortly before their marriage, chaperoned by Mary's sister Jane and her brother Trevenen.
5. Fledborough Church where Thomas Arnold and Mary Penrose were married in 1820.
6. Mary Arnold, by an unknown artist.
7. Rugby School, *circa* 1829.
8. Thomas Arnold, shortly after his marriage, by an unknown artist.
9. Edward, Mary and Susanna Arnold picnicking in the Lake District, in a sketch by Jane Arnold.
10. The Arnold children skating on Rydal Water in the Lake District.
11. Two views of Fox How today.

Notes on the Text

Sources

The Stanley *Life* (1844) and the Hughes novel *Tom Brown's Schooldays* (1857) were formative in setting the dominant nineteenth-century picture of Arnold. They have been discussed in the text at various points, principally on p. 6f and pp. 9ff Stanley makes available selective source material, some of which is no longer accessible in MS, or not easily accessible. If the Stanley–Hughes portraits are at times unbalanced and too influential, there is no case for discarding them. Stanley and Hughes both knew Arnold personally and have something important to say. In subsequent writing the best analysis of Arnold's early years is in Wymer (1953) and some of Wymer's insights have been used in Chapter 1. Another very helpful secondary source is Bamford (1960) despite his tendency to dissolve Arnold's uniqueness in reaction to the effects of the Stanley–Hughes portrait.

MS sources on Arnold still survive: his wife's collection of his table talk, not drawn on greatly in previous studies, and copies of some letters; his teaching notes and the lesson notes of some of his pupils; handwritten memories of him sent to Rugby after his death; his day diary and the more lengthy entries of the night diary. His own printed works are still generally accessible in university and some cathedral libraries.

Notes on the Text

Language, punctuation and references to the Stanley *Life*

It was a characteristic of language in Arnold's time that it was more male-gender oriented than is now the case. Head teachers were usually presumed to be 'headmasters'. Teachers in boys' schools were 'masters' or 'assistant masters', i.e. assistants to the headmaster. The child was usually 'he', 'the schoolboy', etc. Quotations reflecting this have been allowed to stand verbatim without further comment. The obsequious [*sic*] has been kept to a minimum. Arnold, along with other writers of his time, made what would now be regarded as an excessive use of capital letters. In quotations where this occurs, the capitals have usually been replaced by small case letters so as to be less tiresome to the eye, except where capitals would still be used. Where correspondence that appears in the Stanley *Life* is referred to, references are usually by date and not page, so that whichever of the various editions or abridgements is being used, the letter or other reference may be accessed more easily.

Public and state schools in UK parlance

The meaning of 'public school' in the US context is entirely opposite to its eccentric meaning in the UK, where it has come to mean an independent school (i.e. independent from government, centralized or local education authority or school board control) and, therefore, necessarily a fee-paying school. Many of these schools were originally founded as charities for children of members of the public, i.e. the costs were paid by the founding charity, hence the name. But with inflation eating away the foundation monies of 'public schools' over decades or centuries, fees were introduced in time under the headings of tuition (all public schools) and boarding (only residential schools).

This is confusing enough, but the US reader, faced with the phrase 'state school', might logically ask, by analogy with Texas, Virginia, etc., 'which state?' In the UK, 'state schools' is a rather loose term that has come to mean those schools financed by government money and in which no fees are charged to pupils or their parents. The types of these schools and their constitutions vary (in some, religious foundation bodies retain influence and some power), but they must provide free education within the National Curriculum and the periodic government testing procedures, and be subject to government inspection by OFSTED, the Office for Standards in Education.

Introduction

Arnold 1901 and Arnold 2001

In 1901 the Board of Education, forerunner of the present Department for Education and Employment (DfEE), presented every trainee teacher in England and Wales with the new single volume edition of A. P. Stanley's *Life and Correspondence of Thomas Arnold, DD* (first edition, 1844). The preface was written by Sir Joshua Fitch, the Chief Inspector of Training Colleges, himself the author of an earlier book about Thomas and Matthew Arnold, father and son (1897). By 1901 Thomas Arnold had been dead for nearly 60 years. Arthur Stanley, the original writer, had been dead for twenty years. So the subject and the writer of this 780-page 'short' edition were both history. Why was this book chosen? What could be the possible relevance for student teachers preparing to teach primary-aged children in state schools, of the life and letters of a man who had headed a fee-paying, selective secondary school 60 years earlier? Fitch understood this. He had started life as a pupil-teacher in a Southwark elementary school himself, gaining his London BA (1850) and MA (1852) by the hard route of evening study. While commending 'manuals of pedagogy, of method and of school management, and books written more or less expressly with a view to the work of the schoolroom' (1901, p. vi), he felt these

1

to be limited. He believed that student teachers should also be made aware of

> what the most eminent teachers of another age have thought and done, and what is the relation between the discipline and studies of a school on the one hand, and on the other, the claims of citizenship, of professional or industrial work, of the family, of the social organisation and of Christian manhood. This book shows how the career of a schoolmaster may connect itself with the politics, the religious interests, the literature and the corporate life of the community. (ibid., p. vi)

Another century has passed since those 1901 books were presented. To most entrants to the teaching profession in 2001, Arnold is completely unknown, and to those who have heard of him, he is no longer relevant to the preoccupations of state education in the twenty-first century. He has become a piece of independent school history, the head of the school that gave Rugby football to the nation (incidentally, before his time). Few who have heard of Arnold know that he had no interest in organized games, Rugby football included. To others, Thomas Arnold is a footnote in English literature as the father of a Division Two poet, Matthew Arnold. Yet Thomas Arnold's influence in English, Welsh, Tasmanian, Indian and other British colonial education was immense through his own children and through his former pupils, many of whom went on to leading roles in teaching, school inspection and educational administration. His use of the praepostor (prefect) system was widely admired but its influence had largely vanished by the 1960s and 1970s in British schools. Arnold wished to promote 'Christian manhood'. This is a distant concept in a society which sees itself as plural in religions and largely secular in outlook and which is striving to represent women and men fairly in its use of language. 'Christian manhood' would not be seen as an appropriate spiritual ideal by many Christian women or men of the twenty-first century. All this seems to render Arnold both archaic and arcane.

But Arnold was not simply a Titan personality who gripped a Midlands school in a time whose values and language have passed away. He was a thinker and a doer. Arnold had a very clear view of what education was for, what its values should be, both for his pupils at Rugby and for the children whose parents he encountered at the Rugby Mechanics Institute and the staff at Rugby railway station. He was aware that if the Lake District which he loved was a part of England, so also were less lovely Rugby and industrialized Sheffield. Are we more clear than Arnold about the aim of education? To what end is the conveyor belt of mass education currently geared? Do many now read 780-page books or have we accepted a more quick-fix culture, which makes fewer demands on our minds? We seem to have settled for short-term aims. Perhaps we have forgotten, in Fitch's words, 'what the most eminent teachers of another age have thought and done', even forgetting that outstanding teachers existed before 1988 and the Education Reform Act with its National Curriculum and the subsequent government obsession with inspection, testing, recording, school league tables, 'quality assurance', 'school improvement', 'value-added' and 'raising standards' in schools. 'The career of a schoolmaster' no longer self-evidently connects with the politics, the religious interests, the literature and the corporate life of the community, of which Fitch wrote. The range of duties required of schoolteachers is now more narrow and their powers over pupils are more circumscribed. They have to discharge the National Curriculum subjects and Religious Education in a situation in which they can easily be challenged by parental complaint. Teachers are themselves subject to frequent testing and inspection, via direct observation by OFSTED and the published results of tests and examinations of the children they teach.

Fitch's choice of Arnold was a right one, even an inevitable one, despite his being now largely unknown. Few headteachers now can claim to be national figures. Arnold had a vision for Christian education; he was a gifted classroom teacher; he was the father of what is now called 'spiritual, moral, social and cultural development' in schools; he was a leading pastoral figure and head of a boarding house; he was a leader of pupils and teachers and not merely a manager, administrator or chief executive. Arnold's strong certainties in education challenge our assumptions of open debate and clearer resolution, even though his answers can no longer be ours. He was not, as a headteacher or in any other department of his life, a saint. The record is stained in indefensible ways, even by the standards of his time. But he offers a window into some issues which are still being debated and some that ought to be. That in itself would be enough to merit further study of the man. But Arnold does not end there.

Arnold had other personas, as a leading and highly controversial Christian thinker, as a historian, as a devoted if sometimes overpowering family man. These other personas have been largely eclipsed by his educational fame. But they have been seriously addressed here, as any attempt to reconstruct Arnold has to see the whole person. While his family position is essentially a private role, his historical scholarship and his theology were well publicized nationally. Indeed, Arnold first came to the national spotlight by his spirited defence of the emancipation of Roman Catholics from various legal disabilities imposed on them in an earlier era, but still defended by many in his time. He remained in that spotlight as a result of his radical proposals for church reform and his vision for a national church that even now would still be too radical for many Christians. His approach to the critical study of the Bible was ahead of its time and was part of the process of a necessary weaning of Christianity from its dependence on what had been held by many to be an infallible text. He was also able to defend the view that doctrinal difference was not only inevitable but healthy and that the centre of Christianity does not and should not consist of doctrinal uniformity. To some extent Arnold paved the way for a Christianity that was to survive the collapse of certainties in mid-Victorian England and beyond into an eventual 'post-modern' climate, although some of his critics asserted that he helped to bring about that collapse by his 'liberalism'. Arnold's tones on the subject of religion were not always those of the patient teacher; they were more often those of the blistering prophet. He seemed to court the glare of publicity in his violent attack on the Oxford Movement in the Church of England; he believed passionately that it was taking Christianity backwards into priestcraft and medievalism. He was a national figure in religion before he was a national figure in education. Fame at Rugby arose *en passant* and partly as a result of the attack on him in certain newspapers. All this was developing against the less contentious backdrop of his continuing work in history, which was to lead eventually to the climax of his academic career, the return to Oxford as a professor.

Source problems

A. P. Stanley

Like his short-lived contemporaries Anne and Emily Brontë, who survive largely through the filter posthumously created by their sister Charlotte and her friend Elizabeth Gaskell, Arnold's image was established and then subsequently transmitted through two highly influential portraits. Arthur Penryn Stanley's *The Life and*

Correspondence of Thomas Arnold, DD (1845) is written with the reverence of an admiring former pupil, only two years after Arnold's shocking and to later Victorians, exemplary, death. Stanley had worked on it for most of the two-year span from Arnold's death up to publication, taking only a brief holiday in Paris with Charles Vaughan, another celebrated Rugbeian, until it was complete. Stanley was a friend of the Arnold family. His parents were friends and supporters of Arnold. His work was intended as a tribute, not as a dispassionate appraisal of Arnold: 'to have mixed up any judgment of my own, either of praise or censure . . . would have been wholly irrelevant' (1845, p. xviii). 'Stanley's *Life* was in some ways Mrs. Arnold's book about her husband' (Hamilton, 1998, p. 63). But even as an editor, Stanley was obliged to be selective. His criterion was 'not whether I approved or disapproved . . . but whether it was characteristic of him'. He was careful to exclude all detrimental material. Even so, Archbishop Richard Whately (see p. 36) a contemporary of Arnold and friend of the family helped to over-rule Stanley's objections to some letters and sermons. Whately's approval of the final book was warm but qualified. Arthur Clough, another fervent Arnoldian in his young adulthood, felt Stanley was 'very judicious in keeping the right mean between reserve and exposure' (letter to J. P. Gell, 13.7.1844). Rather like the Gospel of Mark in its portrait of Jesus, Stanley was not very interested in Arnold's early years and family background. The one-volume edition disposes of these in 21 of its 780 pages. Arnold's exuberant schoolboy letters home from Winchester receive only passing allusion; 'their unregenerate male adolescence did not harmonise with the final and only posture in which Stanley wished his hero to be observed' (Chandos, 1984, p. 119, note). Needless to say, Arnold's enemies are not represented at length in Stanley's collection, although this is partly because Arnold did not systematically preserve letters that he received.

Bamford attributes Stanley's version of Arnold in part to his own highly atypical pupil experience at Rugby. Stanley entered the school in February 1829 in the fourth form but within six months had been promoted into the fifth and thus to exemption from 'fagging', the requirement on junior boys to serve their seniors. Stanley's peers found him unusual and odd, 'a little fellow in a round jacket', small, delicate and sensitive. But he was never bullied and rarely laughed at, although he was subjected to the 'smoking' ritual (see p. 164). Stanley's mother wrote, 'he never gets plagued in any way like the others; his study is left untouched, his things unbroken, his books undisturbed'. She might not have been told the whole truth, but his 'otherness' is testified to in the writings of his contemporaries in the school. Bamford thinks that Stanley might therefore have been genuinely unaware of the undercurrents of bullying and vice in the school all around him, although his mother's phrase 'like the others' implies that he did know some at least of it. He later described himself as 'utterly ignorant' of the world of *Tom Brown*. Whatever his early period at Rugby, Stanley came under Arnold's spell in the sixth form and the two entertained a mutual high regard for one another from then on. 'No-one else was quite as smitten' with Arnold, in Bamford's words, except perhaps the young Clough. That would account for Stanley's 'rosy view' of Rugby: 'Throughout, whether in the School itself, or in its after effects, the one image that we have before us is not Rugby, but ARNOLD' [Stanley's capitals]. It is certainly the case that a contemporary of Stanley, in a previously unpublished account which appears in full on p. 25, challenges parts of his picture, although this contemporary is less iconoclastic than he believes. Thomas and Mary Arnold visited Stanley's parents at Alderley. They got on well and although, as a pupil at the time, Stanley was dreading the visit, he noted Arnold's 'childlike joy and simplicity' when released from the regime of school life. Stanley was also to defend and protect Arnold in the school (see p. 84f) on one occasion as a sixth former helping to prevent an anti-Arnold riot. So he was certainly among Arnold's strongest supporters: 'I have made him my idol.' When Stanley left the school, Arnold was choked up in saying goodbye to him. So this massive and influential source on Arnold is also one-sided. But no sources are neutral. Stanley preserves some correspondence which is now no longer in the public domain and offers a colourful and real picture of what Arnold's magic could be to some of those who fell under its spell. In 1845 the *Edinburgh Review*, less involved with Arnold than his former pupils, wrote of him:

> He was naturally in extremes. Whatever it was on which he was engaged, he threw himself headlong into it, almost bodily as into a volcano; from whose depths forth he came again – argument and sentiment, emotion and burning words – rolling and thundering, and fused together like lava down a mountain side.

It seems to have been Carlyle who first described Arnold's style as 'unresting, unhasting diligence'. Even Arnold's Jesus was an example of energy and constant exertion (Sermon on Mark 6.31, 1850 edition: 202, where it is emphasized that Jesus and the disciples 'had no leisure so much as to eat'). Arnold can even be portrayed as avaricious. He wrote that 'money tempted me' to stand for Rugby, but he had a rapidly growing family and other dependants (see p. 56f) and was operating in a virtually pensionless society; in the same letter he added 'I should like to try whether my notions of Christian education are really impracticable' (30.11.1827, in Stanley, 1845, p. 86).

Introduction

Thomas Hughes

Another Rugbeian, Thomas Hughes, depicted Arnold's Rugby in the novel *Tom Brown's School Days* (1857). The opening, set in the Vale of the White Horse, Berkshire, appealed widely to Victorian nostalgia for a vanishing rural idyll and Hughes's Rugby is based on sentiment as much as, if not more than, experience. Sentiment for England continued in *The Scouring of the White Horse*, in which he professed an 'intense local attachment, love for every stone and turf of the county where I was born and bred' (1859, p. x). *Tom Brown* is exactly what it claims to be: a novel. But Hughes vigorously defended his portrait of Arnold in the book as the most authentic part of his writing. Moreover, he referred in *The Scouring* to a didactic intention throughout his writing:

> We are sure that reverence for all great Englishmen [sic], and a loving remembrance of the great deeds done by them in old times, will help to bring to life in us the feeling that we are a family, bound together to work out God's purposes in this little island. (ibid., p. xiv)

Arnold was to Hughes one such great Englishman. The Tom Brown Museum website describes the Arnold of Hughes's portrait as 'the kindly Dr Arnold' (www.geocities.com/Paris/Rue/1896/tombrown.html). This was not strictly accurate, as the 'triste lupus' incident illustrates (see p. 124f), but Hughes's Arnold was caring if not always kindly. By the time of writing the preface to the sixth edition of *Tom Brown*, the evidence of battle is clear:

> And what gave Rugby boys this character [of earnestness] ... to this day? I say fearlessly – Arnold's teaching and example – above all, that part of it which has been, I will

TOM BROWN'S SCHOOL DAYS.

BY AN OLD BOY.

Hughes (Thomas)

"As on the one hand it should ever be remembered that we are boys,
and boys at school, so on the other hand we must bear in mind that we form
a complete social body . . . . a society, in which, by the nature of the case,
we must not only learn, but act and live; and act and live not only as boys,
but as boys who will be men."—RUGBY MAGAZINE.

FOURTH EDITION.

Cambridge:
MACMILLAN & CO.
1857.

136

1. Title page of *Tom Brown's School Days* by Thomas Hughes (1857).

not say sneered at, but certainly not approved – his unwearied zeal in creating 'moral thoughtfulness' in every boy with whom he came into personal contact.

Hero worship is entirely natural and justifiable in Hughes, provided the role models are right and that the adoration is transient, leading on from the human hero to the love and worship of God. *Tom Brown* ends on this note:

> For it is only through our mysterious human relationships, through the love and tenderness and purity of mothers, and sisters, and wives, through the strength and courage and wisdom of fathers, and brothers, and teachers, that we can come to the knowledge of Him, in whom alone the love, and the tenderness, and the purity, and the strength, and the courage, and the wisdom of all these dwell for ever and ever in perfect fulness. (1875, p. 306f)

Apart from Arnold's appearance in the book as himself, the boy Arthur may have been in part drawn from Arthur Stanley and there may be other pictures drawn from real pupils (see p. 268).

Hughes's book was attacked by Fitzjames Stephen in the *Edinburgh Review*. Stephen's Arnold was a humourless fanatic who turned lively boys into earnest prigs; Matt Arnold's reply was 'Rugby Chapel' (dated 1857 but possibly written earlier and revised), the elegiac poem in memory of his father. Stanley came to the defence of *Tom Brown* in his 1881 preface to the twelfth edition of his *Life* as a more 'vivid picture of Dr Arnold's career' conveyed by 'the occasional allusions and general tone' of the book than his own. But by 1897 *Tom Brown* was being seen as 'a romance' (Fitch, 1897, p. 104). Fitch could openly discuss the intellectual stress of being a pupil in Arnold's sixth form (ibid.).

Matthew Arnold told Fitch that *Tom Brown* had been praised 'quite enough' as it gave only one side, not necessarily the best, of both the school at the time and Arnold's character. For Chandos (1984, p. 45) *Tom Brown* is a 'compound of romantic fiction and expurgated fact'. Despite this, for 50 years Stanley and Hughes together dominated Arnold's public image, stifling but never eliminating opposing views, until his demise as an icon, symbolized by Lytton Strachey's *Eminent Victorians* (1918), a witty debunking study of Cardinal Manning, Florence Nightingale, General Gordon and Arnold, which reduced Arnold to what Willey (1949) calls a 'high-minded but blundering and conventional prig' by the device of bathos and the subtle misuse of quotation. It was 'a skilful and very readable piece of falsification' (ibid., p. 59). It was also influential.

Later writing on Arnold

Norwood (1929) argues that the Strachey misrepresentation was taken further by Russell, for whom Arnold becomes a sadist and flogger. The strand of Arnold critics continues down to Chandos, for whom Arnold was 'by temperament singularly unsuited to be the governor of small boys' (1984, p. 258). Chandos's Arnold is a successful but unstable demagogue, who gives the rising wealthy middle classes not only a school that they want, but a matching philosophy to castigate unearned privilege in the upper classes above them. Arnold was 'an egoist tormented by a will which craved to impose itself remedially, as he supposed, upon others' (ibid., p. 250). He was subject to 'fits of incontinent rage'. He encouraged 'morbid scrupulosity' among his pupils. In the Rugby Chandos looks at, powered by Arnold's dispatch and diligence, more always seems to be happening than is really taking place. The worst excesses of bullying were put down well before Arnold (*c*.1815) and he changed little, success or failure residing in the authority exercised or abused by the head of each boarding house and the senior praepostor. Chandos argues that despite moral litanies to the contrary, Arnold was ambitious in a quite worldly sense for himself, his boys and the school (ibid., p. 252) and he removed those plodding pupils who were not making good academic progress. Arnold's attack on the lower school (see pp. 170ff) was highly unprincipled:

> We do not know how Arnold, with his tender conscience, contemplated a class of little boys, toiling to achieve what he knew he had himself made it impossible for them to do, by committing them to the charge of men incompetent to teach the subjects required. (ibid., p. 252)

Disagreement with Arnold led to the intimation that the disagreement was with God. Chandos's Arnold viewed his school and boys with distaste, because he disliked the 'evil' state of boyhood. Chandos's Arnold failed because when he appealed to the boys in chapel for money to continue to develop the building (see p. 165), the offertory he received included buttons and cheques for £1000 drawn on the 'Bank of Elegance'.

According to Chandos, Arnold used religion as a medium of control. He was ruthless, arbitrary and cruel. Chandos relates that at one roll call, a boy bawled out his name in the loudest possible tones (he was surely dicing with death in challenging Arnold in public, even in jest) and when questioned claimed that this shouting was due to a nervous disposition. 'Arnold, instead of acknowledging the joke and charging the player fifty lines as its price, solemnly went and consulted a physician to ascertain whether such symptoms could be genuine' (ibid., 1985, p. 260). While this may indicate Arnold's lack of a conventional sense of humour, the evidence is not that simple. Part of his basic approach to pupils at Rugby, which excited much public comment, was to trust what they said (see pp. 140ff). He may therefore have taken the matter entirely seriously, not through lack of humour *per se*, but as a result of his commitment to believe what he was told (see p. 128f). Hamilton by contrast, sees that Arnold's power cannot be put down to mere intimidation: Arnold made the boys not *want* to let him down and he was ready to believe their word (1998, p. 6).

For Bamford the majority of Rugby boys were indifferent to Arnold's philosophy of education; his sixth form produced high-minded prigs and discouraged any real independence of thought (see p. 132f). He conveyed to his 'elect' that they were 'destined for some high mission, but left them without any clear indication what it was' (p. 160f). He was 'like an inspiring but confused military leader' who did not know where his ideas would take people or himself. He did not really understand children at all (Bamford, 1970, p. 5). Bamford's Arnold was not the victim of a hostile world, robbed of advancement he might have had. He set himself against the world and his lack of advancement was due entirely to his own intemperate language and extremist positions. He alienated many. He had a strain of ruthlessness. He was intense to the point of mania. He was tactless and unable to compromise. Moreover 'the mind of this man, usually considered to be the greatest of headmasters, was really interested fundamentally in the world outside the [Rugby School] Close' (Bamford, 1960, p. 212). According to Bamford, 'It was the spirit of martyrdom and religious obsession that exhausted Arnold and eventually killed him' (1967, p. 52). If Bamford is right, the recent disaster in Arnold's personal life (see p. 107), his chronic overwork and the family history on both his father's and his mother's side of fatal heart disease are presumably entirely coincidental as factors in his early death from religious mania. Bamford's Arnold is great in his breadth of vision of society, but comparatively insignificant in his contribution to education.

Introduction

Strachey's Arnold is perhaps one of the best-known portraits. In his own introduction, Strachey admits that

> It is not by the method of a scrupulous narration that the explorer of the past can hope to depict that singular epoch [Victorian England]. He will attack his subject in unexpected places; he will fall upon the flank, or the rear; he will shoot a sudden, revealing searchlight into obscure recesses . . . I have sought to examine and elucidate certain fragments of the truth which took my fancy. (1918, p. viif)

This is self-confessed dilettante history at best, not serious history at all. What Strachey then does is to select, mainly from Stanley, and to provide a cynical, sometimes ridiculing, commentary with the underlining theme that Arnold could not possibly be what he purported to be, even if he had known what that was. This theme should have been Strachey's subject for discussion, not his underlying and unchallenged assumption. His Arnold oscillates between perplexity and peace of mind derived from the assurances of others. But interposed in an analysis of his inward character, readers are suddenly informed that Arnold's legs were 'perhaps, shorter than they should have been' (ibid., p. 210), that behind his firm facial presence there was 'a slightly puzzled look'. Strachey's Arnold did not introduce humane and civilizing customs into the life of Rugby; instead he preferred to apply the Old Testament, with himself playing the part of God.

> [Arnold,] involved in awful grandeur, ruled remotely, through his chosen instruments [the senior pupils], from an inaccessible heaven. Remotely and yet with omnipresent force. As the Israelite of old knew that his almighty Lawgiver might at any point thunder to him from the whirlwind, or appear before his very eyes, the visible

15

embodiment of power or wrath, so the Rugby schoolboy walked in a holy dread of some sudden manifestation of the sweeping gown, the majestic tone, the piercing glance, of Dr Arnold. (ibid., p. 214)

Strachey's Arnold retained classics as the basis of his curriculum because it was the only subject he was any good at and he had invested too many years in studying classics to abandon it. He therefore reinforced 'the ancient system' of curriculum more firmly than ever. But it was morally selected classics. He disliked Aristophanes's morals and never read Juvenal. Under Arnold the public school became more than ever 'a conventual establishment, devoted to the teaching of Greek and Latin grammar'. His chapel performances – the sermons – 'in the plenitude of his dignity and his enthusiasm' are implied to be self-indulgent but highly influential demagogy. Strachey argues that despite Arnold's moral strictures, boys continued to be boys, even in *Tom Brown*, in which a praepostor, Brooke, presides at a fight behind the chapel. But 'a minority of susceptible and serious youths fell completely under his sway, responded like wax to the pressure of his influence and moulded their whole lives with passionate reverence on the teaching of their adored master' (ibid., p. 234). Clough is cited as a key example (ibid., p. 235f): he was found to be gullible again at Oxford under William Ward (see p. 236). Finally, Strachey's Arnold does not die; after a description of the death bed scene he 'passes from his perplexities for ever'.

Can the Arnold of Chandos, Bamford and Strachey be reconciled with the Arnold of Stanley and Hughes? What Stanley, Hughes, Strachey, Chandos, Bamford and others have in common is that their portraits lack balance. Considerable caution is therefore required in reconstructing Arnold's life and values.

The Arnold trail

Cowes, Isle of Wight, was Arnold's birthplace. 'Brummagem', the house in which he was born on 13 June 1795, still exists as Number 43 on the Birmingham Road (Brummagem is itself an old name for Birmingham, although at the time this house was named, the word was better known for its associations with counterfeiting), although it is now renamed Westbourne House. 'Slatwoods' with its 25 acres, to which the Arnolds moved, is now covered by houses. All that remains is Slatwoods Lodge. Whippingham parish church (IoW) contains memorial plaques to Arnold's father and brother. In Laleham the site of Arnold's house (demolished in 1864) is the present primary school, but Buckland's property survives as Muncaster House, now flats, with the house of Arnold's mother and family next door. The parish churchyard of All Saints contains the graves of Arnold's son Matthew and members of Matt's family as well as Arnold's mother, aunt, sister Susanna and baby daughter.

Fledborough Old Vicarage, near Newark, was the home of the Penrose family at the time of Mary Penrose's marriage to Arnold and he visited it on various occasions. One wing was demolished in the 1950s, but what remains is still a substantial house on three floors. There was accommodation for the servants that rectors of that time would have had. The stables, including groom's accommodation, are now known as Rectory Cottage. The village would still be recognizable to Arnold as it still only comprises about fifteen houses and St Gregory's parish church (now usually locked). John Penrose and his wife are buried in the chancel. The Doomsday Book records a church building at Fledborough and much later it was made famous by a rector who performed 490 marriages there by special licence, in a village population of about 60. It had become the 'Gretna Green' of the Midlands. This rector, William Sweetacre, died in 1753 a wealthy man. It was afterwards that the rectory fell into disrepair and was renovated by John Penrose. The River Trent still floods and covers the Holm, although modern flood defences and river diversion have produced some alterations.

In Ambleside, in the Lake District, Fox How, the house built for the Arnolds, survives in private hands at Under Loughrigg beside the River Rothay, about a mile from Wordsworth's house at Rydal Mount. A 'how' is rising ground. This was the family residence in school holidays and of Mary Arnold after Thomas's death. The present gardens are mainly woodland, meadow and 1.5 acres of lawns. Deer still frequent it and from time to time foxes and badgers appear. After Arnold's death the property remained in the hands of his family until the death of his last surviving unmarried daughter, Frances Bunsen Trevenen Whately Arnold, who died there in 1923. The house is unchanged, apart from the addition of garages described by the present owner as 'hideous'.

In terms of the Arnold biographers, Thomas Hughes was a major figure in his own right and is commemorated in the Tom Brown Museum (weekend afternoon opening only) in the old school house at Broad Street, Uffington, the village where Hughes grew up. Some 136 British editions of *Tom Brown* are preserved here, a testimony to its influence. This is the school house that Tom, the son of the local squire, used to play outside and distract the village boys from their work. But the Uffington vicarage that Hughes's grandfather and maternal great-grandfather inhabited is gone. The large parish church survives, with memorial to them. The colony town Hughes founded as 'Rugby' in Tennessee, USA, under the oversight of his brother Warren Hastings Hughes, still exists. Here he aimed to create a classless community based on co-operation, but Little points out (1972, p. 20) that the terrain was unsuitable for the agriculture its economic plan required. It survives reduced in size, but with twenty of the original buildings still *in situ* and about 85 residents. Uffington House, the house occupied by Margaret 'Madam' Hughes, Thomas's mother, is open to the public. Rugby, Tennessee, takes great pride in its history and various buildings are open to the public. A web visit can be made.

One might expect Rugby, Warwickshire, UK, to be the best place on the Arnold trail and in many ways it is. Pevsner aptly describes Rugby as 'Butterfield town' (1966, p. 384) and it is true that Butterfield's striped brickwork is the eye-catching feature of the present Rugby School. But parts of Arnold's school remain: the 'Birching Tower' with its worn step at the entrance, the outdoor cold water pump (though re-sited), part of the cloister and Big School Hall, all of which pre-date Arnold; the head's house with the turret that bore Arnold's flag; the iron swing he had installed for his children in the head's garden, although the wooden support posts are recent; the 'corkscrew staircase' up which he used to run to lessons; his library classroom over the gatehouse (now with a wing added on one side, which changes its tower appearance), although the classroom coal fire place has given way to a central heating radiator and the tables are modern. Fittingly, this room is still used for sixth form classics teaching. The famous kitchen table and chair at which Arnold sat to teach are preserved in the Rugby School Museum at Little Church Street, along with, rather surprisingly, a cast of his hand. If this unmusical man had tried to learn a keyboard instrument he at least had the right shaped hands. The formerly moated island on which Arnold had gymnastic equipment erected is still identifiable in the school grounds. But the Chapel has changed almost beyond recognition since Arnold, mainly through Butterfield's work; the cross which marked Arnold's burial in the vault beneath the altar now finds itself by the chancel in an enlarged building, although the vault which was used no more after Arnold's death is still accessible. Arnold's west door survives, with its text of Psalm 122 in Greek (the Greek Old Testament or Septuaguint):

> I was glad when they said unto me
> We will go into the house of the Lord.

The reclining effigy of Arnold in the Chapel is above that of Stanley, in what has been nicknamed by Rugby pupils 'the bunk bed' memorial.

But in the town of Rugby the *Spread Eagle*, Wratislaw's house, the Mechanics Institute and some of the other places marked on the unclear map of Arnoldian Rugby in Bamford (1960, p. 114) are gone. The railway station at which Arnold conducted services has been rebuilt. Rugby is graced with statues of William Webb Ellis, the schoolboy credited with turning the mass football game at Rugby into the start of the modern one by picking up the ball and running, and a statue of young Rupert Brooke, another Rugbeian. Thomas Arnold, Matthew Arnold and Lewis Carroll (Charles Dodgson) have no statues, although a recent and most attractive monument to Carroll in Rugby Chapel has a picture-frame setting with some of his creations surrounding the inscription. But he was a pupil after Arnold. Thomas Arnold is not quite invisible, but his footprints are fainter, even in Rugby. The real Arnold trail lies elsewhere, in his writings, as we shall see.

1 Outline of Arnold's Life

Home and childhood

Thomas Arnold was born on 13 June 1795 on the Isle of Wight. He was born into the Napoleonic war period. The threat of invasion of England was real, so the island outpost resembled a fortress:

> The Isle of Wight he said was an excellent place to give a child an interest in the war – seeing so many vessels in the roads [shipping lanes] – & perhaps the French ships come in with their colours under the English. (words recorded by Mary Arnold, 19.9.1825)

Thomas was the seventh and final child of middle-aged parents. The Arnold family tree went back to Henry VII, when Arnolds were numbered among the fishing industry in Lowestoft. It would have been very appropriate for Arnold had his earlier ancestors brought back from the Hundred Years War the motto *Me faut faire* adopted by fellow East Anglian Sir John Fastolfe while in France. 'I must be doing' would have been highly suitable for Arnold, as we shall see.

William Arnold, Thomas's father, held the double appointment of Collector of Customs and Postmaster for the island, together guaranteeing a prosperous middle-class position. Life for William had not always been comfortable. William's father had left farming and joined the excise service, meeting his wife in Aylesbury and later being transferred to Poole. Thomas's mother, Martha, was the daughter of a successful business man. The two families knew each other in Aylesbury and as children William and Martha had played together. William had moved to London to be a junior post office clerk and while living there took opportunity to sow the proverbial wild oats, which led to a live-in relationship and an illegitimate son by a woman from Hoxton. Then Martha Delafield arrived as an apprentice milliner at Covent Garden. William acted quickly and 'bought his way out of trouble instead of taking it with him to the altar' (Bamford, 1960, p. 2). William broke off his relationship, made financial provision for the child and set about to win Martha, who forgave him for his lapse. It is hard in a society in which these sorts of relationships are now viewed as a matter of course to imagine the scandal, in middle-class families of that time, that attached to such behaviour and just how far Martha and her family must have gone to forgive William. His ex-partner's feelings are not recorded, but she was labelled 'undesirable' (Wymer, 1953, p. 12) and in early nineteenth-century terms was not presumed to have feelings that mattered. Martha and William were to have a long engagement, eleven years, for reasons of lack of money, partly caused by supporting the son from the earlier relationship. By the time they married in Holborn, on 6 April 1779, William was 32 and had obtained the Isle of Wight post. They moved to 'Brummagem', a terraced house in West Cowes and later to 'Slatwoods' in the less fashionable but more convenient East Cowes. Slatwoods was a family house with 25 acres overlooking the Solent.

It was to be a happy parental marriage. A son, William, was born in 1781, then a daughter Martha, known in the family as 'Patty', to be followed by Lydia, Susanna, Frances, Matthew and finally Thomas. This ever-increasing family, swollen by children and the arrival of Susan Delafield, Thomas's aunt, along with the effects of wartime inflation, were among Martha's major pre-occupations. Many women in her position must have welcomed the menopause. William senior had major responsibilities for authorizing shipping in the busy Solent, for registrations, salvaging, etc. He inducted Thomas into sailing, sea lore, flags and the naval uniforms of different countries. An interest in history and geography was born here and fostered by lessons from his father and Aunt Susan. Fairy tales were discarded in favour of history books at bedtime. Another favourite book of Thomas's was the Bible. Before he was six Thomas had a small library of his own of history (English and Roman) and geography jigsaw cards of English counties, which made a map. All the ingredients of his later studies were therefore present in microcosm. One of the consequences of this early deep reading was that Thomas was inspired to write plays and poems. He wrote a blank verse tragedy before the age of seven, about Percy, Earl of Northumberland, also a hero for the Brontë children. Being a writer was a game for articulate children that many more than the Brontës indulged in. In a pre-radio, -television and -PC age, interests and hobbies were often more literary than is now the case. Perhaps surprisingly, as family entertainment was 'home-made', music and music-making never seem to have featured in Thomas Arnold's interests.

At the same time as these apparently precocious activities, Thomas Arnold was a boy among boys, playing mock battles, re-enacting war victories using toy boats on a pond, romping on the small farm that had been established on the 25-acre holding. The Arnold children were a close family group, although Thomas was especially close to his sister Susanna. The family was not without new scandal. Thomas's eldest brother, William junior, had gone to London to work for a firm of solicitors. By the age of nineteen he had fallen for and married a prostitute, losing his job as a result of absenteeism arising from this infatuation. William senior, who must have had some sympathy for his son's plight in the light of his own youthful adventure, obtained a post for him in customs work in the West Indies, where, conveniently for respectability, his wife died of yellow fever soon after.

But family routines at Cowes were shattered by William senior's sudden death on 3 March 1801 at the age of 55. It was ascribed to angina pectoris, a condition which was to recur more than once in the Arnold family. Weeks of pains that had been attributed to rheumatics turned out to be more serious. He was buried in Whippingham churchyard and a warmly worded plaque in the church notes his 'amiable as well as faithful discharge of his duty in his public station and in his private character' which earned him the warmest 'respect, esteem and affection of all who were occasionally or permanently connected with him in business, society or domestic ties'. Thomas Arnold was never to forget having been made to read to his father a sermon on the text 'Boast not thyself of tomorrow' on the Sunday before his death. Continuity of life through generations was to become a preoccupation of Thomas, perhaps caused by these circumstances. He was not quite six when his father died. Thomas was later to transplant trees from Slatwoods to his new homes, as a sort of link with his family past. Another theme of his later life which perhaps arose from this experience or was boosted by it was the shortness of time, i.e. the time allocated to one's life, and therefore the need to use it to the full. 'Life is before us as a trial time of uncertain length, but short at the longest' as he put it in a later sermon to boys at Rugby ([1832]1850 edition, p. 237).

Apart from the personal loss, with three children in boarding education, two unmarried daughters and an unmarried sister at home, the financial consequences for Martha Arnold were potentially extremely grave. But she was fortunately able to take over the role of Postmistress, half of her husband's work, whose routines she already knew, so that the family's position remained relatively secure. William junior dutifully sent home a monthly contribution from his West Indian salary. Matthew could remain at Oxford. Martha and Lydia remained at home to work the 25 acres. Susanna and Frances could remain at school. Aunt Susan took over the six-year-old Thomas's education alone.

Schooling

In 1803 Thomas was sent to Lord Weymouth's Grammar School at Warminster in Wiltshire, the school formerly attended by his brother Matthew. Warminster was a small school with two staff, a headteacher, Dr John Griffith, a kind man, and a second master, James Lawes, who were both friends of the Arnold family. Lawes was a frequent visitor to Slatwoods and had informally coached Thomas on his visits there. School terms, until the coming of railways, were divided into Long Half (mid-January to mid-July) and Short Half (mid-September until a few days before Christmas). Warminster did not work out quite as planned for this rather precocious and slightly eccentric child. He fitted in well neither with his fellow pupils nor with the adults. He had already developed by the age of ten an ambition to go into the Church: 'I am so attached to that line that I could not endure any other.' He does not seem to have been a particular target for bullying, however, and he spent his leisure time river-swimming, playing fives and an early version of cricket, re-enacting the siege of Troy with a boisterous gang of friends, and cultivating the garden plot to which he, in common with all pupils, was allocated. A naturally retentive memory and the good start he had been given at home meant that the Warminster studies were easily within his intellectual reach. His thirst for classics, history and geography remained unquenchable. Despite the church ambition, Arnold was often absent from morning chapel at school because of his inability to get up early. To this we shall return, as it is one of the barbs fired at the adult Arnold by Lytton Strachey. Even the admiring Arthur Stanley records this problem as 'amounting almost to a constitutional difficulty'. Arnold's much later contribution to a book of family prayers (1842) included the entreaty: 'Let us rise early and go late to rest, being ever busy and zealous in doing Thy will' (ibid., p. 354). Perhaps the opening words were fervently written. Letters home from Thomas were becoming rather impudent; he had outgrown Warminster. 'If he was to be saved from becoming a prig, he must be sent to a bigger school' (Wymer, 1953, p. 25). Griffith and Lawes, both Wykehamists (i.e. former pupils of Winchester, so-called from its foundation by William of Wykeham), recommended Winchester. It was resolved to send Thomas there in the Short Half of 1807.

He was pleased at this move and was admitted as a scholar, i.e. on fees reduced by 75 per cent of what 'commoners' – the other boys – paid. The timing was awkward, as William junior's death in Tobago had recently occurred (1806) and although the reduced Winchester fees were not much higher than those at Warminster, Martha's income was also reduced, having lost its monthly supplement from the West Indies. At Winchester Thomas adapted to harsh, sometimes brutal, school life. He was attacked on his first night as he knelt to pray by his bed, a custom held in low regard by Wykehamists. Boys were required to rise at 5.30 a.m. for 6 a.m. chapel. On four days of the week, three hours' work followed before a half hour for breakfast consisting of 'bread, stinking butter, beer and milk'. Water was often too risky to drink. Daily work was not light and could include up to ten pages of Greek grammar to be learned and recited and 60 sentences of exercises produced before breakfast with subsequent work on Latin verses until midday. The lunch hour was spent mainly waiting on older pupils, one of the duties involved in 'fagging', snatching food for oneself as opportunity arose. Then four hours' work learning Latin poetry, followed by translation and précis work of 40-page passages with a 15-minute break for bread and beer. At 6 p.m. the main meal was served, followed by preparation ('prep') of further Latin before 8 p.m. chapel. At 9 p.m. came bedtime, although boys could work on by candle light to complete their tasks for the next day. Many did, in order to avoid being beaten when 'prep' was tested the next day. Arnold rose at 3 a.m. on six consecutive days to prepare to recite 3000 lines of Homer. He used an ingenious alarm, letting a candle he lit at bed time burn to its end, thus igniting a string which launched a pile of books onto his head to wake him. Winchester made Warminster look like a holiday in contrast. But Tuesdays, Thursdays and Sundays were easier, with reduced formal teaching and some time for recreation.

Arnold was not popular among his peers at Winchester: he had set opinions; he appeared withdrawn or sulky at times; he could also appear blasé. He liked work too much. But if he was not popular, he was not unpopular either. Again, he was not singled out for bullying any more than anyone else, perhaps because of his physical energies and prowess at swimming, boating, fishing, tree climbing and friendly 'skirmishing', mock battles among groups of boys. He never lost this youthful exuberance and practised some of these activities years later, to the surprise and delight of the boys at Laleham and later as head of Rugby. He began to involve himself in directing plays on Saturday evenings. He is also said to have written a play about Simon de Montfort. None of these pastimes suggests a social misfit or reject. There was a willing cast and audience for the plays. He was happy to be involved in 'ragging', nocturnal attacks by members of one dormitory on another which sometimes led to serious damage of property and some human casualties. His letters home suggest that he was fairly happy. Years later, when Arnold was himself a tutor at Laleham, Mary Arnold recorded a conversation about school days (14.9.1825):

> He was talking of the early life of a boy at his first school – & said how wretched it was – & that he supposed very few persons in the station of gentlemen passed any part of their after life so uncomfortably. He said he thought he should make K [a boy at Laleham is referred to here, not Jane Arnold, who was coincidentally nicknamed 'K'] a very good scholar before he had done with him. He took the food well & without its making him sick – I said I thought it a pity he did not go to Oxford. He said he thought it mattered very little about that – some men read more at Cambridge than at Oxford & there were many who were equally idle at both.

He wrote to Hawkins in 1827: 'My own school experience has taught me the monstrous evil of a state of low principle prevailing among those who set the tone to the rest.' In 1808 Arnold demonstrated a sign of later promise in another field: he was chosen as one of the best orators in the school to speak at one of its public ceremonies. A meal of mock turtle soup, veal cutlets, asparagus and marrow puddings rewarded his efforts. This, reinforced with regular food packages from home, helped him to survive the more spartan regular diet of the school. Arnold was not the most able in his form, which may account for his later championing of effort as much as achievement at Rugby, although Chandos is sceptical that he was really sincere about this. But when Arnold asked Henry Gabell, the Winchester second master, to promote him to a higher form, Gabell agreed. Perhaps this was because Arnold was one of few boys to like Gabell and Gabell sensed this.

Among his peers, Arnold was neither a conformist nor a leading rebel. But he did break those rules he did not like, even as a prefect, on occasion playing cards for money, since he saw nothing wrong in it. Real bullying, of which he witnessed much at Winchester, appalled him. His conversation was of Rousseau and religion, social class, revolution, and the Church. He deplored the bad behaviour of royalty, the abuses in the Church including 'the worldly conduct of Christian bishops' and the 'vices and follies' of politicians. These were times of post-Revolution France and of Napoleon, and the great battles. Home was a castle-island, fortified against attack, guardian of the Solent access. The young Thomas, like the young Coleridge and so many others, was excited by the ideals of revolution, the championing of the rights of humankind and the 'good of the people'. He never quite lost this youthful vision, nor its concomitant call to reform abuses in church and society. Alongside this, the desire to join the clergy strengthened. 'Hereafter in mature age . . . I will perhaps more warmly undertake the Cause, and with all the power of my abilities, endeavour to crush and confound the Children of Heresy and Infidelity' (Wymer, 1953, p. 36). This was strong Methodistical language for an Anglican and an early sign of the emergence of Arnold the crusader. 'Cause' was a term beloved of nonconformists for chapel communities and for the campaign for civil and religious liberty. It smacked of 'enthusiasm', a word which then carried a meaning more akin to 'fanaticism' than its present meaning, to many Anglicans. Stanley's record of Arnold's Winchester period is more muted. For him, Arnold was shy, retiring, stiff, formal, with strong and numerous friendships, a critical sense of historical record and happy memories. It was all slightly too good to be true. But whatever the historical detail of the Winchester experience, it was time to move on again.

Undergraduate days

Oxford

In 1811 Arnold went as a scholar to Corpus Christi, Oxford. It was his second choice, after New College, which had stronger links with Winchester. Among his first acts at university was to over-spend on cutlery and crockery for his college rooms, with the result that his furniture had to be hired and not bought. A request home for more money quickly followed. Arnold was pleased to be freed from the regulation and restriction of school life and to be able to explore a new environment, intellectual, geographic and social. Throughout his undergraduate life he continued to enjoy rumbustious outdoor exercise, leaping hedges, vaulting styles and jumping ditches on country walks. In summer he continued the swimming and rowing he had enjoyed as a boy. There were occasional all-night parties in college rooms, wild conversation, games, food and drink. But Corpus Christi was in a phase of studious undergraduates. It was a college with a good family atmosphere, conducive to study. Arnold found the work demanding: a weekly essay to be read for and written; volumes of Latin or Greek to be read then reduced to précis; there were tutorials and lectures to attend. His repeated failure to rise early did not help, even in an undergraduate context where this was and is common, almost a tradition. 'Breakfast' was sometimes taken at noon, after morning lectures, or missed entirely. But as he settled into the rhythms of his new life, he found that he could take the workload more in his stride. Out of lectures he could be found in the Bodleian or the Radcliffe, or working in his rooms, reading classics and also learning French. Brother Matthew, now Classical Professor at the Royal Military College at Marlow, would sometimes visit him in college.

At this time Arnold is described as curly haired, dark and youthful, 'with the air of a cultured vagabond' (Bamford, 1960,

p. 4). University for Arnold, as for most others then and now, provided him with life-long friendships: John Buckland (later to become his brother-in-law), John Taylor Coleridge, the poet's nephew (later to get a First in classics and become a High Court judge), George Cornish, Augustus Hare, John Keble, Trevenen Penrose (later to become a brother-in-law) and John Tucker. John Coleridge had been sent by his uncle, Samuel Taylor Coleridge, a copy of *The Lyrical Ballads* and it was at John's suggestion that Arnold began to read Wordsworth. He found this inspiring and it also brought into his mind images of the Lake District. Arnold was to encounter more of Samuel Taylor Coleridge's thinking via this nephew: the need for a wide base for Christianity; the need to examine the Bible critically; a stress on morals as opposed to 'facts' and science. John Coleridge later summed up his feelings about the time and the group:

> We lived on the most familiar terms with each other: we
> might be, indeed we were, sometimes boyish in manner,
> and in the liberties we took with each other; but our
> interest in literature, ancient and modern, and in all the
> stirring matters of that stirring time, was not boyish; we
> debated the classic and romantic question; we discussed
> poetry and history, logic and philosophy: or we fought
> over the Peninsular battles and the Continental campaigns
> with the energy of disputants personally concerned in
> them. Our habits were noisy and intemperate: one
> break-up [i.e. end of term] party . . . was somewhat
> exuberant and noisy; but the authorities wisely forebore
> too strict an inquiry into this . . . [Arnold] was a mere
> boy in appearance as well as in age; but we saw in a very
> short time that he was quite equal to take his part in
> the arguments of the common room . . . He was fond
> of conversation on serious matters and vehement in

argument; fearless too in advancing his opinions – which, to say the truth, often startled us a good deal; but he was ingenuous and candid and he advanced his opinions which might have seemed to be-token presumption but the good temper with which he bore retort or rebuke, relieved him from that imputation. (1843 reminiscence of events *c.*1812, Stanley, 1845)

Among this friendship group Arnold was perceived as a Jacobin rather than a Tory. His forceful expression of views, a recurring characteristic, must have seemed even more surprising from a 'junior' within the Common Room, but he is said not to have lost his temper or to have felt ill will towards his opponents as a result of extremely severe clashes of ideas and values. Those out-side his friendship group did not always reciprocate the lack of personal venom and these antipathetic feelings were to recur later in his life in response to some of his more vitriolic writing. From the standpoint of middle age, he analysed his own political progress in a letter to Coleridge (24.1.1840):

I was brought up in a strong Tory family; the first impressions of my own mind shook my merely received impressions to pieces, and at Winchester I was well nigh a Jacobin. At sixteen, when I went up to Oxford, all the influences of the place . . . your influence above all, blew my Jacobinism to pieces and made me again a Tory. I used to speak strong Toryism in the old Attic Society . . . Then came the peace, when Napoleon was put down, and the Tories had it their own way. Nothing shook my Toryism more than the strong Tory sentiments that I used to hear . . . I heard language at which my organ of justice stood aghast, and which, the more I read of the Bible, seemed to me more and more unchristian.

If reform began to seem a natural response to Arnold, the whole country was shocked to learn that at 5 p.m. on Monday, 11 May 1812, Spencer Percival, the Prime Minister, had been shot dead in the House of Commons lobby. The assassin was a bankrupt business man from Liverpool who blamed the government for the economic misfortunes of the country. There had been nothing like this since the Civil War and talk of a national crisis quickly swept the country. But for Romantic radicals like S. T. Coleridge and William Wordsworth, the murder was a watershed, after which they could no longer identify with the agitation of the masses. Oxford was not, of course, a manufacturing town like those of the north Midlands and the North, so it was cushioned from events, but the student body discussed them with great vigour.

The student years were years of hard and serious work for Arnold. He preferred history to classics, although Aristotle, Thucydides and Herodotus were favourite writers. Thucydides was to become a post-graduate research interest. Arnold sat his Finals in April 1814:

> I have done with lectures and so on for ever. Henceforth I shall be the Director of my own studies and shall have it in my power to turn my attention entirely to those subjects to which my inclinations naturally lead me.

In later conversation with Mary (20.10.1825):

> He said he did not think he would get a first class degree – there was not power enough, he could not clutch & grasp and grip his books & throw them about as he liked . . . Nobody could give him the art of making his reading in one book bear upon another.

The results came out in late May. Despite his lack of confidence, he had attained a First in Literæ Humaniores. He was not quite nineteen years old. A celebratory walking tour of the Wye valley with Penrose, who had also got a First, followed.

London

While Arnold was enjoying his Oxford years, the home situation was changing. A mysterious paralysis began to afflict his sister Susanna, moving from her right shoulder into the spine. It was beyond the capability of the local doctor to treat. This meant a London specialist, with possibly repeated visits under travelling conditions that would be doubly irksome to someone partially paralysed and in pain. Martha Arnold therefore took the decision to move the family to London and so they moved to Pitt's Buildings, a small rented house in Kensington village in March 1812. The move could not halt the progression of the illness. By the end of the year Susanna had lost the use of both legs and the right side of her body. She was only 25. Much of the rest of her twenty remaining years was to be spent on her back, in a containing bed known as the 'crib'. Susanna was Arnold's favourite sister and her disability strengthened rather than weakened their relationship. She showed exemplary fortitude, teaching herself to write with her left hand. He saw her as a role model for Christian faith in great adversity. So the Oxford vacations were spent in Kensington, which Arnold disliked. It was neither town nor country but 'a mongrel' or 'a vile hole'. Despite this negative attitude, Arnold did not dislike everything about London life. He explored its centre and peripheral villages with Lydia and Frances. He went to the theatre, visited the House of Commons in session, saw the fireworks at Vauxhall Gardens, dined with those of his Oxford set like Keble, Buckland and Coleridge when they were 'in Town'. There were early flirtations with young women. Lydia Arnold, however, was doing more than picnic with her brother in the villages of London. In August 1814 she was married to Lieutenant-General Richard F. W. Lambart, the seventh Earl of Cavan and a war hero. It was a remarkable match. He was a 51-year-old war hero and widower with four children from his first marriage. They had met when he was Commander of the Isle of Wight. Martha Arnold found herself the mother of a countess. She was rescued from the lower middle-class social drift brought about by William junior, who had died in the West Indies in 1806.

There were to be more changes. Within eighteen months of Lydia's marriage, Frances' engagement to Arnold's friend John Buckland was announced. Thomas's sister Martha, 'Patty', married John Ward, his father's successor as Customs Officer. Meanwhile, Susanna's condition was still deteriorating. She could now no longer write. Her left shoulder was becoming paralysed. Martha Arnold and Aunt Susan Delafield were neither young, nor fully physically fit to care for her. Frances suggested they take a cottage at Hampton to be nearer to her. This set the scene for the next move. But while all this was being discussed, Arnold had to sort out a career for himself.

Starting a career: the Oriel Fellowship

His sisters were making 'good' marriages. His brother had a good post at Marlow. What was Thomas to do amid these examples of marital success and upward mobility? Arnold was not fitted by temperament, finance or family position to be a gentleman of leisure. Fortunately his desire to be a clergyman was undiminished. At the time this profession offered both a vocation for the religious and, in the Church of England, a socially very acceptable career. The bishops might be deeply religious men (or not) but they were certainly social barons. Some of the parish livings were very well paid posts, which allowed their incumbents great freedom to study or to visit their people or simply to enjoy themselves, like Jack Russell, who rode to hounds and was a leading socialite at country balls during his 48-year tenure of the living of Swymington in Devon. The obvious route to the Church for a young Oxford graduate would be through an Oxford Fellowship, which would provide him with accommodation and a small stipend until he could be ordained at the age of 23. Two fellowships were vacant at Oriel, Keble's college. Selection was by written examination. So, despite his disavowal of engaging in revision and examinations again, Arnold found himself sitting fellowship examinations in 1815.

The assessment of the examiners was that Arnold's knowledge was deep and his enthusiasm evident, but that he lacked elegance and style and he was clearly not one of the top two candidates on the basis of the scripts alone. At this point one of the Oriel tutors, Richard Whately, intervened. Whately was a figure of considerable personal authority and stature within the university but he was 'dearly loved by the few' (Tuckwell, 1909, p. 61). He and his family were later to become personal friends of the Arnolds. As a child Whately had been an arithmetical genius, a skill that he almost completely lost by the age of nine. His scholarship, massive capacity for mental concentration, candid, almost rude, manners including a total lack of 'small talk' made him something of a living legend. His eccentric dress – a pea-green coat, white waistcoat, stone-coloured short trousers, flesh-coloured stockings and powdered hair, with a white coat and white beaver hat as outerwear – made him a noticeable public figure in Oxford and his clothing was frowned on by the Heads of Colleges as quite unsuitable for a DD. He was known to lecture while reclining on a sofa and smoking a pipe, speaking rapidly and with many gestures. He trained his dog, Sailor, to climb trees and drop from the branches into the River Cherwell to frighten onlookers into thinking he would drown. As Archbishop of Dublin, later, he was to shock and alienate some of his Anglican clergy by establishing a Mixed Education Board for Roman Catholic and Protestant Schools, working with Roman Catholic Archbishop Murray. Whately demanded that his students think for themselves and not merely 'parrot' what they had read. This is perhaps a clue to why he backed Arnold. They also had a common passion for Thucydides. Moreover, Whately was so often right – or at least that was the reputation he held.

Whately argued that Arnold's papers were clearly not the best, but that this was because he lacked good communication skills. These, Whately asserted, would come with time. Where Arnold should be recognized, according to Whately, was in his potential. He would develop further than the other candidates even though they appeared to be currently ahead. If the college wanted someone to bring them glory and credit, Arnold must be the man. This intervention in support of Arnold despite his written examination papers carried the day. Bamford suggests this was unfair, and strictly it was, but this kind of intervention was common at the time and has not entirely died out since. Whately would in any case have retorted that he was simply arguing for natural justice, not legalistic mark scores. Some university job advertisements in our time add that they reserve the right to consider people who have not applied. This can be laudable in some situations, easily corrupted in others. In this case Arnold proved himself within two years, by winning the Chancellor's Latin essay prize and the prize for the best English essay. He did not get the verse prize. Even so, one may presume that his writing style had developed. Whately was right again. The prize essay was published as *The Effects of Distant Colonisation on the Parent State*. It is a clear analysis of both the theory of colonization and the realities (see p. 246), and with Arnold's characteristic high regard for history discusses the matter with reference to Athens, Carthage, Holland and Spain as well as contemporary Britain.

The fellowship offered fee-free study opportunities, a small income, residence in college and a great deal of personal freedom to use or abuse as one chose. The Oriel fellows included some of the university's best intellects of the time: Whately, who later became Archbishop of Dublin (a post Arnold narrowly missed), Edward Hawkins, later to be Provost of Oriel, Edward Copleston, later Bishop of Llandaff and Dean of St Paul's, and Renn Hampden, later Bishop of Hereford. By coincidence, Hampden, whose family were resident in the West Indies, had been sent as a child to be a private boarding pupil of the vicar of Warminster until he entered Oriel in 1811, so he and Arnold had overlapped in the town of Warminster from 1803 to 1807 and had arrived at Oxford in the same year. John Keble was also at Oriel. His later relationship with Arnold as a friend and enemy was partly shaped by Arnold's vehement views on the Oxford Movement. So Oriel was a good milieu for Arnold – a good interchange of minds and ideas within a context of committed work by talented young men. Arnold could therefore work hard and play hard, continuing all the boisterous physical pursuits of his undergraduate and childhood days. Chandos disapprovingly records horse play at Oriel. 'Backs were mounted and chairs and tables upset within the grave precincts of Oriel Common Room itself' (Lake, in Chandos, 1984, p. 266). The picture we have of Arnold is still of boundless energy. But overall there was a serious working atmosphere, which accounted for the dismissal in 1820 from the Oriel fellowship of Hartley Coleridge, S. T. Coleridge's son, for drunkenness, irregular behaviour and 'keeping low company'. S. T. Coleridge's biographer, Richard Holmes, notes that Hartley had 'fallen among saints, who were unsparing in their righteousness' in this 'spartan and intellectually formidable common room' (1998, II, p. 514). But although Holmes captures one aspect of the Oriel atmosphere he is wrong to state that Arnold was a member of the common room at the time of the dismissal;

he had moved on by then. At home were his mother, his aunt and Susanna. There were recurring medical bills to be met. Arnold needed money to send home and he badly wanted to travel on his own account. The fellowship alone would not suffice. Coaching private pupils for the university examinations of 'Little-Go' and 'Great-Go' might be the answer.

But there were many clever young men in search of supplementary income willing to take from a finite pool of private pupils. It was to take more than a year, with an accumulation of debts to discharge, before Arnold started to make money out of coaching. Moreover, the pay was small and not always easy to get. Eventually work with five pupils enabled him to reach a financial break-even point. Money could be sent home and also saved for travel. He toured the battlefields of Waterloo, visited northern France, Belgium, Germany, Luxembourg and in 1818 found a place and a person that were to prove formative: the Lake District and a meeting with Wordsworth. The year 1818 was also one of decision. The old childhood ambition to be a clergyman was now nearing fruition. His undergraduate and post-graduate choices had been geared to that end. To be a clergyman and help to reform the Church was Arnold's greatest wish. But he began to worry about whether he could in honesty 'subscribe to', i.e. agree with, the 39 Articles. These were held to be the defining essence of Anglicanism, a list of doctrines that especially showed how the Anglican Church was free from Roman 'error'. If Arnold could not 'subscribe' to these, could he go ahead with ordination into the Anglican clergy? Perhaps he was not, after all, suited to the career he had always wanted. This was a time of reconsideration and consulting the opinions of friends whom Arnold valued: Hawkins, John Coleridge, Whately. Their view was that his doubts would disappear as his understanding of scripture and theology increased. Not entirely convinced, Arnold consulted the Bishop of Oxford. The bishop agreed with his friends. On

20 December 1818, Arnold was ordained deacon in Oxford Cathedral. It was as easy as that; no ordination course or theological college preparation. An interview with the bishop was sufficient. The professionalization of the Anglican clergy was not to happen until after Arnold's death. But Arnold's difficulties did not decrease and he was to write in 1839 on the twenty-first anniversary of his ordination as deacon, 'I had enough and more than enough of scruples and difficulties, not before only, but afterwards for a long time' (to Stanley, 20.12.1839).

A post-ordination career

Because the mere fact of ordination did not dissolve Arnold's doubts, he was left with the dilemma whether to engage in a full-time church position and allow himself to rise the ladder of preferment, to dean of a great cathedral or to bishop or even archbishop in Ireland or England, or whether to pursue a different career, with his ordained status at the periphery rather than the centre of his work. More immediate was whether to be ordained priest as the next stage of the ordination process. Arnold felt he needed a further term at Oxford to sort himself out, but at the end of this time he was no clearer than before. His misgivings about the 39 Articles were no less. How could one allow oneself to rise through the Church with these doubts, especially if with the passage of time they increased rather than decreased? He therefore felt obliged in conscience to seek another career. The armed forces seemed unattractive, although he had a brother-in-law who could have 'pulled strings' on his behalf. It was then acceptable for friends and family to help in one's 'preferment', i.e. promotion. Arnold felt law and medicine, both very socially respectable alternatives, to be entirely unsuitable. In law one might be retained to defend criminals one knew to be guilty, which would constitute 'moral nastiness'. He felt medicine was bankrupt in terms of philosophy and seemed to be based on empirical guesswork. 'How ignorant are we of the causes of disorder, of the real influence of air, of infection, and of that strange phenomenon of diseases incident generally to the human frame.' Another possibility was to take private pupils in a bigger way, not on an hourly basis for examination 'cramming' but full-time. This might be combined with a small or low paid parish post. Cornish, Buckland and Tucker were all set on this. Arnold's friends urged on him the idea of 'schoolmastering'. Arnold, in reaction to the loss or at least deferment of his lifetime ambition and subsequent loss of personal momentum, was still unsure about teaching as a career. He held that everyone has a role, a part, to play in life, but discerning his own was extremely difficult. Might it be to instruct the young? He simply did not know.

At this point he was influenced by John Buckland, now his brother-in-law as well as friend, and Edward Hawkins. Hawkins told him very frankly that he thought he was 'quite unsuited' to be a parish clergyman, perhaps because he would offend the influential members of his congregation by his outspoken doubts or apparently radical politics. He would be far better making a contribution to the field of education, itself in need of reform just as much as the Church. Buckland was conducting a small school at Hampton which was flourishing in a room in the vicarage. He wanted to expand. He wanted to found something that would be better than either private fee-paying lessons with the local parson, or what were seen as the corrupt grammar schools. His idea was to form a 'preparatory' school, to prepare younger boys for public schools or older boys for direct entrance to university. The idea was new. Two age groups implied two classes and two teachers. Would Arnold consent to be the second teacher in partnership with Buckland? Arnold would be given the older pupils, freedom to design his own syllabus and total control of his house.

Expenses and profits would be shared and the rates would be 10 guineas for enrolment, then 70 or 80 guineas per annum according to the lower or upper class the boy was in. Boys would be resident with the masters and their families and provide their own towels, knife and a silver spoon and fork.

Arnold readily consented – it must have seemed at least a temporary solution to his dilemma – and the partnership began in the summer of 1819. Hampton was discarded as the best site for the school, since two houses were now needed. Extensive searches in Kent and Surrey failed to satisfy. Finally they settled on a long lease of two houses in Laleham, a village near Staines, near the present intersection of the M3 and M25 motorways. Arnold described it as 'a quiet village, and not at all infested with cockneys and with no coach passing through it . . . being situated on the Thames it is very convenient for pleasant walks and for bathing and punting'. Arnold and Buckland would have to repair and renovate the houses themselves as cash was too scarce to pay others. Arnold's house belonged to an East India captain, but it was in better repair than Buckland's, which had damp and was on level ground nearer the river. Buckland, on the other hand, was the better DIY person of the two. Arnold was now a house-holder, with a job. But he also had a debt, £1000, incurred by a necessary loan to set up and equip the school. It was a considerable sum of money for the time and the interest rate was an inexorable 5 per cent per annum. He invited his mother and family to move in with them. That could be congenial, help with the boys, and reduce the expense of their maintaining a separate establishment. Martha and Aunt Susan arrived by chaise. Susanna had to travel in her crib by boat along the river so as not to be jolted. Arnold was now 24. This was to be the real start of his work.

Laleham

The first year

Arnold's routine was quickly established. The boys and Arnold were up by 7 a.m. A snack of bread and butter and home-produced milk was followed by lessons from 8 till 9 or 9.30, then breakfast. The subjects were classics and divinity with later history and geography added and from 1823 mathematics and algebra. The teaching method was a mixture of 'lectures', class lessons and individual tutorials to test the pupils on their learning. Further teaching lasted from 10 a.m. until about 2 p.m., which marked the 'dinner' break. This was taken at Buckland's house, about five minutes' walk away. Tea afterwards was taken at 6 p.m. in Arnold's drawing room, with his mother, aunt and sister. The young men then did 'prep' till 9 p.m. leaving Arnold

2. The house at Laleham, near Staines, where for close on nine years, from 1819 to 1828, Dr Arnold conducted a small private school before obtaining his appointment to the headmastership of Rugby.
— *from a photograph taken soon after Arnold's death*

the evening free. He toured their rooms before retiring himself.
Byrne and Churchill (1937, pp. 12ff) have an unreferenced sec-
tion on daily life at Laleham, with its weekly compulsory bath on
Saturday evening. Waistcoats were removed for outdoor games.
The River Thames was used for swimming. A large spartan play
area provided the only place for informal games for those who
finished their half-day's work early.

Laleham village seemed unpromising, with a small population,
widely scattered housing, and three inbred families called Hart-
well as the main educated occupants. These intemperate Tories
seem to have had the effect on Arnold of changing the Toryism to
which he had returned at Oxford back to Whig sympathies. He
found the countryside flat but charming and threw himself into
rescuing the garden. It inspired him to write

> God is the Tree and sound the Root
> Whose Produce is so fair a Fruit:
> Grows there elsewhere a Fruit like this?
> Then all my Troubles I dismiss!
> Servants of God! With you I go,
> Whose lives your Master's Warrant show.
> (Adamson, 1989, p. 62)

At first he could mention 'some very pleasant families' locally, no
doubt encountered at church.

The Anglican church of All Saints was staffed as a 'chapel of
ease' by the vicar of Staines, who was delighted when Arnold
and Buckland offered to alternate in conducting the Sunday
services there and help in the Sunday school. In the latter capacity they replaced an alcoholic woman who was on occasions
drunk in school. Recalling Arnold's pleasure in the improvement in the Sunday school, Mary records him saying one
evening:

> It is just as absurd to expect to teach children by scorn as it
> would be to enslave grown men by forms – & there is a
> great deal of mischief done by both these things . . . When
> he had been commending a plum pudding at dinner he
> said. Bad pastry is like bad poetry – good for nothing – it is
> quite a luxury and should be had good or not at all.
> (13.11.1826)

The church building had a history which would have appealed
to Arnold: Norman pillars, Elizabethan brickwork, a pre-
Reformation altar slab with incised crosses and over the west door
a large 1811 oil painting by G. A. Harlow depicting Jesus walking
on the water and reaching out to Peter, in a scene of awesome
darkness. The church was conveniently on the road between the
two houses. Arnold and Buckland would have conducted matins
and perhaps evensong, as the regular Anglican Sunday services
then (holy communion was a rarer event); their diaconal status
meant that they could not celebrate communion without a priest.
Arnold does not seem to have been immediately convinced that
the role as teacher would be his life's work. He regarded Buckland
as more successful and committed and he turned down the offer
of a teaching post at Winchester, writing

> I know myself very unqualified to fill [the post] . . . Success
> in my present undertaking is of course doubtful: Still my
> chance is . . . tolerably fair, not indeed of making my
> fortune but of earning such an income as shall enable me
> to live with economy as a married man.

This is hardly a statement of confident commitment to a life's
work. Yet the work at Laleham could not be too oppressive.
Arnold's pupils did not reach double figures. It was hardly a
school in any modern sense of the word. He was more like a

private tutor than a 'schoolmaster' except that where a private tutor resided in a wealthy pupil's home, Arnold's pupils resided in his. It was, as we shall see, the activities that Arnold added to this work which made his Laleham period as filled as Rugby later was. Fitch (1900, p. 17) was quite wrong to see it as 'comparative solitude' or 'retirement' and Stanley's description of it as 'tranquil' is also inaccurate.

Marriage

If Arnold was uncertain in his profession, in his personal life he made a clear decision; in his first month at Laleham his proposal of marriage to Mary Penrose, sister of his friend Trevenen, was accepted. 'Tre' and 'Pen' are both Cornish prefixes and the family came from strong Cornish stock. Mary's father, John, was a clergyman and a son of the parsonage. She was born in Carwythenack ('Crannick') in Cornwall in 1791, making her nearly four years Arnold's senior. Like Thomas she had enjoyed a happy family childhood, with a move in 1801 to Fledborough, a small village between Newark and Gainsborough, near the confluence of the Rivers Maun and Trent. This was a living her father had held in plurality with his Cornish ones since 1783, but had paid for a curate to run. This curate was John Wootton, a local schoolteacher from Tuxford and also curate of Dunham. Holding plural livings was common practice of the time and a way of augmenting the parson's income. Taking on a local curacy, effectively part-time, was often a way of supplementing the schoolteacher's income. Fledborough was in flat, flood-prone fields, a village of half a dozen houses and a ruinous rectory which could flood with the rising of the Trent. A rectory had been on the site from *c*.1200, but the building into which the Penrose family moved dated from 1736. They had to renovate and extend what remained. It must have seemed a stark contrast to Cornwall. The family settled well, sustained by their inner life and also that the first impressions were worse than the reality. It was good dairy country. The river could in some ways substitute for the sea. The natives were friendly, perhaps delighted at last to have another resident rector unlike his scandalous predecessor (see p. 17).

Arnold made a short visit to his friend Trevenen at Fledborough in the New Year of 1819. The warmth between him and the family was mutual. There was laughter, conversation, fun, walks and rides. By midsummer, Arnold was in love with the dark-haired, fresh-complexioned Mary. Her diary entries of the time reflect a lively, humorous and very fresh, attractive style. He had no income – Laleham opened one month later – and the £1000

3. Fledborough Parsonage in time of flood. It was here that Mary Penrose spent much of her childhood and later met Dr Arnold for the first time.
— *from a sketch by Jane Penrose (circa 1811)*

debt. A proposal of marriage could therefore mean an inauspicious interview with Mary and then with Penrose Papa. This was not the case, however. Mary accepted him. It might be cynically remarked that in a society as restricted as Fledborough and coming on for 29 she would not get many other offers, but the evidence suggests that on the contrary it was love and not desperation that prompted her answer. Arnold related that 'Mr P. did not say a word to recommend me to wait [for better finances before marrying]; but on the contrary said he was much pleased with my plan of working out my fortune for myself.' Both families exchanged happy letters but it was to wait until the thaw in the winter of 1820 before Mary could be brought to Laleham to meet her future mother-in-law and family. Her reverend father brought her, reinforced by her sister Lydia and her brother Trevenen who came across to join them from his curacy at Eton. Mary broke down at the ordeal of meeting Martha, Aunt Susan, Susanna and the others, but quickly recovered and they had a very successful week in which everyone got on well: 'Our two families met in strength at the dinner table. I think there could not have been a happier party; none seemed strangers to one another, but as if they were already related.' Arnold got on very well with his prospective father-in-law. The whole week gave Arnold new impetus to make a success of the job.

But two more family deaths now influenced him strongly. His brother Matthew, now a chaplain to the armed forces at Gosport, drowned while sailing in Stokes Bay, aged 35. Then Uncle Joseph Delafield, Martha's brother, died suddenly of a heart attack. Arnold was now, with the role by custom passing down through males, 'head of the family'. This gave him an added sense of responsibility for the family dependants and unwaged. He decided that a marriage that summer would be the best course of action and the availability of the house next to the Bucklands meant that he could rent it for his mother, aunt and sister. Events

4. Dr Arnold and Mary Penrose (*left*) on a picnic shortly before their
wedding, chaperoned by Mary's sister, Jane, and her brother, Trevenen.
— *from a drawing by Lydia Penrose, sister of Mary Penrose*

moved quickly. There was a wedding to arrange, the house to be
redecorated, his relatives to be moved, their new house got ready
and a cook to be engaged for Thomas and Mary. Arnold retreated
from the bustle of all this to spend a long visit at Mary's home,
culminating in a quiet wedding ceremony performed on 11
August 1820 at Fledborough by John Penrose. Arnold was 25.
Mary was almost 29.

The later Laleham years

Arnold returned to work at Laleham reinvigorated. The marriage
was to be a very happy one. Mary proved a 'hit' with the pupils.
Both families had provided good models for matrimonial harmony and close family life. But marriage also gave Arnold a career

5. Fledborough Church where Thomas Arnold and Mary Penrose were
married by Mary's father, the Revd John Penrose, the incumbent.
— *from a Penrose family sketch (circa 1820)*

incentive to succeed and reasons for looking ahead. He now had a
wife, as well as adult dependants in his own family. Soon he
might have children. If teaching were to be his course, on what
principles should he conduct his professional work? He wanted
to make Christianity the basis of his educational work. A God-
fearing citizen was worth more than a merely clever one. It
quickly became clear that Arnold preferred the plodding pupil to
the clever one, although his later opponents questioned this. But
how could one reflect that in education? How could religion rise
above being a *subject* of teaching and preaching and become a
way of living for young men?

The small pupil numbers allowed for a degree of closeness
in the pupil–teacher relationship which was not possible at

Winchester. In the afternoons Arnold would join with the boys in all the pursuits that he had delighted in during his own childhood and undergraduate days. Pole jumping in the back garden, or Campus Martius as Arnold called it, was added to the repertoire, which also included mock battles, river swimming in the tranquil setting of the nearby Thames, games of 'Red Indians', etc. He said, 'I spear daily, as the Lydians used to play in the famine, that I may at least steal some portion of the day from thought' (Goulburn, 1856, p. 49). There is evidence of energy. Mary records (3.9.1825): 'I was remarking on his looking so well . . . He said he felt quite elastic – just like a horse . . . impatient to be off.'

At the evening dinner at Buckland's house he would sit with and join in the chatter at the boys' table. The pupils continued to be welcomed into his own drawing room for 'tea', a light supper after studies ended at 9 p.m. This included chatter, chess, backgammon and other indoor activities. He wrote to Cornish: 'I felt completely for the time a boy as they were.' But he was never completely a boy as they were. There was a seriousness:

> H = [*sic*, a pupil] asked him if he liked chess. He said –
> 'No, I think chess is a great waste of good intellect – one
> might write four pages of sermon at the expence [*sic*] of
> understanding which is bestowed on a game of chess.'
> (Mary Arnold, 6.3.1826)

In the classroom Arnold was also developing the technique that would distinguish him at Rugby. He was careful to explain and to answer questions, neither of which was a typical manner of teaching then, but his later famous ire was aroused when confronted by idleness. He was willing to expel, even with such small pupil numbers, but took the view that 'lenity' (lenience) was rarely wasted.

By the summer of 1823 Arnold was invited again to apply for a vacancy at Winchester. It was the post of 'usher' (second master) and would have meant that he would probably have been seen as the head designate of the school. But he was happy at Laleham. There were nine pupils with him, but the boarding and tuition combined fee for one year was 200 guineas per pupil. In 1827 and 1828 he turned pupils away. More importantly, he was in sole charge there. This meant that, if one is an Arnold supporter, it gave him the chance further to test his experiment of Christian education in circumstances he could control, or if one is critical of Arnold, it can be seen as permitting his demagogic qualities to continue in a situation he could entirely dominate, as opposed to obeying someone else at Winchester. One of his Laleham pupils, Bonamy Price, who later moved to the staff at Rugby, wrote of Laleham:

> It was a place where a newcomer at once felt that a great and earnest work was going forward. Arnold's great power as a private tutor resided in this, that he gave such an earnestness to life. Every pupil was made to feel that there was work for him to do – that his happiness as well as his duty lay in doing that work well . . . A strange joy came over him on discovering that he had the means of being useful and thus of being happy . . . His hold over all his pupils I know astonished me. It was not so much an enthusiastic admiration for his genius, or learning, or eloquence which stirred within them; it was a sympathetic thrill, caught from a spirit that was earnestly at work in the world.

These were productive years for the Arnolds in other ways. Jane Martha was born in 1821, Matthew on Christmas Eve 1822, Thomas in 1823, in 1824 a daughter who survived only a few days; in 1825 Mary (junior); in 1826 Edward Penrose and in 1828 William ('Willy') Delafield. All these children were given family nicknames by Arnold as babies or toddlers: Jane was 'K'; Matthew 'Crab'; Tom, 'Prawn'; Mary, 'Bacco'; Edward, 'Didu' and William, 'Widu'. Jane quickly showed something of her father's wilfulness or strong character, on one occasion refusing to curtsy to her mother despite admonitions and being made to stand in the corner. It brought to Arnold's mind 'how truly is our pride our original and besetting sin from the very first'. Many years later 'K' was probably the outspoken 'Fausta' in Matt's poem 'Resignation' (begun 1843, revised in 1847). In family letters, if not 'Crab' or 'Crabby' (see p. 66) he tended to be 'Mat.' (rather than Matt). 'K' could be strong-willed and could appear harsh, and the sister–brother relationship with Matt was to have its peaks and troughs. With the children, too, Thomas continued his revels, teaching them to bowl a hoop, to swim and to tend their garden patches as he had done at school. There were pranks as well, including early morning running around the house removing the bedclothes of the sleeping children. He set the syllabus for their governess and it included Italian. But when the children were intended to be serious, serious they had to be, just like Arnold's pupils. Arnold also spent time with Mary every day and visited the 'other house' of his mother, aunt and sister. From 1823 he also began to visit the poor people of the district, extending his curate's role further. This included a weekly prayer meeting with a homily at the workhouse. Together with Mary he visited the sick of the area. While all this was going on, after children and pupils were in bed, Arnold was working on a Lexicon of Thucydides. It took ten years and three volumes to complete. By 1822 he was also working on a history of Rome from Gracchi to Trajan. This was a series of articles, later published in book form. Arnold sent his drafts to critical referees and spent many hours in painstaking revision and checking on the basis of

6. Mrs Arnold, née Mary Penrose.
 — *from a contemporary painting*

their comments. He learned German in order to read German books on ancient history.

All this is a reflection of astonishing energy, even in a young and active man, and it is a record of a very full life. 'Tranquil' is, as has been suggested, exactly the wrong term to describe the Laleham time. But Arnold did take a break – rest would not be the right word – in the holidays, frequently visiting London, to see Coleridge, in particular, and Oxford to see Whately and Hawkins, or Sidmouth to see Cornish (who by 1839 had been elected to the Exeter Diocesan Board of Education) or the Lake District to meet Wordsworth again and to meet Southey for the first time. First visits were made to the West Country, to Yorkshire and Edinburgh. There were holiday visits to Fledborough and the Isle of Wight, France, Germany and to Italy several times. These visits were not always wonderful for Mary, who was often pregnant or nursing small babies. Sometimes he had to go alone. At home there was holiday gardening. The holidays were as active as the terms.

Arnold's mind was also maturing and developing in these Laleham years. His reading of history convinced him that humankind too infrequently learns the lessons of history; that the case for Church reform was even more urgent, that he longed to write about 'Christian Politics', the application of the gospel to humankind as citizens. He did not start the book, but he developed the ideas in his Laleham sermons. His preaching style was not formal and stylized, as was the convention then, but direct. He seemed to be preaching an impossible ideal, or was it revolution? It was a strong gospel for a village congregation. Some thought he was unsettling what they considered to be Christian belief. His approach to education was also becoming clearly defined. Mary records a conversation:

In talking of unbelief he said it was nothing but a love of

wickedness beginning in indifference – to the Bible and of course leading directly to a hatred to [*sic*] it & a wish to prove it untrue – as interfering with the practice of evil. He said that considerations of this kind made an awful thing to think of one's children as they advanced in life – and he said it was within the last three years he had been struck in almost all the books he saw with the want of Christian principle to be formed in them . . . There was only one thing with regard to his pupils that he could promise – & carefully endeavour to maintain, that they should never hear from him any sentiments but those of a Christian. (8.9.1825)

He also began to review his first efforts in history with the confidence of adult scholarship:

When he came up from his work he said he had been looking up his old Thucydides while below. I asked what he meant – and he said 'the translation w^h [which] he had made of some of it while at Winchester just before his election at Corpus, entirely for his own amusement with notes critical and historical and he was a good deal amused to find that a great many of his own notions were right – of how things are to be understood 'but there was this difference that then I timidly expressed my opinion that the Books were wrong about it – while now I should say confidently that which they said was nonsense.' (Mary, 20.3.1826)

Arnold was blissfully happy as the Laleham years passed, apart from one thing: money. He had chosen to limit pupil numbers in his house, but he had not chosen to limit the numbers of his own children. More pupils might alter the character of the school.

London University was newly opened (1827) and Arnold wrote to offer his services as professor of history. Many such posts were part-time and that was what he hoped to combine with Laleham.

Then came the event that altered his destiny. John Wooll, the head of Rugby School, announced his intention to resign after 21 years in post. In September 1827 Arnold received a letter from Hawkins urging him to apply for the vacancy. He turned it down. Although the money worries would be solved by such an appointment, he doubted 'how far I am fitted for the place of headmaster of a large school'. He added that he objected to a post which limited his freedom of action; more expulsions would be needed to tame public school abuses than school trustees would welcome:

> [they] regard quantity more than quality . . . Yet I could not consent to tolerate much that I know is tolerated generally, and, therefore, I should not like to enter on an office which I could not discharge according to my own views of what is right.

Here we see high principle, or unbending dogmatism, according to whose side one is on. What is clear is the finality of Arnold's refusal.

The move to Rugby

Whately did not accept this refusal and wrote an appeal to Arnold. Arnold, however, understood from other sources that the head was expected, although not legally required, both to be a priest and to possess a doctor's degree and he was only a deacon, without a doctor's degree. He was not prepared to consent in either case. Whately still did not accept this answer and was joined by Hawkins in further pleading. Arnold, who by allowing

the discussion to continue had perhaps revealed that his mind
was not entirely closed to the matter, allowed his name to go
forward four weeks after Whately's first appeal. He wrote to
Cornish words that were quoted against him by later opponents:

> I was strongly urged to stand, and *money tempted me* [my
> italics, but see p. 56], but I cannot in my heart be sorry to
> stay [Laleham] where M and I are so entirely happy. If I do
> get it, I feel as if I could set to work very heartily, and, with
> God's blessing, I should like to try whether my notions of
> Christian education are really impracticable . . . When I
> think about it thus, I long to take rod in hand: but when I
> think of the . . . perfect vileness I must daily contemplate
> . . . When I could no more bathe in the clear Thames, nor
> wear old coats and Russia duck trousers, nor hang on a
> gallows, nor climb a pole, I grieve to think of the possibility
> of a change; but as there are about thirty candidates, and I
> only applied very late, I think I need not disquiet myself.

There were actually over 50 applicants, including several people
in headship posts already. Seven, apart from Arnold, were
eventually to find a place in the *Dictionary of National Biography*.
Selection was on the basis of application and testimonials and,
collectively, the applicants offered about 1000 testimonials to
the school's twelve selectors. Interviews formed no part of the
process. Whately's intervention had helped Arnold earlier in his
career (see p. 36); it was now to be Hawkins, whose testimonial
as Provost of Oriel launched him into Rugby. If Arnold were
selected, Hawkins declared, he would change the face of education throughout the public schools of England. It was later seen
as prophetic. Arnold, whose experience must have made him an
outsider as a candidate, was offered the job, at £113 6s 8d per
annum plus £2 per pupil for every pupil within ten miles of

Rugby and a free house with the job which could serve as a boarding residence for up to 50 pupils, with associated boarding fee income. Arnold himself was told that the Hawkins reference or 'character' got him the job (letter to Hawkins, 28.12.1827, 'Sir H. Halford told me [it] had weighed most strongly in my favour'). But telling the news of their pending removal to the Arnold family in the other house at Laleham would not be easy. Nor was it entirely easy for Arnold himself, who wrote that he had been regarding Laleham as 'too much of a home'. Arnold's later critics were to make much of the phrase 'I long to take rod in hand' when this letter was published after his death. To them it was evidence of his sadistic tendency. It seems much more likely that the phrase was used merely to mean to take up the duties of a schoolteacher in the established biblical tradition of 'spare the rod and spoil the child'.

There were eight months ahead to prepare for the new post. A January 1828 visit to the school took place at the invitation of Dr John Wooll, the incumbent head, and the Arnolds travelled via Oxford, spending a night with the Whatelys. There was great curiosity in the school and the town but Mary was able to write to her invalid sister-in-law, Susanna, that the school seemed to be in decline and that everything in terms of the house and place was 'on a quieter and more moderate scale' than she had expected. It was not going to be too grand, or too great a transition and she added that they were 'most kindly received'. The kindness did not prevent her from collapsing on the way home and having to be left with the Whatelys to recover. It was the consequence of nerves and another pregnancy. The interest in the Arnolds within the town was more than curiosity as, with the local population of 2500, the school was by far the biggest employer and it was in the town's interest to acquire a head who would keep pupil numbers up. By March, Arnold had formulated an aim for the new work at Rugby:

a most sincere desire to make it a place of Christian education . . . to form Christian men, for Christian boys I can scarcely hope to make; I mean that from the natural imperfect state of boyhood, they are not susceptible of Christian principles in their full development . . . and I suspect that a low standard of morals in many respects must be tolerated amongst them. But I believe that a great deal may be done. (2.3.1828, from Laleham, Stanley, 1845, p. 88)

It was to be the Laleham experiment, re-run in a full school setting, and the unpromising setting of a public school of the time.

Arnold was still unsure about his status as a deacon and not a priest in full Anglican orders. He discussed this with John Wooll, presumably as he respected Wooll's understanding of the likely view to be taken of this by the trustees. Wooll took the view that the trustees would not interfere with what they would view as a matter of conscience. In any case, he might have added that Arnold's status as deacon had not prevented his appointment. But Arnold was wondering whether there might be an advantage to the school in his having the entitlement to administer the sacrament of communion in the school chapel. That would require ordination as a priest. It is strange that he was thinking of this as an issue, as the school had a chaplain who was licensed to do exactly that, but it is an early indication of Arnold developing his views of what he wanted his role as head of Rugby to become. Arnold critics later hinted that he would not wish to defer to someone his junior in every other respect in the public services in the school chapel. Whatever the deeper motives, Arnold chose now to consult William Howley, Bishop of London. He was rapidly reassured and ordained priest by Howley on 1 June 1828. By November he was also Doctor of Divinity, although, to Mary, calling him doctor sounded 'strange, almost ridiculous'.

Amazingly, not all the trustees had yet met Arnold in person, and he returned to Rugby with Buckland in early July to meet them and to inspect the building developments for his house. The trustees had listed in writing how the school was conducted and Arnold gave an immediate response that too much time was being spent on classical prose but that his intentions were 'not so violent as they seemed to imagine with regard to changes'. In fact, his views on curriculum were reassuringly conservative. Four meetings took place in which the trustees seemed to offer Arnold a free hand to develop the school, which must have reassured him about leaving Laleham, while reserving the right to dismiss him, an issue which was later to reappear. The next day – the last day of the school year – he sat in on the examination of the sixth form in the morning and met teaching staff in the afternoon. A final dinner with the trustees followed in which, embarrassingly, the venison was so bad as to be rejected from the table. Arnold returned home to Laleham to pack.

They left Laleham on 5 August 1828. Jane ('K') had a face 'quite swollen' by crying. Arnold visited every family in the small village to say goodbye; Mary's diary records that she was not strong enough to do this. They were all so upset at leaving the place and the 'other house' with their remaining family that they forgot to take Spot, the dog, who was restored to them by the local bricklayer, chasing the coach by another route, with Spot running beside his horse. Arnold arrived as head at Rugby School with his family by stagecoach in August 1828, his furniture having arrived in advance by the Grand Junction Canal. The journey to Oxford, the overnight changing point for the Rugby coach, took eight hours. They had booked the whole Leicester coach from Oxford to Rugby for the next day.

We left our beloved house this morning in Layton's coach, fourteen in number, i.e. Miss Rutland, ourselves, six children and three housemaids. George and Elizabeth. We started about a ¼ before nine, and at Hounslow we waited till the Oxford coach came.

Arnold wrote one of his final letters from Laleham to Tucker, that they had left the Laleham house 'sadly desolate; all the carpets up, half the furniture gone, and signs of removal everywhere visible. And so ends the first act of my life since I arrived at manhood.' The first day was fine but the second day saw rain. But the house and servants at Rugby were ready, so unpacking could begin at once. Within less than a week Arnold had interviewed each of the teachers individually and had surveyed the buildings, discussed the gardens and made laundry arrangements for the boys. Unpacking was largely completed. Term started three weeks later.

7. Rugby School, *circa* 1829.

The pre-Victorian years at Rugby, 1828–36

Arnold's work in education and theology are discussed in detail in Chapters 2 and 3 respectively. In what remains of this chapter, the emphasis will be on the life of Arnold and his family during the Rugby years, which were to end with his premature death in 1842. But although Arnold died before a number of his projects were complete, these are the significant years, the years of opportunity, to test out his ideas on education, the years of prophecy, to speak out about theology and the Church as he saw them, and the years of maturity, to refine his position both as a national figure and professor of modern history. Arnold was 33 when he took up his duties at Rugby. There were 116 boys on roll at the school and six assistant teachers when he started. The head was expected personally to teach the sixth form, which was common practice at that time.

Many public schools were a byword for disorder and the pupils were often only just contained by the severest of disciplinary measures. There was often an underworld of vicious bullying and illicit behaviour among pupils themselves. Abuse was a way of life in some schools, from teacher to pupil or from older pupil to younger pupil. Induction rituals into public school life could be a terrifying experience for boys newly taken from their family life at home. Boarding situations held the possibility of all sorts of abuse, including sexual, during the non-structured times of the week. The 'Rugby rebellions' were still within living memory in the town. These had taken place between 1770 and 1818, on at least two occasions requiring soldiers to quell them. In one example in 1797 the head, Henry Ingles, known to pupils as the 'Black Tiger', caught a boy firing a pistol at the windows of his housemaster. It was not a toy gun. The source of the gunpowder was traced to a local tradesman, Rowell, who had entered the purchase as 'tea' in his shop logbook. The boy was flogged and his friends smashed Rowell's windows in a rather illogical reprisal. Ingles decreed that the cost of this damage should be carried by the fourth and fifth forms collectively, demonstrating an example of the perennial truth that if teachers punish whole classes for the offences of some members, they will unite all the pupils, good and bad alike, against them. The pupils drew up a protest, declaring that they would not pay. Ingles threatened mass floggings in return. Their response was the use of a petard to blow up the door of the head's study (in his absence), then the following day to smash more windows and make a bonfire of desks and books. When a mixed force of special constables, farmers with horsewhips, a recruiting party of soldiers and local malcontent youths who fancied a scrap with the privileged boys of Rugby arrived on the scene, and the Riot Act was read by a magistrate, the revolting pupils retreated to the island in the 'Lake' in the school grounds. Here they were captured from the rear by the soldiers, who had to wade the moat to do it. Floggings and expulsions followed.

But Arnold's immediate predecessor John Wooll passed on a reasonably ordered school by contemporary standards after a tenure of headship from 1810 to 1827. Indeed, if flogging were to be seen as an indication of determination to create order, Wooll must be held to be at least satisfactory. On one notorious occasion he flogged an entire form of 38 boys in fifteen minutes, perhaps adding new meaning to the phrase 'strength to your arm'. On his arrival, Arnold immediately brought to the school 'an image of vehement righteousness' (Murray, 1996, p. 7). There is more than a hint of this in the firm jaw, the set eyes and the slightly wild hair in the 1839 portrait by Thomas Phillips (see cover). Arnold took headship very seriously as a high calling. But although he was never the sort of person to merge into the background, his beginnings at Rugby were not sensational. He was carefully taking the measure of the situation as it was at Rugby.

On the first Sunday of term he merely contented himself to check the register in Chapel and to note that the boys behaved well. They were perhaps also taking the measure of him. He wrote that this first official school occasion vividly brought back to his mind his own school days. The day after, Monday 1 September 1828, Arnold sat down on 'an undignified kitchen chair at the little table' in the Upper Bench room, not elevated at the common teacher's dais of the time, to teach the sixth form. Every lesson was to begin with the class and Arnold standing for prayer. A 'mesmeric look' (Wymer, 1953) around the class preceded, to see that all were suitably seriously inclined. This was to become the new standard start to Arnold's classes. On the second Sunday of term, he preached a short 'sermonet' of about fifteen minutes in chapel. Its manner was immediately impressive to pupils and a sign of things to come. In a letter to a newly appointed teacher he wrote what was to become a famous dictum: 'The qualifications which I deem essential to the due performance of a master's duties here, may in brief, be expressed as the spirit of a Christian and a gentleman' (Stanley, 1845, p. 107). How he tried to achieve his aims and to what extent he succeeded is the subject of Chapter 2. But by 1832 he had succeeded in creating a team sense among the staff and among the praepostors (prefects). They were 'right behind' him. The damaging gap between staff and head that can undermine so much of the work of a school did not exist at Rugby. But his feeling for boys remained a 'tough love', i.e. he seems to have genuinely cared for them, but this was not always known beyond the intimacy of the sixth form or some of the members of his boarding house or his occasionally emotional pleading in chapel. The Laleham practice of inviting pupils to tea with the family continued and *Tom Brown* provides a reverential account of the warmth of the welcome (1857, p. 152f). East declares 'how kind and gentle he was, the great grim man, whom I've feared more than anybody on earth' (ibid., p. 277). To others 'the Doctor' was to remain simply an awe-inspiring and distant figure, tinged with Old Testament qualities of wrath. As we shall see (p. 137f), his early years at Rugby had a definite element of purging about them.

While Arnold was settling himself into Rugby and Rugby was coping with his way of doing things, matters did not stand still in his family. Thomas ('Tom'), his son, was taken ill with a life-threatening liver complaint in Arnold's first term. While Mary and the governess took turns to sit up day and night with Tom, Arnold had to carry out his teaching duties. He wrote a prayer at this time which included the lines:

> Spare us the blow, if such Thy will –
> But if the bitter cup must fill –
> Teach us to drink and thank Thee still.

Tom recovered. Matt, even at six months, had been described by Arnold as 'backward and rather bad tempered'. Probably this latter trait came from Arnold himself. But Matt was also experiencing difficulty walking, requiring the wearing of leg irons for more than fifteen months and possibly accounting for the nickname 'Crab' or 'Crabby', a less cruel name in its contemporary culture context than it would be now. When these irons were abandoned at the age of four, both his legs were misshaped. It remained unclear, even then, whether the irons had helped or hindered his development. Both he and Tom began to develop a stutter. Arnold critics were to blame the overpowering paternal presence for this. There were other childhood scares: William fell into the fire but was saved by the prompt action of a servant. Matt fell off the sofa and caught a nasty gash on his head on the carved clawed feet of a nearby table. Later his arm received a very nasty phosphorous burn which threatened to become infected and could therefore have proved fatal. Baby Walter had a violent attack of 'inflammation' and had to be bled frequently. It left him 'much reduced'. All survived. Arnold was very conscious that the time might be short, writing in 1830: 'The deaths of my two brothers, who neither of them outlived my present age, ought to be sufficient to remind me that health, even in a far more robust frame than mine, is no security' (cited in Hamilton, 1998, p. 23). He had other reminders. Martha, Arnold's mother, became ill back at Laleham. Buckland, who had remained with the Laleham school establishment, summoned Arnold back in April 1829. He arrived too late. Martha died on 14 April, aged 78. Then in September Arnold had to rush with Mary to Fledborough, where her father, John Penrose, was seriously ill. A series of minor strokes had led to two major ones. The Arnolds arrived while he was still alive, but unconscious. The funeral was conducted by Keble. Then in August 1832 Susanna Arnold, his invalid sister, suddenly died, ending the many years of frailty and decline. It was a blow for Arnold:

> I never saw a more perfect instance of the spirit and power of love, and of a sound mind; intense love, almost to the annihilation of selfishness – a daily martyrdom for twenty years during which she . . . never talked about herself . . . inheriting the earth to the very fulness of the promise, though never leaving her crib, nor changing her posture. (6.9.1832, to Whately)

The simple tombstone reads: Susanna, third daughter of the late William Arnold Esq., of Slatwoods, Isle of Wight, April 4, 1787, August 22, 1832. Mary Arnold had herself, following a 'most virulent sore throat' given birth prematurely to a daughter, who lived just seven days (her tiny gravestone reading 'F. T. Arnold, May 1832'). The mother's life too had been at risk. This left Aunt Susan Delafield, who was herself now, 'decayed sadly in her mind', the sole survivor of the family group from 'the other house' at Laleham. Arnold regretted the passing of a portion of his life with these members of his family and was to note the very common human feeling in such situations that material possessions, 'pictures and china, and books, and candlesticks &c' from this period of his life, now took on a special significance with the people gone. Aunt Susan herself finally died in 1836, her eightieth year, joining the others (including the Arnold's baby daughter) in Laleham church yard, in a series of modest graves which were eventually to be faced by the grander ones of Matthew Arnold and his family. Thomas felt 'visibly brought into that generation whose time for departure comes the next'.

John Penrose left Mary £1800, a considerable sum of money for the time. Arnold could have appropriated this, as the Married Women's Property Act was not then on the statute book and husbands could lay hold of their wives' capital. But Arnold urged her to invest it as security in case he should die or become disabled and lose his own income.

Perhaps he felt surrounded by mortality after the spate of family deaths, for he took out a £5000 policy with Rock Insurance, a massive sum with a correspondingly high premium. He also made a will, with John Coleridge and Trevenen Penrose as executors and gave a private letter to Penrose 'To be opened after my death', which also suggested using his sermons and other writings as a basis for supplementary income for his dependants. He wished each member of the family to have something as a personal memento, regretting that he had had nothing like this from his own father. At this point his ambition was if, possible, to retire from Rugby in fifteen years' time (1844) at about the age of 50.

But if the early Rugby years saw family contraction in the older generation and Arnold's own generation with the death of his sister Susanna, they saw further family expansion in the generation below and the continuance of the family nicknames, with the birth of Susanna ('Babbat' or more fully 'Babbat Apbook') in 1830. Next came the short-lived daughter, whose birth in 1832 threatened Mary's life. Then came 'Fan' (family name 'Bonze', but full name Frances Bunsen Trevenen Whately Arnold) in 1833 and finally Walter ('Quid') in 1835. Mary could then rest; indeed her energies were so depleted that apart from a daily ride and helping Arnold in his regular visits to the poor of Rugby, Mary took no regular form of physical exercise. She had brought nine children into the world. She did seem to respond well to homeopathy, however. They enjoyed the 'pony walks' and talk together, Arnold striding ahead, leading the white pony on which Mary sat.

The education of his own children now began to occupy Arnold's thoughts more. He drew up their syllabus personally. For the older ones it included arithmetic, French, geography, German, Greek, history, Italian, Latin and scripture. It was a more modern curriculum than was allowed to the boys at the school. By the time they could walk, the children were expected to partake of some of this programme. A governess carried out the actual teaching, which also included learning a Bible passage and all or part of a hymn each day. Arnold tested his children on Sunday evenings and rewarded good results with small toys he knew they wanted. But with his own children and with the Rugby boys, Arnold had lost none of the playful side of his nature. Clad in his oldest clothes, tattered and disreputable as they were, he still indulged in walking, riding, gardening, swimming – often with 'K' at a favourite place in the river that they called Roly Poly – and playing cricket. He was known to shin up the elms in the Close at the school and his regular practice of running up the 'corkscrew', i.e. circular, staircase to his classroom was quickly established. If the door were kept open the assembled sixth form would hear him coming. He believed these various exercises helped his appetite, relaxed him after school work and

8. Thomas Arnold shortly after his marriage to Mary Penrose.
— *from a contemporary painting*

ensured a good night's sleep. Many years later, Tom Arnold (junior) recalled his father within the family:

> Stern though his look could be – and often had to be – there was a vein of drollery in him, a spirit of pure fun, which perhaps came from his Suffolk ancestry. He was not witty, nor – though he could appreciate humour – was he humorous; but the comic and grotesque side of human life attracted him strongly . . . In a sense we were afraid of him; that is, we were very much afraid, if we did wrong, of being found out and punished, and still worse, of witnessing the frown gather on his brow. Yet in all of us on the whole love cast out fear; for he never held us at a distance, was never impatient with us, always, we knew, was trying to make us good and happy. (in Bamford, 1960, p. 209)

For Hamilton (1998) Arnold had facetiousness but not humour. But Arnold had to begin to look beyond the stage of home education for his children with a governess. He was nervous about exposing his own children to the potential evils of boarding school life although he thought that 'the trials of a school are useful to a boy's after character' and so Matt was sent in 1831 at the age of nine to Buckland at Laleham. It had the advantage of small pupil numbers and provided a setting which Arnold knew well and a tutor of whom Arnold strongly approved. It was a reciprocal arrangement: John Buckland was enrolled at Rugby in 1832 and his brother Matthew followed in 1836. But Matt Arnold did not prosper at Laleham and came across as neither clever nor hard-working. K wrote of it as 'a really bad and injurious school' and Matt felt confined by the 'detestable little gravel playground, which we never left except on Sundays'. Arnold's early letters to Matt at Laleham show a kind but unyielding sympathy with his difficulties:

I am sorry, my own Crabby, that you are in trouble about your Greek Grammar – it puts me very much in mind of my own trouble when I was first put into Phaedrus. You cannot think how many impositions I got, and how many hard knocks – but still the end was that I learned Phaedrus, and so the end will be that you will learn your Greek Grammar . . . Work away, Crabby, and do your best, and be my own true Boy, and I shall always love you very dearly. (Hamilton, 1998, p. 19)

E— *takes out of his Pocket his Bread and Meat and* M— *her Bread and Cheese, and* S— *ditto . . .*

9. Edward, Mary and Susanna, three of Dr Arnold's children, picnicking on Fairfield in the Lake District.
— *from a sketch by Jane Arnold, the doctor's eldest daughter*

The other Day upon the Ice
Once or twice or even thrice
She tumbled, up again she got
Steady footed she is not.

10. The Arnold children skating on Rydal Water near Dr Arnold's holiday
home of Fox How, in the Lake District. Mary Arnold falls.
— *from a sketch by Jane Arnold*

It still did not work out, even though Matt was praised as 'a grand
Crab' for his progress in poetry. Buckland was glad to return
Matt home to Arnold in 1833 where, with Tom, he was taught
by a private tutor. This 'temporary' arrangement was to last for
more than a year, until the two boys were sent together to Winchester on the last day of August 1836. Arnold was as nervous as
they were and composed a special prayer for the occasion of their
leaving. He had some idea of what lay ahead for them. Matt
wrote a poem about his departure. It is astonishingly redolent of
the mood of his later matured writing:

73

One step in life is taken
And we must hurry on
And cheer our onward path as best we may.
And if a moment's space we stay
The world around seems all forsaken
And we – deserted and alone . . .

Do Thou, O Lord, be present still!
And aye direct us with Thy guiding hand
That as we labour up life's toilsome hill,
Or with a slower step descend – we may be found
Mid all the storms that shake the world around
Not to have built our Temple on the sand.

The poet was fourteen years old. Winchester did not work out well. Thomas Arnold worried about the problems of supervising 130 boys there in one house and the mutually corrupting influence of boys. He continued to worry that boarding education could weaken the ties with one's family, replacing love with more distant respect. Within a year, Matt and Tom returned to Rugby, this time as pupils. They could now live at home. Edward Penrose Arnold ('Didu') and William Delafield Arnold ('Widu') were to follow their brothers into Rugby School in 1838 and 1839. For Jane, 'K', there were no possibilities of extending her education. But she had been a good pupil at home:

> When Jane was young, I used to teach her some Latin with her brothers and that has been, I think of real use to her, and she feels it now in reading and translating German, of which she does a good deal. (letter to Hartley Coleridge, 2.1.1841)

Another letter from Fox How, undated, provides a window into

Arnold family life. It was not printed by Stanley because Arnold's wishes at the end had not been realized:

> Jane's mind between 13 and 14 is opening fast . . . & I think she is labouring to make God the centre of her world; the boys are of concern . . . this I suppose will be so, but I trust that they show a fair promise of good hereafter; their intellects are very good & active & they are loving and obedient – but their great Trials are to come. . . . Mary is not good at her book, to use a good old phrase, but she is loving & generous & mirthful as a bird. Little Susy at four years & a half is every one's darling – meek and obedient, & so lively and strong and active; & the little Baby is beginning to walk alone . . . I feel as if I could wish never to go out of the valley any more – but to live between Winandermere [*sic*] & Grasmere till my bones went to Grasmere's churchyard, to lie under the yews which Wordsworth planted there, & to have the Rother with its deep & silent pools passing by – yet I know well that life is not given us for such dreams, & I feel no [helplessness? Writing unclear] in my occupations, & no despondency though neither have I any sanguine hopes of doing good.

Arnold knew the extreme practical difficulty of providing intellectual education for girls but he supported it strongly in principle as the degree examination 'concentrates one's reading so beautifully'.

While Arnold was busy teaching and running the school, organizing and overseeing his family, indulging in national controversy about theology, planning sermons, counselling pupils, writing to former pupils ('one of the freshest springs of my life'), corresponding with parents, meeting former Oxford friends, coaching recent pupils for Oxford entrance, one might have thought that his time was fully committed. But this was not the case. He took a personal interest in the circumstances in which their servants lived, even to inspecting their rented rooms in inns and intervening to get them a better deal if necessary. He and Mary visited the elderly and sick in the town. He tried to establish and then continued to raise funds for a dispensary for free medicines for the poor in Rugby. There was a newspaper venture, after the style of Cobbett, *The Englishman's Register*. It quickly collapsed, but not before the editor of the *Sheffield Courant* had spotted the journalistic talent of Arnold, as someone who saw and felt the effects of a rapidly industrializing society. He was engaged to write for the *Courant*.

The foreign holidays continued: France, Germany, Italy. 'K' was taken to the Isle of Wight to see Slatwoods, her grandparents' former home. In the summer of 1831 they did a Grand Tour of Britain with four of the children, Bacco, 'K', Crab and Prawn, which took in Derbyshire, Yorkshire, County Durham, Northumberland, Holy Island, Edinburgh and Perthshire, returning via their beloved Lakes and a visit to the Wordsworths. The Wordsworths and the Arnolds got on well, walking, dining and discussing with each other. The Lakes also became a venue for Christmas holidays. By 1833 the Arnolds were so much in love with the area that they decided to buy a holiday home there as a retreat from Rugby. That Arnold needed a retreat from the job, but also the place, was clear in a letter to Whately:

> We have no hills – no plains – not a single wood, and but one single copse: no heath – no down – no rock – no river – no clear stream – scarcely any flowers . . . nothing but one endless monotony of inclosed [*sic*] fields and hedgerow trees. This is to me a daily privation; it robs me of what is naturally my anti-attrition . . . the positive dulness of the

country about Rugby makes it to me a mere working place. (1.2.1833)

This may not have been entirely fair to the Rugby area – 'there is nothing fine between us and the Ural mountains' – and it was written during the March controversy (see pp. 139ff), but it is clearly how Arnold felt about it at that time. He had enjoyed walking in its meadows when he was newly appointed but in later time he was to lament the stripping out of 'many an old wild and tangled hedge' and their replacement by a 'cut and stiff fence of stakes'. Wordsworth recommended Fox How, above Ambleside, on the Rydal valley, as the base for buying land on which to build the house of retreat, a quarter of an hour's walk from his own house at Rydal Mount. Arnold bought the estate and Wordsworth agreed to keep an eye on the builders in Arnold's absence at Rugby. It was a site with stunning views, near the River Rothay.

In the spring of 1834, the house 'Fox How' was complete and the first family visit took place during that summer holiday. Dorothy Wordsworth arrived with a rug she had made as a house warming present. There were six bedrooms plus two for staff, large public rooms including a schoolroom for the children and a very spacious study for Arnold. Five acres were turned into a garden. The holidays were active times with the children for Arnold: sailing boats on the tarn, climbing, walking, ice-sliding in winter, shooting snipe, gardening, running, swimming, picnics. Indoors were debates, charades and acting. Praepostors and teachers from Rugby were occasional guests. But Arnold never inspired over-familiarity; Clough could not imagine 'anyone calling "the Dr" Tom, even at Fox How' (letter, 8.8.1836). There were written house rules for the 'Dogs' [children], including:

1. That all Dogs do strictly observe hours: to wit, that they be downstairs to breakfast by ½ past 8 o'clock, and in to dinner

11. Two views of Fox How today.

by 5 o'clock, and in the house to tea at 8 o'clock, not to go out again.

2. That Dogs Didu [Edward] and Widu [William] do not fish, nor go out rowing or sailing without a man, nor go on walks without the elder Dogs . . .

4. That all Dogs bear themselves reverently and discreetly towards Dog K [Jane] – not barking, biting or otherwise molesting her, under pain of heavy judicum with many smites.

'K' remembered these as happy days, 'Pappy' reading family prayers, daily (holiday) lessons from 10 till 12, errands, walks to Ambleside to collect the post, cross-country rambles, the fun and family games, the table 'crammed till it can cram no more', and finally sinking happy and exhausted into bed at night. There was even a *Fox How Magazine*. Arnold looked forward to retirement to Fox How, 'if I live', although he worried about what would become of 'poor little Walter' if he retired before his schooling was complete. 'Pappy' felt some guilt about the paradise at Fox How 'in these most troublous times, it seems more than is allowable to be living, as we are here, in a place of so much rest and beauty'. He hoped that the sense of natural beauty would not eclipse the sense of moral evil. But Arnold found the mountains spiritually inspiring, like the Psalmist:

> I often used to think of the solemn comparison in the Psalm 'the hills stand round about Jerusalem; even so standeth the Lord about his people'. The girdling in of the mountains round the valley of our home is as apt an image as any earthly thing can be of the encircling of the everlasting arms, keeping off evil and showering all good. (Willey, 1949, p. 80)

Arnold loved to 'lift up mine eyes unto the hills, from whence shall come my help' (Psalms 121). But the affection for Fox How and the pleasures of gardening – Arnold threw himself into mowing the considerable lawns – did not prevent travel further afield. A letter of 1835 notes that it was unusual for the Arnolds to spend as long as two weeks of the holidays in Rugby. This unusual holiday fortnight at Rugby was partly to enable Arnold to keep up his holiday reading programme in the mornings. In 1837 the Isle of Man and Ireland were added to the Arnold list of places visited.

But life was not all family fun, reading and Rugby. Arnold had become known well beyond the confines of the school and the town. In 1829 the first volume of his sermons appeared in print, followed in 1830 by the Thucydides lexicon. The sermons went into a second edition in 1830, although that did not stop the loyal 'K' from buying copies for her siblings in an effort to boost 'Pappy's' royalties. He started his Roman history, which was eventually to run to three volumes. He was aided by a good reading speed and the appearance in his dreams of some of the scenes which he was researching, an unusual talent in a historian, although necessarily subjective (see p. 148). It helped his talent in writing and especially in the classroom for bringing history to life. He 'saw' the death of Julius Caesar, the destruction of Jerusalem in AD 70 and other ancient history scenes in this way. Mary records a conversation about writing:

> He asked what I should like him to undertake [when his history was completed]. I mentioned ecclesiastical history but he seemed to think it would be too great a work – & to doubt to be able to render it useful . . . I said I should have particular pleasure in putting by for our Children's use what he had gained by his evening toil – he said that it would not be much, but still it was something to think that it was formed between the hours of nine and ten . . . He

said he should like to make a recipe for a good mind just as you would for a plum pudding – of the different ingredients. & how to proportion the quantities. Of course it would differ in some degree according to the subject – but still a good deal might be alike for all . . . 9 tenths of a man's reading, or somewhere about that proportion, should be in works relating to particular facts – & the other tenth in works of the very highest philosophy in which he included the highest sort of Poetry – among writers in this class he mentioned Aristotle, Plato – Bacon – some of the best parts of Johnson – & Pascal – Happily he said there were a good many from whom to select but the numbers must be few when compared to the other class & for this plain reason that any Tom Noddy might write a Book which might give you useful knowledge about some particular facts while he could never write poetry or philosophy – it was a clear waste of time to be reading niggling essays on issues. (12.10.1825)

By 1835 more sermons had appeared, Thucydides was in its third edition and the Roman history was in progress; the first volume appeared in 1838. He set himself to learn Hebrew in 1835. All these were uncontentious, but his writing on religion was combative and strong. It will be discussed in more detail in Chapter 3. But a brief summary is needed here to explain Arnold's persona beyond the walls of Rugby at this time.

In 1828 Arnold had written a pamphlet, *The Christian Duty of Conceding the Roman Catholic Claims*, in defence of Catholic emancipation from the old legal disabilities against them. He viewed the Church of Rome as far from incorrupt, but was motivated by the feeling that 'to do national injustice is a *sin*, and that the clergy, whilst they urge the continuance of this injustice, are making themselves individually guilty of it' (letter to J. Lowe,

16.3.1829, his italics). It produced outrage. 'Yet I know I did not write it with one atom of unkindness or violence of feeling . . . and what I said of the clergy I said in the very simplicity of my heart' (letter to Cornish, 2.9.1829). It may have cost him the Archbishopric of Dublin and all further advancement in the Church of England. He was offered a non-residentiary canonry at Bristol Cathedral in 1831 at £600 a year, but declined it on dual grounds that the distance from Rugby meant that he could not officiate there and that in any case it would be a bad example when he was stopping his Rugby teachers from combining their work with local curacies. Even with the short-lived *Englishman's Register* (1831) Arnold could write that he had 'got a gallows at last, and am quite happy', i.e. he knew it would come under public attack. In another letter he says 'it will be a pecuniary loss, it will bring me no credit, but much trouble and probably some abuse, and some of my friends look on it not only coldly, but with aversion' (2.5.1831, to W. W. Hull). His anonymous pieces in the *Sheffield Courant*, which also reproduced for a wider audience some of his pieces in the *Register*, were politically disturbing to many. In these he attacked the labelling of factory workers as 'hands' as symbolic of their value to the owners. 'Their hands are attached to certain mouths and bodies which must be fed and lodged . . . as cheaply as possible.' This led to the creation of slums. He lamented that no one cared for the 'heads and hearts' of the 'hands', neither employers nor government. Tories, politicians in general, 'half-heathen clubs . . . utterly unlawful for a Christian man . . . close brotherhoods' such as Freemasonry; friendly societies; the state of the Church of England and its clergy as a real 'stumbling block in the advancement of Christianity', all these came under the sharp attack of Arnold's pen.

In *The Principles of Church Reform* (1833) he pressed the case harder. Mary Arnold urged him to tone down his writing. It made him enemies among those who did not know him. It also cost him friendships. Keble had been viewed as launching the Oxford Movement in his Assize Sermon of 1833. Arnold attacked the Oxford Movement repeatedly in a whole series of private and public writing reaching its climax in 'The Oxford Malignants', an anonymous article in the *Edinburgh Review*. The title was not his, but it expressed his sentiments perfectly. They were cast as formalizing, Judaizing fanatics, 'ever the peculiar disgrace of the Church of England'. His authorship became an open secret which nearly cost him his job. Even his friends were uneasy. Cornish thought his views on Catholicism arrogant. Coleridge thought the *Sheffield Courant* pieces did not become the head of a major school and advised Arnold to avoid acrimony and get on with his real job, running a school. Hawkins thought the pamphlet on church reform had been dashed off without proper consideration. Arnold was hurt by both the latter comments. He felt that his views were deeply and carefully considered and that his writing did not interfere with his job. He wrote to Coleridge that 'I can truly say that I live for the school.' 'I claim a full right to use my own discretion in writing upon any subject I choose, provided I do not neglect my duties as master in order to find time for it' (letter to Hawkins, 29.5.1829). This contrasts with Arnold's slightly milder position a year earlier when Rugby lay in the future:

> I owe it to Rugby not to excite needless scandal by an isolated and uncalled-for publication . . . When I am fully decided on a matter of consequence I would speak out as plainly and boldly as your heart could wish. (letter to W. W. Hull, 29.7.1828)

He could not stop himself writing and campaigning, however, as he revealed to Susanna: 'The paramount interest of public affairs outweighs with me even the school itself . . . I must write a pamphlet [about the cause of the poor] in the holidays, or I shall burst' (November 1830).

There was also writing addressed more locally: a *Tract on the Cholera* for the inhabitants of Rugby (1831) in which Arnold, in common with many thinking people of his time, exercised a lay interest in public health matters and in the cause of better sanitation, as Patrick Brontë and other clergy did in their own localities. Cholera had reached Newbold, a village two miles from Rugby and Arnold closed the school term early, as a precautionary measure. But in 1832 Arnold convened a meeting at the *Spread Eagle* to celebrate the passing of the Reform Bill and make arrangements for a celebratory public dinner, a common nineteenth-century institution to mark major events such as the later arrival of a railway. This meeting led to a letter to the press criticizing the political stance of the head of a prestigious school.

Unfortunately for Arnold, and fortunately for his critics, an incident then took place for which Arnold alone can be held fully responsible, but it made him very vulnerable in the outside world. In 1833 he flogged a fourteen-year-old boy called Thomas March for what on the surface was a very minor offence, the inability to pass an oral test on a piece of 'prep'. To make matters worse, the boy was physically weak (his ailments included a hernia), the flogging was severe even by standards of the time and he was absolutely innocent of the offence of which he had been accused, as he had repeatedly emphasized to Arnold before the beating (for a full discussion of this case, see pp. 139ff). That was ammunition for the Tory *Northampton Herald*, which attacked Arnold from then on, using every chance to campaign against him, including the raising of the school fees at Rugby in 1834. Other newspapers began to sense that there were newsworthy doings at Rugby.

The newspapers were able to continue their campaign of vilification when Arnold found himself in the glare of publicity again when the regular occasional custom of mass trespass and catching of fish by boys at the river, which had grown to their using drag nets and making massive hauls, came to a head when a gamekeeper failed to apprehend seven boys, fell into the river and was brought directly by his employer, Boughton Leigh, to the school to demand instant retribution. Arnold's examination of the sixth form revealed that no one knew or was willing to name the offenders. He used an identity parade to reveal them. Only six were identified and they were immediately expelled. The school was in uproar. The boys held that they had 'rights' to fish that had been allowed or at least unchallenged for generations. The fifth and sixth forms met together in a very ugly mood to discuss what was to be done. This time 'the Doctor' had gone too far. A 'right' which was theirs by custom and tradition had been removed, etc. It gave Arnold's enemies in the school a chance for agitation. Another Rugby school rebellion was a real possibility. Only appeals by three of Arnold's best supporters in the sixth – Stanley, Vaughan and Lake – turned the tide – but only just. Arnold, however, saw no matter for discussion, concession or conciliation and stood before the whole school and said: 'It is not necessary that this should be a school of three hundred, or one hundred, or of fifty boys, but it *is* necessary that it should be a school of Christian gentlemen.' *The Times* reported the affair. Arnold was a national figure.

Then came controversy at the Rugby reading room. The cost of newspapers (about 7d in the then penny currency) made them beyond the pocket of aspiring working-class readers, so many new towns provided reading rooms and took out subscriptions to leading newspapers. The violent mutual denunciation of Tories and Whigs in these newspapers offered entertainment as well as, occasionally, education. It was natural for Arnold, as the local headteacher, to be on the committee that selected the newspapers. When *John Bull,* a strong Tory newspaper that attacked Arnold and had very recently attacked Whately, disappeared from the subscription list of the Rugby reading room, questions were asked why. In 1835 Arnold proposed that the *Northampton Herald* should also be banned. The Tories opposed the ban and told Arnold to sue the paper if he objected to what it published about him. But eight of them walked out of the committee meeting in protest at what they called the violence of Arnold's language on the subject. This left Arnold, seven of his staff, his doctor, the Rector and Arnold's friend William Wratislaw, a local solicitor. The matter was put to a vote among these remaining members of the committee and the *Northampton Herald* was duly banned. Even the Whig *Northampton Mercury* was uneasy about the way in which its rival had been disposed of. *The Times*, which had yet to get past Arnold's censorious eye, recorded that 'this blundering Arnold takes everything out of season'. The Rugby Tories finally resorted to opening a rival reading room.

Then Arnold made a two-day journey from the Lakes to Rugby in 1835 to vote publicly for the Radical candidate for Parliament, a Captain Gregory, rather than the Whig or the Tory. The Radical's platform had a ready appeal to Arnold: reform of church and state. Gregory wanted bishops removed from the House of Lords, something Arnold did not support (see p. 209). The Tory candidate was a son of one of the Rugby School trustees and the father of a Rugby pupil, so although Arnold's vote was a statement of principle, it was hardly tactful, as secret ballots had not yet arrived. It was more ammunition to *John Bull*, which argued that Rugby parents should ask:

> Am I performing the part of a father in exposing my son to the fascination of such talent as Dr. Arnold possesses, when I know he will be taught the language of heresy and be

nurtured up in the cradle of Radical Reform?
(Bamford, 1960, p. 76)

The *Northampton Herald* pitched in with warnings about 'the plastic mind of youth' becoming 'biased in faith and politics' and that Radicals should be 'dreaded and denounced as instructors of our children'. The attack moved to an attempt to prevent Arnold from voting at all in Rugby, on the grounds that he was not a freehold property owner there, but occupied a house owned by the school. His only defence was that Wooll had voted before him and so there was precedent and custom for the practice, but Arnold's case was not upheld and his name was removed from the register of voters.

Speech Day 1835 provided more problems for Arnold, this time from Tory Old Boys and supporters of the school, led by Boughton Leigh. In such situations former pupils often feel loyalty to the head under whom they studied and many of these were Wooll's former pupils, not Arnold's. Leigh, the outraged landowner in the fishing dispute and the leader of the Tory group involved in the reading room protest, had plenty of reason to dislike Arnold. At the dinner at the *Spread Eagle* that followed speech day, Leigh objected, surprisingly, to the Loyal Toast (to the king) on the grounds that if it could be made by Radicals (he meant Arnold), all of whom were presumed to be republicans, the toast had become meaningless. Leigh skilfully proposed a new toast: Church and King, to express loyal support to both in their present, i.e. unreformed, state. It was intended to place Arnold as an ordained clergyman in the Church of England in the public position of denying monarch and Church or appearing to concede Tory claims. Arnold's supporters recognized what lay at the heart of this proposal and shouts of 'No insult to the Doctor' were quickly parried by shouts of 'No insult to the King'. It seemed as if the whole formal dinner would break up and that even violence might occur, until Macaulay, a Rugbeian, who was the head of Repton School, called out in a loud voice a toast to the Queen. This was impossible to ignore. The act of the whole gathering rising and the respectful silence surrounding this uncontentious toast had a calming effect. Litchfield (see p. 142) was sorry that Rugbeians could not offer the trustees the same congratulations for Arnold's religious principle as they could on his moral virtue, private character and classical achievements. Leigh agreed to drink to Arnold's health 'as a private individual, but not as the instructor of Rugby school'.

A new institution in the Rugby calendar, a Founder's Day dinner, was held in October after the Easter speech day rumpus. The impetus seems to have come from Arnold's opponents and it was a matter of speculation as to whether he would attend. Not to do so could be construed as disrespectful to the heritage and tradition of the school. To attend could provide another opportunity for a public attack on him. Once again the *Spread Eagle* was to be the venue. Arnold did appear, but only eight or nine other guests turned up. *The Times* ascribed the low turn-out to Arnold's presence at the event. It was possibly right. A letter to the *Northampton Herald* stated that 'more than a hundred would have attended if it had pleased the autocrat to have remained at home' (14.12.1835). Arnold did not attend another public dinner at the *Spread Eagle* again.

John Bull then picked up the case of another expulsion. It was claimed that two praepostors had held a junior boy against a wall, banging his head, after which a third beat him savagely with a large knotted blackthorn stick, yet it was the junior boy who was expelled. Was this the right way to run a school? Was Arnold backing a gang of bully boys against the weaker ones in order to impose his authority? The incident was not as simple as presented (see pp. 143ff for a fuller account) but it contained sufficient examples of lack of judgment in the matter on Arnold's part to fuel his enemies, especially when he refused even to discuss the matter with the expelled boy's father. While this case was going on, the trustees took the unusual step of issuing a statement. It was not framed with this particular case in view, but it did affect the subsequent appeal (p. 144). Granted the various controversies in which their head was engaged, it is a remarkable statement of support:

> We, the undersigned Trustees . . . are glad to have an opportunity of expressing our entire satisfaction with Dr. Arnold's management of the School. Many of the young men who have proceeded to the universities from Rugby School have distinguished themselves, and done honour to Dr. Arnold's system of education; and we believe that the discipline of the School has been conducted upon most humane and liberal principles, and on this conviction we continue to repose entire confidence in Dr. Arnold. (23.3.1836)

The *Northampton Herald* then returned to the attack with a piece on 'Dr Arnold's Revolutionary Prize Books'. Arnold chose and presented these prizes at his own expense, but he had included one about the French Revolution of 1830. Tory fears about a repetition or glorification of the Terror were easy to revive. Journalists scouring for anti-Arnold ammunition read the book. It contained a passage about a child of twelve shooting dead a soldier and telling a later investigation that he (the soldier) had insulted him and that either he or the child should die. Children shooting their elders! This was in a presentation school prize, personally selected by the headteacher. Arnold retorted that the matter was one of history, not morality. Bad incidents could equally be found in Cicero or the Bible. The *Northampton Herald* followed with an attack of which this was part:

Not thy angry resolve – nor thy changing decrees
Not thy toadying serfs – nor thy trembling trustees
Nor thy rod clotted thick with an innocent's gore [March]
Nor thy letters that pierce parents hearts to the core
Not expulsions of children too youthful to reason
Nor thy Prize-books explaining the beauties of treason . . .
Not thy pen dipped in gall, which gave Satan his cue
Though it lost thee a mitre, in *Scotland's Review* . . .
(25.11.1837, Bamford, 1960, p. 125)

Arnold took legal advice from Coleridge about whether to sue the newspapers for libel, but Coleridge's view was that as a clergyman he should not take action in a court. Arnold conceded to Hawkins that it would be 'better to bear it' than go to court. The 1836 speech day dinner had by now arrived again. The *Spread Eagle* had changed hands, to a supporter of the *Northampton Herald*, but Arnold had already decided to hold the official meal at the school. Arnold's supporters were eager to attend the school dinner but his opponents decided to adjourn after the speeches to their own dinner at the *Spread Eagle*. There was therefore no confrontation of the sort that had earlier occurred, although two separate dinners for the head's supporters and opponents were hardly an edifying spectacle for him or the school. The separate dinners were to continue. Bamford (1960) argues that at this point the press campaign against Arnold had run out of steam. If so, Arnold was about to give it its best weapon so far.

It was Arnold's involvement in the Hampden case that led to a vote of censure against him instigated by Earl Howe in a private meeting of the school's trustees. Prime Minister Lord Melbourne (Whig) wished to promote Whig clergymen to bishops. But there were only two possible people from Oxford: Arnold himself and Renn Hampden, then Principal of St Mary Hall. Arnold was suspect as a 'loose cannon' who would give ammunition galore to the Tories, although Melbourne kept him in mind until 1835. Hampden, 'an ugly, stolid, dull man with a heavy manner and a harsh voice' (Chadwick, 1971, I, p. 113) was therefore the only possible bishop. But before he could be promoted, the death occurred of the Regius Professor of Divinity at Oxford. Archbishop Howley sent Melbourne a list of five candidates, on which Hampden's name did not appear (see pp. 215ff for a fuller discussion of this affair). Archbishop Whately and Bishop Copleston (both Whig sympathizers and fellow Noetics of the Oriel common room) lobbied for Hampden, so Melbourne wrote to offer him the Chair. Newman, Pusey, Keble and Golightly opposed Hampden on grounds of heresy. Chairs of Divinity could then legitimately be subject to these challenges. Petitions were raised against him. It was not publicly known that the king had already approved the appointment. When it did go public, the opposition continued unabated. At last Arnold pitched in with 'the Oxford Malignants', a blistering attack on all the 'Newmanites'. The Tory press copied extracts as evidence that Arnold was unsuited to a bishopric. This is why Earl Howe tried to remove him from Rugby. The statutes of government of the school meant that he could have been removed without any legal right to defend his position. The trustees meeting was leaked to Arnold by one of his supporters; he had not been told of it, still less invited to attend. Arnold had three times refused in writing to tell Howe if he were the author of 'The Oxford Malignants': 'I cannot and do not acknowledge your right officially, as a trustee of Rugby School, to question me on the subject of my real or supposed writings on matters wholly unconnected with the school' (27.6.1836). The trustees split 4–4 but as their constitution allowed for no casting vote, the matter had to be dropped. Despite this, Arnold was very settled at Rugby and could record that in their dealings with him, the trustees were 'as civil as usual'. They must have been torn. He was raising pupil numbers, income and the school's national profile, but not always for the good. At times he seemed to thrive on controversy. He would have liked to be Bishop of Oxford (letter to Whately, 16.5.1835) but was very happy at Rugby, except that he wished to devote more time to writing:

> I have got a very effective position here, which I would only quit for one which seems even more effective; but I keep one great place of education sound and free, and unavoidably gain an influence with many young men, and endeavour to make them see that they ought to think on and understand a subject before they take up a party view about it . . . I think my love of tuition rather grows on me.

Arnold also acquired a high profile in the new London University. He accepted a seat on its senate (1836) with alacrity. He quickly proposed that a study of one of the gospels or epistles of the New Testament in the original Greek should be a compulsory part of the course for every candidate in Arts. He was clear that this was part of the complete and liberal education which an Arts graduate should have and that in a Christian country a liberal education without an element of the Scriptures must necessarily be incomplete. But the other senators saw this as too much like the tests that they prided themselves on London having abjured (it was planned to cater for Jews and atheists as well as Christians) so his proposal was defeated, although an optional study in the field became the precursor of the AKC (Associate of King's College) and other certificates. Arnold resigned over the matter in 1838. Clough wrote to J. P. Gell that Arnold's stance must have seemed 'a great novelty in that godless place . . . It must have been a very grand thing to see him get up among all those people and declare that they must do something to show that they were Christians and that it was a Christian University.' (15.1.1836). But Arnold's tone and the content of much of what he said made him appear to those outside Rugby a vitriolic, even dangerous, influence on youth and his clarion call for church reform almost certainly lost him a bishopric. Yet he neither entirely fitted the label conservative or radical. Arnold was at times a radical conservative; at others he seemed a conservative radical. He was not a party man. Nor, as his opponents feared, was he deliberately abusing his position in the school to propagate his controversial views among the boys. At the same time, those boys who greatly admired him were bound to be sympathetic to his views. It is easy to see how his enemies could assume that he was proselytizing.

The final Rugby years, 1837–42

The winter of 1836–37 was the most savage on record since 1799 and, before that, of 1658. The family stayed at Fox How for the Christmas holiday, but, surprisingly, experienced no snow or rain, nor were they victim to the local influenza outbreak. Arnold wrote that 'greater peace and happiness' would have been impossible to enjoy than this break. It was a refuge from the controversies in which he was involved. In the middle of Long Half, April 1837, his spirits were low; in a letter he described himself as sad and dull. By December he was showing evidence of having modified his political views, writing that the last six years had taught him what Roman history should have taught him before, that when an aristocracy is not totally corrupt, its strength is 'incalculable' and survives political change. This means that the 'great amount of liberty and good government enjoyed in England is the security of the aristocracy'. He dared to voice this in *The Courant*: 'I say plainly – and I beg not to be cried down unheard – that this great means of blessing are the Aristocracy and the Christian Church.' But it was perhaps a sign of the non-party aspect of Arnold's position. At the same time he could write with some support for Chartism, that the real evil which lay at the basis of their agitation was

> too deep for any human remedy, unless the nation were possessed with a spirit of wisdom and of goodness, such as I fear will never be granted to us after we have for so many centuries neglected the means which we have had. (letter, 10.5.1839)

In 1839–41 he wrote a series for the *Hertford Reformer* on Chartism and on Church and State. But he did not support the Chartist solution.

Thus, 1838 was in many ways a watershed year. It marked a decade of his rule at Rugby. There was a crop of academic successes at Oxford and Cambridge by Rugbeians, which was to be sustained over the following years. And 1838 also saw the publication of his *History of Rome*, maintaining his presence in the field of scholarship. There was also a concern about health, or at least an unwillingness to take it for granted. The Rome Preface records Arnold's intention 'if God spares my life and health' to continue the history up to AD 800 (1838, p. viii). The railway arrived at Rugby in September 1838. Boys could now enrol from further afield. A three-term year, with shorter terms than Long Half and Short Half could now be contemplated as a result of easier travel. The arrival of the railway was not without pain for what had been a quiet town, and the revels of the navvies in the Market Place were a source of scandal and concern. For Arnold they were an opportunity for crusade and he protected the boys (some of the older ones might have engaged in willing conflict with the navvies), wrote to the company, visited the men themselves at work and for once gained *en passant* good feeling in the town. A Mechanics Institute followed the arrival of the railway; Arnold appeared here as a regular lecturer. He rejoiced to lecture on history, with charts he had himself produced to illustrate the themes. He had visited many of the European places about which he was speaking and could provide first-hand anecdotes. Religious services by request at the railway station were to follow with extension lectures in Lutterworth.

But in 1839 Arnold appeared in further public dispute, defending a case in Chancery which was about the very heart and purpose of the school. It was brought because, contrary to the foundation deeds of the school, he had starved the Lower School out of existence by a policy of dissuading parents from sending their sons and also by appointing two completely unsuitable teachers to carry out the work. It cost him the friendship of his old Radical ally in earlier battles, William Wratislaw, the Rugby solicitor, two of whose own children were personally involved in this fiasco. Even Arnold admitted that his actions looked 'like the old charge against masters of Foundation Schools, that they discourage the Foundationers, in order to have boarders who pay them better' and that his 'old friends' of the Tory newspapers would use it to attack him. They certainly did. Arnold did not endear himself to many Rugby residents by this course of action and they were delighted when he and the trustees lost their expensive court defence. The full details of the case appear on pp. 170ff. But surprisingly, for a high profile national court judgment against him, the public clamour in the Tory press died down fairly quickly. Perhaps this was because it was seen as very much a local controversy. Or it had less sensational value than a misplaced flogging or expulsion. More likely, as it had no political or religious background, it was therefore less newsworthy.

Despite this, the tide of popular opinion began to move with Arnold rather than against him. He began to be seen as a public hero and not a public enemy. He was able to polish his reforms of the school, reducing the Fifth in size from 38 to 24, better to enable training and preparation for their coming role as praepostors. A school magazine was established which, under Clough, Stanley and others, quickly set a high tone of production. 'I delight in the spirit of it,' wrote Arnold. A formal debating society replaced a very disorderly 'levy' meeting of sixth formers. A drama group was created, enthusiastically supported by 'the Doctor' and his wife. The lodging houses in which boys used to board had by now all been replaced by school boarding houses. The worst excesses of bullying, roasting fags, blanket tossing, etc., were things of the past. He could report the largest numbers so far on roll, a sign of undiminished parental confidence, with 36 in his own form. The small teaching room must have been tightly packed.

The changed public perception of Arnold was marked by a visit to the school in 1839 of William IV's widow, the Dowager Queen Adelaide. She was a contemporary of Arnold (1792–1849) and is described in *Chambers* as worthy but dull. But she was also Queen Victoria's aunt and her visit reflected approval of Arnold as an educator on the part of the establishment. In the presence of Earl Howe and other dignitaries, Her Majesty took Arnold's arm and was shown the quadrangle, the chapel and an impromptu special game of Rugby football at her unexpected request, the 75 boys of School House versus the entire rest of the school (225). School House won 2–0, one goal being scored by Tom Hughes. The dowager queen graciously met Mrs Arnold and the Arnold children in their drawing room. 'K' wrote a lot about the day in her diary. Blessed with this royal seal of approval, the trustees can only have been pleased with their 1828 appointment, even if it had been rather a rollercoaster ride at times.

Soon after the royal visit, Arnold received a communication from Sir John Franklin of the Colonial Office, on behalf of the government, to ask him to undertake the appointment of the head of a new school or university to be established in Hobart, Van Diemen's Land (Tasmania). This person could influence

12. Dr Arnold, accompanied by his two sons, Matthew (the poet) and Thomas – both of whom are now praepostors at the school – shows Queen Adelaide, widow of William IV, a game of football at Rugby.
– from a drawing by Jane Arnold, the doctor's eldest daughter

education throughout all the colonies in that part of the world – who should it be? That Arnold was engaged as a consultant is another sign that he had 'arrived' in the eyes of the establishment. There is a possibility that Arnold may have considered such a post himself. His geographical interests were as old as he was. The idea of shaping education in a new world was an appealing one. It might be Laleham and Rugby again on a bigger scale. In 1829 he had written about investing his first £1000 in Swan River, western Australia, and building a house and school there to work in after he 'shut up shop' at Rugby (26.10.1829, letter to Tucker). In 1836 he had written to the governor designate of Van Diemen's Land that if he were to be made a bishop or the principal of a school or college, he 'could be tempted to emigrate with my family for good and all' (20.7.1836). It would be a moral crusade, to help transform a colony sown with 'rotten seed' and 'morally tainted in its origin', i.e. by convict deportations, of which Arnold disapproved strongly. Even in 1840 he could write of being made a bishop in New Zealand, perhaps wistfully, perhaps in jest. He had a friend in Edward Stanley, Arthur Stanley's father, by now Bishop of Norwich, although it was recognized that in the UK the best church preferment Arnold could hope for would be a deanery.

Perhaps he felt too old at 44, only five or six years short of his original target retirement date; he then owned 200 acres of land in both Australia and New Zealand, along with railway shares and shares in the USA to try to provide retirement income. He had difficulty extracting the dividend payments on the US investments. Perhaps he was too attached to Fox How. Perhaps he was considering new opportunities within the UK. Or perhaps there is a big difference between a dream and the real opportunity to carry it out. Whatever the reason for not putting himself forward, his recommendation was John Gell, a Rugbeian ex-praepostor. Arnold was to send him letters of advice when he was in post. Arnold's letter informing Gell of his recommendation was written in the classroom during Lesson Four with Gell's sixth form brother writing Greek verse close by Arnold's side. 'He [Franklin] wants a Christian, a gentleman and a scholar.' These would have been exactly Arnold's own criteria. The appointment was ratified by the government without question. It was a sign of Arnold's status as an educator.

In 1839 Arnold decided to reduce his very considerable and still growing workload. He announced his intention to lay down his duties as head of School House: 61 boys signed a petition against this, which still survives in the archive at Rugby (see pp. 162ff). He relented. But 1839 was a difficult year within the school, with a long-standing feud between the sixth and the rest of the school, which ended with various expulsions, including two from within the hallowed sixth itself. Also in 1839, Arnold was received by Queen Victoria in a private audience in London. Presumably Aunt Adelaide's report had gone higher. The only record of what took place comes from him and it is cryptic: 'I was amused by the novelty of the scene.' If Arnold was more acceptable to the establishment as an educator, his views would not have found favour in every department. He opposed the 1840 opium war against China as an attempt to make the government of China import a 'demoralizing drug' which 'we, for the lucre of gain, want to introduce by force'. He also opposed total Sunday closure of the railway in the name of Sabbath restrictions he saw as more Jewish than Christian, but he wished to restrict trains to one each way per Sunday so as to allow railway staff most of the day as a holiday (letter, 19.2.1840).

Things were also moving in Arnold's career outside Rugby and in his family. His sisters Lydia and 'Patty' were now both widowed and had moved to the district with their children. Frances had sent two of her sons to Rugby. Three of Arnold's own children, Tom, Matt and Edward, were now pupils. Matt and Tom worried him because they seemed too boyish and irresponsible. He wondered whether some time in the colonies would help them to mature. But in 1840 Matt astonished him by winning the sixth form poetry prize with 'Alaric at Rome', and then, with the help of Lake as a tutor, a scholarship to Balliol. He was one of two selected from 30 after four days of written papers and a lengthy viva. Arnold would have been even more surprised and thrilled had he lived to see Matt become a Fellow of Oriel, 30 years after he himself had done, and eventually Professor

Sir

    We, the Undersigned, have heard with regret your intention of giving up the School-House: we venture to say that the personal regard we feel for you would make us extremely lament your leaving us: and we humbly hope that this Expression of our feelings may be allowed some weight in influencing your determination.

April 29th 1839.   Signed.

H. Dorat.
A W Walrond
I. R. Moorsom
H. L. Bevan
G. E. Hughes
T. Walrond
J Mackie
A R Nevill
C Hutton
A J Ormerod.

13. The petition of 1839 to persuade Arnold not to give up School House.

CE & G Barnard
J. Yeadon.
W. Evelyn.
D Bennett
J Wynne
H. Whately
C Munro
S Sandes

H Skipwith
E Shapland
W P Adam
R Inser
J Hughes
R Skipwith
J Lea
W. Wingfield
F. Wingfield.
W Franklin
C J Willoughby.
J Foster
J. White
C Thruston
H McSween
H Blunt
H Woodrow.
A. G. Day
J G Holloway
B Bright
E Smythe
W Attfield
E Amphlett
Hayes

D Miller
G C Taylor
H Sharp
J Davies
C Hobhouse.
A. Wothesley
J N Fellowes
J J C Olivier
A Crowder
E Thomas.
G Wolley
A Turnbull
H. Jeffreys
H Algar
J Smith
A Belebar
J Fenwick
J J Findlay
G Franks
G Rennie
J Monson
J Pochin

of Poetry. Arnold decided that if he could see Matt and Tom through Oxford financially, he might then afford to retire. That would mean an 1842 departure. In 1840 Arnold was offered the Wardenship of Manchester University by Melbourne, the Whig Prime Minister. Bishop Stanley was one agent behind this. Arnold refused, giving as grounds that the duties were unclear and that he did not feel able to do justice to the size of the job as he saw it. The income was also small and Arnold felt it would make completing his children's education difficult.

There was a sort of timelessness about Arnold's current existence, despite its many pressures. He could often write letters during Lesson Four, the last afternoon lesson, while the sixth were engaged in a writing exercise. In one to John Gell, he describes himself sitting in

> that undignified kitchen chair, which you so well
> remember, at that little table . . . at which you have so often
> seen me writing in years past. And, as the light is scarcely
> bright enough to show the increased number of my grey
> hairs, you might, if you looked in on us, fancy that time
> had ceased to run. (8.3.1841)

To Seton Carr (5.10.1840): 'I am writing this at Fourth Lesson, as usual, and the lower row are giving up their books, so that I must conclude.' Other correspondence was with scientists and scholars. There could be some delay, as unclearly addressed letters were occasionally delivered to Rugeley (Staffordshire) not Rugby (Warwickshire). For philological purposes Arnold was trying to learn Sanskrit and Slavonic. His own writing for publication was therefore in haste, but still based on reading, careful thought and sometimes correspondence to test ideas with other scholars.

Professor Arnold

Long Half 1841 was a difficult year in the school. Three pupils died, one from 'pressure on the brain' (meningitis?), another from fever and another having been sent home 'in a delicate state'. Four other boys had nearly died. Pupils were evacuated to the Fox How area (the sixth form, who lodged in local farm houses) and the Leamington Spa area (the others, except local Rugby boys). The summer vacation trip for 1841 was to Italy, France and Spain with Mary and the two older boys. In 1841 the death of Dr Nares, the Regius Professor of Modern History at Oxford led to a new opportunity. There were no heresy tests for history professors. Melbourne offered Arnold the post. This time Arnold did not refuse and wrote to Hawkins that although the money would help his retirement, he would have been tempted to Oxford for no money at all. Arnold had behind him a significant publications list, not all modern history, including encyclopaedia articles, three volumes on Thucydides, an unfinished *History of Rome* and thirteen articles on 'the social condition' published in the *Sheffield Courant*. His intention was to stay on at Rugby and lecture in Oxford on an occasional basis, until such time as he might retire from the headship. The income might supplement his other investments as a basis for retirement while providing for those of his family still dependent on him. Importantly to Arnold, the post would still allow time for Fox How. But before Arnold gave his inaugural lecture on 2 December 1841, another event in the life of the family took place in October: Matt's departure for Balliol. It marked 'the first separation of our family, for . . . all our nine children have hitherto lived at home together, with very short exceptions, but now it will be so no more'. Many modern parents will appreciate the pathos of these Arnold regrets.

Despite fears that he would use his Chair as a pulpit from

which to denounce Tractarianism, leading to a gladiatorial audience of about 400 – ten times the average inaugural number – in eager anticipation in his first lecture series, he consciously adopted a manner of forbearance and restraint. Arnold held them spell-bound in a packed Sheldonian Theatre. He sought to lecture 'neither hostilely nor cautiously, not seeking occasions of shocking men's favourite opinions, yet neither in any way humouring them, or declining to speak the truth, however opposed it may be to them'. The whole tone of the series is one of humility and this was possibly increased by Arnold's awareness that unlike some professors, he was not in a position to research and study full-time. He felt academically vulnerable. Mary, Jane, Matt and also Rugbeians Stanley and Clough attended the inaugural. He left Rugby at 5 a.m., reaching Oxford at noon. The Arnolds returned to Rugby at 11 p.m.; he had marked sixth form exercises on the journey both ways while it was light. The lecture series was a defence of the study of modern history as defined by Arnold (see p. 244). He returned to complete a series of eight lectures over two weeks, this time renting a house in Beaumont Street, with the Arnold family also in residence. After the lectures, in the company of his family, along with Stanley, Lake and Clough, Arnold would pursue some of his former walks, visiting Bagley Wood, Shotover, Horspath, Cumnor, Elsfield and the valleys behind the Hinckseys. On one social occasion he met Newman (2.2.1842) and found him unexpectedly pleasant company.

The Chair in Modern History must in many ways mark the zenith of Arnold's work, his acceptance back in Oxford and the recognition that it gave to his scholarship, coupled with his acceptance by the establishment as a, or 'the', leading British educator. 'Everybody was very kind and certainly it satisfied me that in returning to Oxford I was going to no place full of enemies.' There were other excitements in planning. Matt had showed more talent, only narrowly missing the Hertford Latin Scholarship. Tom was about to enter University College. 'K' was to be married in June to George Cotton, a Rugby teacher from 1836, whose monocled 'moral thoughtfulness' pleased the Arnolds. They might also have seen his professional talents. He was to become head of Marlborough and a future bishop. Not everyone agreed; Wordsworth wrote of him 'a more unattractive youth . . . I never saw'.

Meanwhile Arnold was nearing a personal meeting with Thomas Carlyle (1795–1881). This perhaps unlikely duo had been corresponding, with Arnold failing in 1840 to solicit support from Carlyle for a society intended to gather together sociological evidence about the condition of the poor and persuade the upper classes to involve themselves in the issue. Carlyle, however, was disinclined as he felt such societies often failed in their aims and might even exist simply to glorify their members, but he expressed a rather passive sympathy for the sentiment behind Arnold's idea and the two continued correspondence. Carlyle, who felt that the contemporary form of priesthood was unfitted for the times, also shared Arnold's dislike of the Oxford Movement, which in typically Carlylean rhetoric he had dubbed 'strange Centaurs, spectral Puseyisms, monstrous illusory Hybrids, and ecclesiastical Chimeras' (in Knights, 1978, p. 79). Carlyle had published *Sartor Resartus* ('The Tailor Retailored') in 1834, originally in magazine instalments. The labyrinthine style which embraced German and English and the multi-layered and at times almost impenetrable text had as one of its messages that the negating Everlasting No was pitted against the constructive imperative of the Everlasting Yea, which demanded submission to the will of God and an active commitment to work – both themes that struck a chord with Arnold, although it was far from clear what 'God' and 'work' precisely meant to Carlyle. They also shared a common interest in history; Carlyle's *On Heroes, Hero-Worship and the Heroic in History*

105

appeared in 1841. Carlyle had written an essay on Chartism (1839) which grappled with the 'Condition of England' question. Although Carlyle was sceptical about the power of societies such as Arnold proposed, he was genuinely interested in Arnold's work.

Family life continued with all its vigour and Arnold's day book records it in outline for 1842:

> Feb 11th Friday
> Left Oxford, & arrived safely at Rugby . . . Getting Things in Order. Mr Fenwick dined with us.

> February 13th Sunday
> No Lectures; Chapel at 11 & 4. Preached on S.Mark X.21,22 Sermonet. Mr Fenwick dined here. Walrond at tea . . .

> February 15th Tuesday
> Heard the Twenty in Virgil
> Aristophanus. –
> Dogs' Day Skirmish. – K. Tom, Bacco, Babbat, Skraltit [? Unclear writing] & Corus
> Pelting at the Clay Pit. Babbat's eye hurt.

> February 17th Thursday
> Went up to London. – in Downing Street. at the Brewhouse. – Tavistock Square. – Went on to Coventry by mistake and came back in a Fly.

> February 20th Sunday
> Lectures at 10 and 3
> Went to the Railway at 10 ¾.–
> Chapel at 4. – Preached on Galat. III.1
> Summit in Hall. –

March 3rd Thursday
Flogged Clarke for a Lie.

March 15th Tuesday
Exd [examined] Lower Remove. Put up Gill, Owen, Coke. Aristophanus – Composition. Went to Lutterworth with M. Dined at the Gurney's. – Lecture on History at the Mechanics' Institute. W. Buckland came.

Local walks were a frequent diversion. On one occasion there was a walk to the Dunchurch turnpike, on another a 'beautiful pony walk beyond Dunchurch on the path towards Thurlaston'. Pony walks feature often, e.g. 'Pony walk with Willy to Toft Hill'. Arnold records 'Walk with Cotton', 'Deep snow . . . Took only some turns in the School Field', 'Long walk with Didu and Widu to Shawell. Disaster of Widu's Garments. – ', 'Walk with Babbat to the Coltsfoot', 'Walk with Crab by Lawford Mill', 'Bathe at Waterfall [April 25, early in the year for river swimming] with Tom'. A Slatwoods revisit found him reflecting to Mary:

> Slatwoods was deeply interesting. I thought of what Fox
> How might be to my children forty years hence . . .
> [Slatwoods is] the only home of my childhood, while to
> them Laleham and Rugby will divide their affection . . .
> – I had also a great interest in going over colleges at
> Winchester, but I certainly did not desire to change houses
> with Moberly [the head of Winchester]; no, not situations,
> although I envy him the Downs . . . [and neighbouring
> ancient British history sites]. And [next section crossed
> out] I think also, but this I would not say publicly, that I
> envy him. But when I look at the last no [number] of the
> Rugby Magazine or at V or S [Vaughan or Stanley] . . . , I

envy neither him nor any man. Thinking that there is a good in Rugby which no place can surpass in its Quality be the Quantity of it much or little.

Arnold returned to Rugby from his Oxford lectures in the Lent Term of 1842 to the shock news of Jane's engagement being broken off by Cotton. Cotton was still fond of Jane, but he had come to the view that he did not love her and that therefore it could not be right for the marriage to go ahead. It was a complete shock to Jane. She collapsed into a depression in which she would neither eat, sleep, nor speak. Arnold and 'K' were especially close. From the age of 18 she had been his *de facto* personal assistant and confidante. This trauma took place in the same week that Carlyle was due to visit Rugby. He arrived on Friday 13 May. With Arnold's mind less than focused on the task, they toured Naseby battlefield together. There is even the suggestion that in his confusion, Arnold showed Carlyle the wrong site.

On the following Tuesday, Arnold collapsed following a walk with Mary. This itself was a bad sign for a man who in 1836 could write that he had had only one day in bed since 1807 (letter to Hawkins, 23.11.1836). However, a 'slight attack of fever' had occurred in 1840 when he was prescribed three days' strictly inactive bed or sofa rest and several days upstairs afterwards. It helped his high pulse rate to recover. He admitted then that he needed the Christmas holidays at Fox How to bring him back to something like full strength. Now (1842) for five days he was in bed again with a 'light fever'. He was in no doubt that it was 'brought on by my distress and anxiety about dearest Jane'. Even Stanley, who would not admit family matters or criticism of Arnold into his *Life*, notes a mysterious 'accidental cause, into which it is not necessary to enter' that possibly hastened Arnold's death: this was definitely it. Arnold's commonplace book, the mixture of day diary and appointment planner which records his school work, tersely lists the events:

April 23rd Saturday . . . The Whatelys all arrived from Ireland
April 24th Sunday . . . Archbishop preached for me.
6 May School Day Round with Cotton
May 15th Sunday
. . . Sad discussions about Cotton. Wrote to him.
May 16th Monday
. . . Went up to Town with dearest M and brought down our K. – Saw Lydia and Bunsen.
May 17th Tuesday.
Exd [Examined] 4th Form. – Dearest K. & [? unclear] went to Fox How. – Aristophanes. Composition. Pony walk with Stanley. – Unwell and went up Stairs afterwards, & remained there.
May 18th Wednesday
Up stairs all day. – Unwell, & distressed about dearest K.
May 19th Thursday
Still unwell. The Whatelys came and were most kind
May 20th Friday
Still up Stairs. – weak & harrassed. – Saw the Whatelys severally.
May 21st Saturday
Still up Stairs. – went down in the evening & afternoon for a little while . . .
May 22nd Sunday
Still up Stairs in the morning. Went to Chapel in the afternoon. Grenfell did duty for me. – Lecture at 7.
May 23rd Monday
In at second lesson. Homer. The Whatelys went. Did not go out. Livy. Greek verse.

May 24th Tuesday
Whole Holyday – Wet Day. – Sat at home very quiet. –
cleared out my closets.
May 25th Wednesday.
In at first lesson. – Thank God! Herodotus. French and
German. Composition in my Room. Walk with dearest M.
in School Field.

With characteristic determination, Arnold had risen from his bed
to teach, confiding to Mary that he felt 'quite a rush of love to
God and Christ' and that he hoped to be 'softer and more gentle'.
He was unsettled. Fuller night diary entries marked a humbler
pattern, as if a change had taken place in him. He might be
expecting to die.

May 22 – I know that my senses are on the very eve of
becoming weaker, and that my faculties will then soon
begin to decline too . . . Is there not one faculty which
never declines, which is the seed and seal of immortality;
and what has become of that faculty in me? What is it to
live unto God?
Tuesday evening, May 24 – . . . Strengthen me to bear
pain . . . Strengthen my faith, that I may realise to my
mind the things eternal – death, and things after death,
and Thyself. . . .
May 29 . . . O Lord, save me from idle words . . .
May 31– Another day and another month succeed . . .
I would wish to keep a watch over my tongue, as to
vehement speaking and censure of others . . .
Thursday evening, June 2 – Again the day is over and I
am going to rest. O Lord, preserve me this night, and give
me strength to bear whatever Thou shalt see fit to lay on
me, whether pain, sickness, danger or distress.

But if this seems sombre, and to Bamford it borders on 'religious mania' (1960, p. 171), Arnold was busily looking forward to summer at Fox How, writing to the children who had gone on in advance of him, while he was finishing term. He seemed to have recovered and apart from cancelling a planned lecture in Oxford was swimming and partaking in all his usual exuberant activities. The last week of term saw the fifth form examination, the school speeches, the visit of the examiners from Oxford and Cambridge and former pupils en route home from the universities calling in. On the last day the morning was spent examining boys on history, in preparation for which he had stayed up late the night before, finishing the paperwork of the term, distributing prizes to departing boys and saying goodbyes. There had been an afternoon swim in the river and a walk in the garden with Mary. Characteristically on Arnold's last evening he hosted an end of term supper at 9 p.m. for sixth form boys who were members of his House. He is said to have been in high spirits, looking forward to Fox How. Finally, he checked the School House accounts. An earlier praepostor's view of the last night and day of term throws light on the activity:

> I dined at Arnold's, and had a very pleasant evening. Then followed all the misery of the last night – noise, noise, noise of preparing and wishing good-bye, &c., till twelve o'clock and after; followed at two o'clock by the still greater noise of going. After my two hours' sleep, I had a busy morning of breakfasting with my tutor, of paying off window-bills, &c., &c., packing up &c., &c., and so on till twelve o'clock, when I dined out, and returned to the school at three o'clock calling over [registration], wished the fellows good-bye and waited for the coach till four in the school field. (Clough, to his mother, December 1835)

It must have been more tiring for Arnold, who personally scrutin-ized pupils' travel arrangements. His last private diary entry before retiring to bed illustrates the earnestness which his opponents so derided and his supporters admired:

> Saturday evening, June 11th. – The day after tomorrow is my birthday, if I am permitted to live to see it . . . How large a portion of my life on earth is already passed. And then – what is to follow this life? How visibly my outward work seems contracting and softening into the employments of old age. In one sense, how nearly can I now say, 'Vixi' . . . And now I thank God that, as far as ambition is concerned, it is, I trust, fully mortified; I have no desire other than to step back from my present place in the world, and not to rise to a higher. Still there are works which, with God's permission, I would do before the night cometh . . . But above all, let me mind my own personal work, – to keep myself pure and zealous and believing, – labouring to do God's will, yet not anxious that it should be done by me rather than by others, if God disapproves of my doing it.

Shortly before 5 a.m. Mary was wakened by Arnold tossing and turning in bed. He was far from well. He complained of pain across his chest. He said he had experienced it more mildly the day before while walking and before and after swimming. The pain seemed to pass down the left arm. Mary, who in the light of the family history feared an angina attack, called Elizabeth, one of the servants, and gave him salvolatile. This was 'smelling salts', ammonium carbonate in alcohol, commonly used to revive faint-ing or semi-conscious people. She started to dress to send for help. Arnold, who must have been alarmed and was very well aware of his own family cardiac history, suddenly quoted the words 'Jesus said unto him: "Thomas, because thou hast seen, thou hast believed – Blessed are they which have not seen and yet have believed."' At times he seemed in great pain and shortly after he remarked to Mary that if he had only been as used to pain as 'dear Susanna' he could bear it better. It was not only Arnold's symptoms but his manner that alarmed Mary. The doctor was urgently sent for and taking up her prayer book to read him a psalm, Mary was asked by Arnold to read Psalm 51. He repeated the twelfth verse, 'O give me the comfort of Thy help again, and stablish me with Thy free spirit.' It was a strange irony, for in a sermon on Genesis 34.30 many years earlier Arnold had attached 'little value to the prayers that can be said . . . to anyone, when the stroke of death is on him' for the state of trial is then over. But he did hope that 'the lesson of death' can be learnt in life. 'Even a day's loss of appetite, a day's or a night's restlessness, a day's want of interest in our common business and amusements, does but speak in gentle language what we must one day hear in thunder' (*Sermons* 1850 edition, p. 296f). He was ready.

Meanwhile the young doctor, Bucknill, the son of Arnold's usual doctor, arrived at 6.45 a.m. Arnold was lying on his back with a rapid pulse and a flushed appearance. Arnold asked after Bucknill senior and said that he did not wish to disturb him so early in the day. He described his symptoms and then before Bucknill could answer his question as to what it was, the pain resumed. Bucknill told Arnold it was a 'spasm of the heart' and prescribed brandy, hot water bottles and mustard poultices. Bucknill asked Arnold if he had ever fainted, had difficulty in breathing, or severe chest pain. Had any of his family died of disease of the chest? Yes, Arnold's father, aged 53. Was it suddenly fatal? Yes, suddenly. Arnold then asked Bucknill: was heart disease very common? Where did it occur most – town or country? Why? Is it generally fatal? 'Yes, I am afraid it is.' Bucknill left to fetch medicines.

Mary ran to fetch Tom and Arnold joked with him about his temporary deafness of the evening before. Then in a quieter voice he told him to 'thank God for me! I have suffered so little pain in my life that I feel it is very good for me. I do *so* thank God for giving me this pain.' It seems that not surprisingly, the young Tom did not understand the seriousness of the situation. Mary started to read the Prayer Book Exhortation for the Visitation of the Sick, Arnold saying 'Yes' at the end of many of the statements. The doctor now returned and applied more of the same medicines. Arnold told him that if the pain returned as severely as before, he did not know how he could bear it. He repeated the question and received the same answer about the likely outcome of the attack. Thinking that he might still recover and that there was no more to be done immediately, Mary went down to the study taking Tom. Bucknill was left in the room administering laudanum to Arnold. They had just got downstairs when the servant, Rowland, yelled for them to come back. Arnold had had another massive spasm and lost consciousness. He was still breathing. The other children who were at home were quickly summoned; five had gone ahead to Fox How. The older doctor arrived. But Arnold did not regain consciousness and died shortly after, round about 8 a.m. The shock for his family, and for the pupils and staff at Rugby, was immense.

Arnold died on the eve of his forty-seventh birthday, and the end of his fourteenth academic year at Rugby. He was buried under the communion table in the school chapel on the following Friday by Moultrie, the Rector of Rugby. The following Sunday the family took part in holy communion at the same altar and heard read Arnold's Easter sermon for 1841, 'Faith Triumphant in Death'. A school service took place on the first Sunday of the next Half. For Matt, seeing the body of his father was the end of an era; as if 'all that they had ever known was contained in that lifeless head'. For Clough, Arnold 'was for a long time more than

14. Tom's visit to the tomb of Dr Arnold.

a father to me'. Arnold had combined the earnestness of the evangelical, a catholicity of churchmanship which was rarely equalled before the twentieth-century ecumenical movement, a willingness to confront the gospel with modernity well in advance of most of his contemporaries, social concern that extended beyond the children of the comfortably off, scholarship in history and theology, outstanding and memorable classroom teaching, active pastoral care, personal religious devotion and a vision of education with Christianity at the centre, not the periphery. He was not to find an equal, and his influence on the public schools and on their twentieth-century imitators, the grammar schools, was immense. His giant stature as an educator eclipsed his very considerable significance as a religious thinker. The time has come to reappraise his significance for the twenty-first century.

2 Arnold the Educator: Laleham and Rugby

While Arnold was nearing thirteen years old as a pupil at Winchester, Samuel Taylor Coleridge delivered on 3 May 1808 what was to be the most celebrated lecture of his Royal Institution series. The subject was education. It was both a reflection of the growing public interest in the topic and also a boost to it. The lecture lasted for two hours and ten minutes and was played out to a packed theatre and gallery. In typical Coleridgean manner, the entire lecture was a digression and veered between metaphysics and melodrama (Holmes, II, 1998, pp. 130ff). Education was a controversial and popular subject and was to remain so in British debate for the next 200 years. Bell and Lancaster had recently set up their rival school systems. Rousseau's principles for education were being debated. Public school abuses and problems were already being publicized. Coleridge spoke about the 'disgraceful punishments' in his own time as a pupil at Christ's Hospital School. His life was 'embittered by the recollection of ignominious punishments' he had received as a child. The audience was deeply moved. The education of the poor should be the responsibility of the state, he argued. Dramatically throwing down Lancaster's book on the table, Coleridge attacked the punishments imposed on children for their failures in rote learning in the Lancastrian system. These included the shackling of legs, being trussed in sacks, being made to walk backwards in corridors

15. Head's House, Rugby, from a contemporary photograph.

and suspension from the classroom ceiling in 'punishment baskets'.

> No boy who has been subjected to punishments like these
> will stand in fear of Newgate or feel any horror at the
> thought of a slave ship . . . My experience tells me that
> little is taught through contest or dispute, but everything
> by sympathy and love.

Education should 'lead forth' by love and imagination. It should work by love and so generate love, habituate the mind to intellectual accuracy or truth and it should 'excite power'. The lecture was a mixture of Coleridgean magic and moonshine but it made his fame in London and beyond. What Coleridge dreamt of in education did not remotely correspond to the experience of the boy Arnold at the time, nor to the prevailing practice in public schools, but the adult Arnold admired S. T. Coleridge, critically, and as a later friend of the Wordsworths must have known their mixed feelings about Coleridge.

The 1885 *Dictionary of National Biography* entry for Arnold argues that there was 'nothing startling' in his reforms, 'nor was there anything recondite in his system' (*DNB*, 1885, p. 114). But the 'TW' who wrote the article was Theodore Walrond. He had the advantage and disadvantage of being a former Rugby star pupil for much of Arnold's time there (entering in 1834 aged 10) going on to become head boy, member of staff and unsuccessful candidate for the headship in 1870, which might account for his testiness in the *DNB*. More recently another biographer presents Arnold as of no original educational significance, writing that 'the mind of this man, usually considered to be the greatest of headmasters, was really interested fundamentally in the world outside the [Rugby School] Close' (Bamford, 1960, p. 212). What made Arnold original in education was his 'single-minded, fierce determination to turn out Christian gentlemen' (McCrum, 1989), 'his unwearied zeal in creating "moral thoughtfulness" in every boy with whom he came into personal contact' (Hughes, 1857, 1994 edition, p. 16). But he did not believe that this could be done by extra religion classes or more compulsory chapel services, but by what would now be called whole-school ethos.

Arnold wrote before taking up his post at Rugby of his hope to make the school 'an instrument of God's glory, and of the ever-lasting good of those who come to it' (28.12.1827, Stanley, 1845, p. 86), hardly a half-hearted statement by one whose real interests lay elsewhere, unless one interprets it as a pious cliché. For Bamford, Arnold's distinctiveness lay merely in the powers of allowing the sixth formers to flog younger boys and in the cultiva-tion of an intense religious attitude among boys (1960, p. 189). The former was not original, even if the latter was. Arnold himself wrote to John Coleridge:

> You need not fear my reforming furiously . . . but, of my success in introducing a religious principle into education I must be doubtful . . . To do it, however imperfectly, would far more than repay twenty years of labour and anxiety. (29.8.1828)

In *Tom Brown*, Hughes notes that:

> the Doctor, than whom no man or boy had a stronger liking for old school customs which were good and sensible, had . . . come into the most decided collision with several which were neither the one nor the other. . . . and when he came into collision with boys or customs, there was nothing for them but to give in or take themselves off; because what he said had to be done and no mistake about it. (1857, p. 113)

But even 'the Doctor' was not invincible, as we shall see (pp. 123ff, 135f). Reviewing Arnold within the gallery of Rugby heads, Rouse assesses his significance as his aim 'to infuse a Christian spirit into the existing system, so far as this should prove to be possible' (1898 [1909], p. 222). This is an extremely accurate summary of the Arnold project at Rugby.

Headteacher and manager

John Percival, who was later to be head at Rugby and Bishop of Hereford took this view of Arnold:

> The dominating idea of his Rugby life was that a head master is called of God to make his school a Christian school, an idea which has no doubt been enthroned in the hearts of multitudes of other schoolmasters, both before and since; but he was determined to make it a new power in the world through the intensity with which he nursed it as a prophetic inspiration, and preached it in all his words and works with a prophetic fervour. (in Fitch, 1897, p. 109)

Arnold's view was that:

> The management of boys has all the interest of a great game of chess with living creatures for pawns and pieces, and your adversary in plain English the devil, who truly plays a tough game and is very hard to beat.

Arnold identified six 'evils' which might exist in a school. These were: 'direct sensual wickedness', comprising drunkenness and sexual abuse (he did not speak explicitly about the latter but the allusions are clear); 'systematic falsehood', when lying becomes

the accepted practice of the great majority of pupils and is tolerated by all of them; systematic cruelty such as bullying, especially
of pupils reluctant to join in 'the coarseness and spirit of persecution' all around; 'a spirit of active disobedience' in which all
authority is hated and rules deliberately flouted; 'general idleness', where the tone of the school is such as 'to cry down any
attempt on the part of any one boy or more, to shew [*sic*] anything like diligence or a wish to improve himself'; finally there is
the bond of evil, 'a prevailing spirit of combination in evil and of
companionship; by which a boy would regard himself as more
bound to his companions in ties of wickedness, than to God or
his neighbour in any ties of good' (in Bamford, 1970, pp. 86ff).
In a sermon these evils are described slightly differently: the false
tongue; the violent hand; the proud or sensual or covetous
thought; the indolent temper; the unkind or selfish or unjust
action (Sermon on Genesis 34.30, 1850 edition, p. 298).

Rouse (1898) argues that Arnold wished to elevate teaching
from the training of the intellect to the training of character and
that this is where his success would lie. In the academic achievements of their pupils, Rouse argued, other heads such as Butler
could rival Arnold. For Arnold, education did not *include* spiritual development; its whole aim *was* spiritual development, which
he understood as the Christian path to Christ. But if these were
visionary aims, there were also practical objectives. Arnold used
to take each form for an occasional lesson. There was also a
monthly examination by viva which Arnold conducted in each
form. These examinations formed the basis of half-yearly reports
to parents. *Tom Brown* records a strongly life-like occasion when a
boy who was said to be a favourite of Arnold's but had neglected
his 'prep' was asked to construe 'Triste lupus, stabilis' and began
by guessing 'the sorrowful wolf'. But 'triste' is neuter and so
cannot agree with 'lupus', which is masculine. The passage comes
from Virgil's *Eclogues* 3.80 and means '[something] dreadful' or

'[something] ill-omened'. Virgil's character Damoetas says roughly in context: 'A wolf is bad for flocks, rain is bad for corn, gales are bad for trees – and Amaryllis' temper is bad for me.' Arnold's temper must have resembled that of Amaryllis and the guess was indeed ill-omened for the boy:

> A shudder ran through the whole form, and the Doctor's wrath fairly boiled over; he made three steps up to the construer, and gave him a good box on the ear. The blow was not a hard one, but the boy was so taken by surprise that he started back; the form [i.e. bench, not the assembled class] caught the back of his knees, and over he went onto the floor behind. There was a dead silence over the whole school. (1857, p. 143)

'The Doctor's' temper was volcanic. Even Stanley can write of 'that ashy paleness and that awful frown' which warned of Arnold's rising anger. His own children knew it. There is no doubt that Arnold appeared awesome to those boys outside the charmed circle of the sixth form and School House. Rouse calls his effect on the junior boys one of 'extreme fear' (1898 [1906], p. 230). But the terrifying aspect of Arnold can be over-stated; many other heads of the time appeared to their young charges in a similar light.

However, despite Hughes, the extent to which Arnold eliminated vicious events in the Rugby School underworld is disputed. 'Singing in Hall', which could be a terrifying ordeal for new boys, continued. They had to stand on a table, holding a candle in each hand and sing a song, while being pelted with crusts of bread and other missiles, in theory for singing a wrong note. The ordeal ended with the initiant pledging the house by downing a mug of salt and water stirred by a tallow candle. Arnold made inroads on some customs. He attempted to ban the school beagles pack and eliminated the keeping of guns for hunting. He prevented the hiring of horses by boys for steeplechasing at nearby Dunchurch and tried to stamp out the associated gambling. But he also knew 'when to see and when not to see' and on another occasion allowed the school to watch the steeplechasing (but not to take part). In *Tom Brown* after a singing night with lots of noise and beer drinking 'and nobody the worse for it', presumably a fictitious comment since adolescents were involved, the Doctor 'sees nothing' at the night prayers.

Arnold did succeed in reducing the extent of fights between

16. The Fight, from *Tom Brown's School Days*.

boys and regulated the occasions of them; he reduced the poaching and vandalism practised against local farmers and restricted the extent of fagging. But he seemed to accept the customary and possibly inevitable view that in a 24-hour schooling situation in a boarding establishment, some territories could not be policed and that therefore one had to try to bring the wrong mind to the right mind by persuasion as the only means of advance. Alcohol abuse was never entirely eradicated under Arnold and the harmful public water supplies meant that in Rugby and many other schools tea (with its requirement for boiled water) and beer were the two staple drinks. One illicit custom practised by the school 'Cocktail Club' was to save the beer from supper, mix it with spirits purchased in the town and drink the resultant potion hot. This 'club' continued until finally suppressed in 1845, under Tait's headship, with expulsions which included those of two praepostors. Hughes, in a letter written later than *Tom Brown*, described a common alcoholic escapade which continued throughout Arnold's time, the production of a very potent home brew. It was made from a dessertspoon of powdered rice, added to the same of Demerara sugar with half a salt spoon of powdered ginger and two raisins in a wine bottle. The rest of the bottle was filled with water and left until the raisins rose to the top (three days), then the ale was drinkable. The cork had to be wired down well – kept longer it could explode.

Teachers

With one exception, Arnold's teaching staff were ordained, in accordance with the custom of the time. Arnold significantly raised the status of his teachers by raising their salaries so that they were not obliged to take on local curacies to make ends meet. This allowed them more time for the school and therefore produced an increased professionalism in teaching which was to influence other schools. It paved the way, unwittingly, for the reduction of ordained teachers after Arnold, since the income was now sufficient in itself to live on. The schoolteacher became less an educated person who was dabbling in teaching, church work and perhaps other activities, more a professional in the service of a single institution, the employing school. Arnold also allowed the housemasters their boarding house profits, reckoned at about £15 per annum per pupil. Thus a housemaster might earn £1500 per annum, a very considerable sum for those days. Arnold's own estimated income, at the end, was about £4000 p.a. In comparison, a schoolteacher (not a head) elsewhere might get £400. Arnold believed that the teacher still needed to be ordained in order to acquire a proper social status to the task, although he made an exception in his own school for the talented Bonamy Price, who was imported from Laleham. He also believed that ordination, though not necessarily a mark of the highest character, was likely to guarantee avoidance of the worst sort of character. Teachers should set a moral example to their pupils. If these were not all original ideas, they were very effective reforms. The teacher should also be a continuing learner: 'If the mind once becomes stagnant, it can give no fresh draught to another mind; it is drinking out of a pond instead of from a stream' (20.3.1839, Bamford, 1960, p. 177). The teacher was to be like a university tutor, requiring a restlessness of mind 'in the state of a running stream', and the continual pursuit of further learning for oneself. 'He is the best teacher of others who is best taught himself.' Linked with this was the desirability of travel, in order to gain new vistas, mental as well as topographical. No one should graduate with a First and live off it for the rest of his working life; continual further study would refresh and develop the teacher's learning and would benefit pupils through enhanced teaching. Of course, a liking for children was essential: 'he who likes boys has probably a daily sympathy with them; and to be in sympathy with the mind you propose to influence is at once indispensable' (in Bamford, 1970, p. 103). Holidays were seen as an essential means of refreshing the health of teacher and pupil alike and for diversions in the literal sense, turnings aside from school work and preoccupations. Arnold's view was that teachers should remain in post for no more than fifteen years, after which they would be out of touch with the scholarship of a new generation in the universities. Staff meetings were held regularly, replacing Wooll's offer of a daily individual meeting with him for which teachers had to take the initiative. Staff meetings were not democratic, because Arnold remained clearly in charge of the school, but they were genuinely consultative. Arnold insisted that the greatest single factor in the success or failure of teaching a child was the teacher.

Praepostors

The practice of making older boys praepostors, prefects, was almost universal in the public schools, as was the granting to them of significant powers, including the power to use corporal punishment. Most public schools could not be run without praepostors, as there were simply insufficient academic staff to cover all the duties needed in a boarding school setting, especially in those schools where teaching staff did additional jobs outside the school, such as local curacy work. The theoretical defence for this practice was that being accorded such responsibility was a training ground for those responsibilities of adult life they would be expected to shoulder on leaving the school. At worst it could be a licence for bullying or exploitation. A conversation at Laleham recorded by Mary Arnold gives an insight into Arnold's readiness to use praepostors:

He spoke with approbation of the Winchester system of

the higher boys being tutors to others – & said that he had never known an instance of their not attending to their pupils. . . . [He said] there is but one kind of knowledge of the greatest importance for all men to obtain – and that is the knowledge of our duty . . . Speaking of intellectual excellence he meant when it was applied to some useful end – for as to the love of intellectual pleasures when cultivated only for their own sakes, he thought no better of them than he did of an inclination for turtle & venison. (21.9.1825)

Where Arnold went further than many of his contemporaries was to take the theory of praepostors utterly seriously, placing great emphasis on the role of praepostors, both for their own training and for that of younger boys. Strachey notes that Arnold took this existing 'mere disciplinary convenience' and converted it into 'an organ of government'. His praepostors had almost the status of teachers. He therefore gave them great trust and expected complete loyalty in return: 'When I have confidence in the sixth, there is no post in England for which I would exchange this; but if they do not support me, I must go.' Bamford says he treated them 'like gods', that no case against them was ever considered. This is simply not the case, as there were examples of the expulsion of praepostors. They were expected to be examples to the rest of the school in speech and behaviour. They were the leaders of Rugby pupil society. One praepostor, 'D.E.R.' wrote rather high-mindedly in the *Rugby Miscellany* soon after Arnold (1845) that the sixth form was:

an aristocracy of talent and worth, created by neither birth, interest, nor personal strength . . . [It turned] those who should otherwise have been the ringleaders in every disturbance into an organised and responsible nobility, with power, privileges, and a character of their own to preserve. (Rouse 1898 [1909], p. 292).

The theory was not unique to Arnold, but perhaps the extent of the application was. Praepostors in all schools were a real power base. But Arnold worked with them to advance his own aims. They were not a power base independent of the head. Rouse argues that what Arnold did was to attach significant duties to the role of praepostor, where before there had been mainly privilege (1898 [1909], p. 224). Praepostors had the power to punish more junior pupils. A 'study licking' meant three strokes of the cane. A more serious 'hall licking' was administered in the presence of the sixth form. When questioned by a praepostor, a boy's word had to be accepted, but woeful would be the punishment if he was later found to be lying. Clearly, the system could be subject of much abuse, but Arnold was determined that praepostors should act responsibly and well. He defended the theory: 'a strict system is not therefore a cruel one'. In cases where fagging worked, it gave a younger pupil some help, occasional advice and protection from an older one.

Four praepostors were invited to dine with the Arnold family in each week of term time. Arnold wanted his praepostors to possess not only the right behaviour but the right mind. The seriousness of Rugbeians at Oxford attracted comment, both favourable and unfavourable. There were weaknesses in this system: not all praepostors could cope with their responsibilities, or, if they were over-conscientious like Clough, they had to live with the dreadful fear of failure under the Doctor's all-seeing eye. When Clough arrived at Oxford in 1837, aged eighteen, having won almost every prize Rugby could offer, he was already emotionally worn out by the years at Rugby even though, or perhaps because, he had been integrated into the Arnold family life by 'the Doctor', aware that Clough's own parents were away in the

USA for much of the time. Clough himself records in a letter to his mother the sort of practical incident a praepostor might be involved in:

School House Rugby, Oct 15th

I am just come out from a's [*sic*, i.e. Arnold's] two hours second lesson and feel rather over-inclined to talk about any thing that comes into my head . . . I dare say you will want to hear about the annoying affair which took place in the School not long ago, so I will try and tell you the truth about it, as shortly as I can. One of the tradesmen in the town one day came and told me that he suspected 3 boys in the School of stealing things out of his shop. I asked these three boys, and upon two of them confessing and the third telling rather a suspicious story of [crossed out, indecipherable] about the matter, I went & told the case to Dr. Arnold. On further investigation being made, it was discovered that 8 boys had been engaged in such practices for two or three days before it was discovered: and had taken property to a considerable amount out of various shops besides robbing one or two orchards. Three of the boys are above 14 years old, and these were expelled; the rest were quite children and were not expelled, but only sent away from the School for two years' time (in one case of a worse character than the rest, three years') with permission to return, if the parents' [*sic*] chose . . . provided that they can produce testimonials of good behaviour during the interval. One of these younger culprits is a boy from Chester named Hassall, I sho^d [should] suppose, son of the late mayor there: – another is a relation of the Newcomes of Ruttin being a grandson of old Dr Hughes, the Canon of St Paul's (or Westminster?)

whom my father will know: the rest are all boys living with their parents in the town. Such is the case. I do not for my own part think very much of it, nor do I conceive it as a thing which should really make anyone think decidedly ill of the School, or indeed decidedly lower his opinion of its merits. Such things are sometimes unavoidable among little boys and are more to be regarded as men regard storms or earthquakes than anything else. One cannot prevent a bad boy occasionally coming to the School, nor can one be surprised at his example taking considerable effect among little boys. If any great lowering of the tone and feelings of the bigger & higher fellows were to take place, it would be definitely worse and more to be lamented.

Another drawback of the importance of praepostors was that for those boys who left the school at the end of the Fifth there was no taste of paradise, of personal teaching by 'the Doctor', of the final grooming for responsibility in the world. The privileges of juniors fagging for them were not allowed. But Arnold did raise the status of the fifth form, as the sixth-in-waiting, by exempting them from fagging. Even so, they did not complete the Rugby character-building course and attain its full benefits. 'Tom Brown', on the other hand, could look back as an Oxford undergraduate on his own part 'in the ruling of 300 boys, and a good deal of responsibility' (Hughes, 1861, p. 39). The strength of this as argued by Rouse (1898 [1906], p. 224) is that whereas the custom in many schools had become for heads to rule them with savagery, like despots in a conquered state in which teachers were seen as the natural enemies of pupils, with the older pupils as leaders of a slave organization in which the strong ruled the weak, pupil differences being settled by brute force, Arnold used this pupil-rule system as the mainspring of his organization, but with himself in control of the older boys, not leaving them as client kings in territories into which he did not venture. He treated them as young gentlemen, not as necessary evils required in the task of subduing the school. He did not materially change their role, but he gave them dignity, a sense of responsibility, even partnership with him. However, *Tom Brown* actually admitted, perhaps unintentionally, another weakness in this system and that is the vacuum created when a strong sixth form leave the school, to be replaced by weaker personalities and then bullies in the fifth form step into the gap.

Gover (in Chandos, 1984, pp. 261ff) recounts an anecdote that shows that Arnold could exert great pressure on praepostors, not always justifiably, to conform to his view of things. Gover as a

17. Flashman bullies Tom, in *Tom Brown's School Days*.

sixth former had dined at the *Spread Eagle* with a recently left Old Boy and another sixth former. Gover drank one sherry and one port, with tea after the meal. They returned to school late, having stayed to listen to a lecture about the microscope being given in the inn. But on return to the school their housemaster, Roger Bird (see p. 140f), reported them to Arnold for lateness. The boys gave Arnold a full account of what had happened. He expressed regret that 'such circumstances might have led you into excess'. Gover was not content to be rebuked like this and replied that he had drunk no more than he would have done at his father's table. Arnold, challenged in this way, paused and replied that 'abstinence is better than moderation'. Gover, feeling unjustifiably criticized, repeated his account of the meal. Arnold repeated his criticism. The interview ended inconclusively. A few days later, Arnold detained Gover after class. He said he was grieved by what had happened, but the two sixth formers could express their regret by partaking the following Sunday in the communion service, at which attendance was always voluntary. Gover felt that doing this would imply admission that he had behaved wrongly. His fellow sixth former took the line of least resistance and attended the service. Gover did not. A few days later Arnold raised the matter with Gover again. He reproved Gover for not showing any sorrow and therefore set him a written imposition. He 'seemed to impose it reluctantly, with pain to himself'. Gover did the task and handed it in. Arnold seemed to wait, brows uplifted, for further apology or evidence of contrition. Gover said nothing. Arnold took the imposition from him. The next Sunday's sermon, in which no one was mentioned by name in accordance with Arnold's regular practice, was on the relations which must exist in school life to the law and the necessity of subjection to it.

To Chandos this incident provides evidence of Arnold's bullying tendency to require conformity, 'a boy being pressed by a man to do violence to his own understanding of truth and falsify his own conscience for the sake of another's version of "righteousness" '. Arnold left no account of his side of the matter, as he was hardly likely to do for what in his daily work was so minor an incident. We therefore cannot assess the tone in which Gover responded, nor be certain what Arnold's real concern and displeasure were. If Gover's response about what he would do at home was, or seemed to be, truculent or insolent, as pupils can sometimes appear when defending their position under stress, Arnold's comment about abstinence would be at least understandable. In a boarding school situation some concern for late returns from off-campus events is entirely justifiable. Perhaps Arnold's suspicions led him to play himself into a corner he could not get out of; most schoolteachers at some time manage this in pupil interviews or interrogations. It is not uncommon that when teachers handle a situation badly, pupils at the receiving end feel that they have 'got it in' for them. On the other hand, it must be readily conceded to Chandos that like many people who possess religious or moral certainty, Arnold found it hard to admit the validity of divergent views.

Fagging

Arnold accepted that fagging was a necessity in providing for 'regular government' and avoiding 'the evils of anarchy' in schools and believed that a large boarding school cannot be adequately governed without a system of fagging. It can check bullying and keep order. It prevents misrule by the physically biggest pupils. But he said it 'requires to be watched' to prevent abuse. There were two types of fagging in Arnold's Rugby: school fagging and house fagging. School fagging meant performing duties such as scoring, umpiring, etc. on the sports field, on an *ad hoc* basis if selected after roll call. In some school matches a party

of powerful players took on the whole school and every boy who
was not a 'cap' had to stand in goal during a Big Side match. The
rules in these engagements were not rigid and there was a high
risk of injury. By 1843 the rules did at least ban attempts to
throttle or strangle during the course of a 'maul'. A first-hand
description of football at Rugby by William Arnold survives (in
Rouse, 1898 [1906], pp. 266–70). House fagging was more
onerous than school fagging. The 'fag of the week' had to rouse
the others at 6.30 a.m. Then after first lesson the fag had to go
into town to buy any luxury foods required by the fag's praepostor and cook them. Then the praepostor's study had to be tidied
and thoroughly cleaned. Later in the day half a dozen fags prepared toast in Hall for tea (toasting forks were banned). Then
came a duty for those selected to wait by a fireplace in the
corridor for any praepostor who wanted supper serving.

Another fag's eye view is provided by a letter home from new
entrant E. H. Bradby in 1839. He joins a form of 46. There were
still initiation rites on entry.

> 27.10.1839 . . . Last night I had to mount upon the Hall
> table and sing my song. I sang 'Mrs John Prevot' . . . It is a
> very nervous thing to have to mount upon a table and sing
> before about 39 boys; if you don't sing well you are floored,
> and have to sing two the next Saturday . . . This week I
> was 988 [the week's mark total in the form] and only 3
> from top . . .

The top places in the class are unstable as boys are moved up and
down in rank order after frequent testing. Bradby said his prayers
in his study and not a public room; even Arnold's Rugby was
not so spiritual that safety could be guaranteed for private de-
votions performed in public. Clearly, Arnold could not change
everything quickly, nor did he try to. Hughes again:

> Arnold had not time, in my first years there, to stamp out
> the old heathenism which he found at Rugby, and the
> private prayers question was still acute, . . . dominated by
> two notorious bullies who set their faces against the boys
> kneeling by their bedsides. [When one did so, they] held
> him down on his knees and 'slippered' him. No other boy
> interfered . . . and the praepostor of their room had not
> come up, as it was before 10 o'clock. (writing in 1896,
> recalled in Self, 1909, p. 17)

Bradby disliked school dinner, 'lumps of pudding and dabs of
fat'. His first impression was that 'the fagging is a mere nothing. I
have only been fagged once, which was to carry a book for a boy
to his house' (this was school fagging) but his tasks increased over
time. His praepostor invited him to sit by his fire in winter 'and
the mere fact of knowing him prevents one from being bullied'.
He writes to his mother that:

> five praepostors . . . have been sent away for being drunk
> and kicking up a row at a calling over [registration] . . . I
> remembered your good advice and did not clap them as
> many did, but remained quite quiet, as likewise the other
> day when Cotton (our master) came into School, some of
> the boys hissed at him, but I got out from among them as
> soon as I could . . . Three of them – among whom was
> Arnold's son were 'coached' [i.e. flogged], and have had
> very long and heavy punishments.

Which of Arnold's sons was flogged? There is no clear answer. In
1839 William entered the School, aged 11; Edward had entered,
aged 12, in 1838; Tom had entered, aged 13, in 1837.

Rewards and sanctions

Arnold awarded prizes for effort as well as achievement, all at his own expense, 'a great many books in extremely handsome bindings' (A. H. Clough). He was very keen to praise pupils who did not find learning naturally easy, but who made substantial effort and progress. The prizes for 1842 included Latin Prose, English Prose, Latin Verse (subject: Vulcanus), English Verse (subject: The Victory of Suffering). Half-holidays for the whole school rewarded a scholarship to university by a sixth former. He also rewarded pupils by his verbal and non-verbal cues as to his response to their work. The public schools of the day existed in a climate where corporal punishment was widely but not quite universally accepted and often adminstered with something approaching savagery. The twenty-first century finds difficulty in understanding the nineteenth century in this respect and sees physical punishment sometimes too clearly as sadism. It clearly sometimes was, as Dickens's school narratives could testify (see p. 174f). But physical punishment for boys at least was an accepted part of family as well as school life. When there was controversy, it was usually about the severity of it, rather than the practice *per se*. In accepting its necessity, Arnold was just a teacher of his time; he did not accept that it was degrading and he felt it was in some contexts less of an ordeal for the pupil than a long, repetitive, written task such as lines. However, Arnold's use of it in the March case alone (pp. 139ff) could be said to call into question the whole practice.

Arnold recorded that he was pleased not to have to resort to flogging for some time after he arrived at Rugby, although this may have been the 'honeymoon period' in teaching, when teacher and pupils are weighing each other up. He viewed flogging as unsuitable for older boys and as something that should be reserved for the most serious offences: lying, wilful disobedience and persistent idleness. Impositions, 'lines' and extra duties were used at Rugby as alternative punishments for more minor offences. It seems clear (Rouse, 1898 [1906], p. 228, footnote 1) that Arnold applied to the trustees in 1831 for permission to introduce the sanction of solitary confinement for certain offences and the idea that pupils should reflect on their mis-doings and soberly prepare for a different path, in isolation with-out the support of their peers, would have appealed to him. But the trustees did not agree. In the light of Arnold's contract (see p. 61) it is unclear why he asked them at all, unless he feared opposition to so new a step in the annals of the school.

The ultimate sanction and one which is still easier to apply in an independent school than a state school is expulsion. It is now-adays euphemistically referred to as 'permanent exclusion'. Before he went to Rugby, Arnold was quite clear that he viewed the expulsion of the hardest cases a necessary and neglected task in the public schools. Trustees would not want to lose their fee income. He was committed to expulsion as a method of rooting out the worst cases of pupil behaviour and removing those unlikely to benefit from their place in the school.

> Sending boys away is a necessary and regular part of a good system, not as a punishment to one but as a protection to others. Undoubtedly it would be a better system if there was no evil; but evil being unavoidable we are not a jail to keep it in, but a place of education where we must cast it out, to prevent its taint from spreading. (Bamford, 1970, p. 105)

He was prepared quietly to expel the worst trouble-makers (the bully Flashman was characteristically dispatched without cere-mony first thing in the morning after his final offence) and to advise the parents of pupils making no progress to withdraw them, despite the fears of his trustees that numbers in the school would reduce. In fact they rose. 'Till a man learns that the first, second and third duty of the schoolmaster is to get rid of unpromising subjects, a great public school will not be what it might be, and what it ought to be' (ibid., p. 127). If this seems harsh in a climate more sensitive to the special needs of children, it must also be set in a context in which 'dull' children were sometimes retained in their schools as a source of income, despite their deriving no benefit from their presence (especially taking into account the mainly classical curriculum), and their being the butt of bullying or at least a source of laughter and ridicule among their peers. But it is in the application of sanctions that teachers are often at their most vulnerable to the outside world and in the public glare of the media. So it was to prove with Arnold in two cases in which his judgment was, to put the mildest connotation upon it, weak in the extreme.

The March case

Stanley presents Arnold as averse to flogging, except for the offences of lying, drinking and habitual idleness and then only among the younger boys, but by 1833 he had fallen foul of the Tory *Northampton Herald* for publicly flogging a fourteen-year-old boy called Thomas Gonne March with eighteen strokes for persistent lying. Even Hughes concedes Arnold's ire was well known and that there were discernible signals: 'the Doctor's under lip was coming out, and his eye beginning to burn, and his gown getting gathered up more and more tightly in his left hand' (Hughes, 1857, 1994 edition, p. 142). The March case represents what has to be seen as the most serious misjudgment in the treatment of a pupil of Arnold's career within Rugby School. It provides plenty of evidence for those who want to depict him as a sadistic flogger, or a tyrant unfit to be in charge of children.

Needless to say, the matter is not raised in Stanley's *Life* and although even in *Tom Brown* Arnold loses his temper (see p. 123), there is nothing on this scale. At the same time, the twenty-first-century mind is revolted by any notions of severely flogging children, whether guilty or not, whereas the nineteenth-century mind accepted flogging as a natural part of public school life.

Part of the background to this case has to be seen in Arnold's attempt to infuse honesty into the code of school life. 'He believed a boy's word as he believed a man's; and if he was sometimes deceived even then . . . yet the greater number of boys were ashamed to tell him a lie' (Rouse, 1898 [1909], p. 226). In the school underworld it was said that it was a pity to lie to 'the Doctor', because he always believed you. In our society, where a recent minister could defend being 'economical with the truth', lies have become a socially acceptable self-defence mechanism. But to Arnold they were manipulative, deceitful, even wicked. He would have had great sympathy with the Quaker concept of 'plain speaking'.

As has been noted, Arnold would examine pupils in the various forms of the school regularly. The form teacher would give him a note of the work done and another member of staff would go with him to help in the questioning of pupils. On this occasion the accompanying teacher was James Prince Lee, later to become a celebrated head himself. On the basis of misinformation supplied in a note from Thomas March's teacher, Roger Bird, Arnold began to examine the boy on a translation passage he was supposed to have prepared from Xenophon's *Anabasis*. The boy immediately explained that they had not yet reached that point in the book. Arnold's famous thunderous frown appeared and he re-checked the note. Bird was not present in the room. Arnold informed March that the note said that they had indeed reached that point. March denied he had been told to prepare this. Lee was sent to check the note with Bird. One can imagine the atmosphere in the form, with 'the Doctor's ire' a well-known and greatly feared event. Prince Lee returned to say Bird was right and March was wrong. The Reverend Roger Bird had been on the staff for thirteen years at this point (he served from 1820 to 1840, leaving to become vicar of Combe Bissett, Wiltshire), having previously been a Fellow of Magdalen. Arnold accepted his reply without further investigation. He rounded on March, calling him 'Liar! Liar! Liar!' March continued to defend his innocence. From Arnold's point of view the evidence against him was total. It existed in writing. He had verified it. What he did not do in the heat of the moment was to check with the other pupils in the room. We must presume they were too frightened to interrupt him to confirm March's story. Instead, March was flogged, not for failure to do the 'prep' but for repeated lying. He was given eighteen strokes. The lesson proceeded, although presumably Arnold could not have examined the next boy on the same passage, or he would have received the same result. One can vividly imagine what the next boy to be questioned must have been feeling while this flogging was proceeding. March was a weak boy, with a hernia, and was absent from class for the next two days, recovering in his boarding house.

It was bound to emerge, however, that Bird had made a mistake. When it came to light, Arnold was filled with remorse – at that time he would not have been as fearful of litigious parents or suspension by his governing body as would now be the case – and he visited the boy's class to apologize in public. Not content with that, he presented a public apology to the boy in front of the entire school. By now, of course, the March parents had learned what had happened and they removed him from the school. Arnold wrote an apology to them. Perhaps surprisingly, March was returned. The press got hold of the story while Arnold was in the Lakes in mid-January 1833. It was recalled that Wooll had never given more than twelve strokes and that was for rebellion and that in his day there was a 24-hour delay in administering major punishments, to allow the heat of the moment to cool. This would have undoubtedly saved March. The press attacked Arnold, not for the use of flogging *per se*, which was accepted as a matter of course, but on the basis that if lying produced this punishment, what must more serious offences incur? Would he flog boys to death? But for Arnold there was no more serious offence than lying. He insisted that he would trust what his pupils told him, a radical departure in education, to which they generally responded well. Breach of trust was to him breach of the most basic relationship between teacher and pupil. He expected no less of himself: it would be foolish and inconsistent for a person to live like a heathen and profess to believe as a Christian (*Sermons*, 1832, 1850 edition, p. 278). By 1854 William Arnold could write that in the great public schools 'the gross notion of its being fair to deceive a master . . . is quite exploded' (*Oakfield*, p. 229). This is certainly an over-statement, but it is a testimony to Arnold's influence.

The March affair was a problem entirely of Arnold's making, unlike many of the problems that arrive on the desk of headteachers. But his handling of it showed serious professional misjudgement that need not have been made and cannot be glossed over. Or rather, it was a case of anger prevailing over judgement. Arnold knew that self-control was one department of Christian living in which he needed to improve. The staff wrote a letter to the press in defence of Arnold, signed by all except curiously Bird. The press attacks continued through February. Arnold's attempt to gag the man whom he thought was their main informant failed spectacularly. This was another mistake. His letters to this man, Francis Litchfield, Rector of Farthinghoe, were forwarded by him to the newspaper. Litchfield was a Tory, hunting, hard-drinking parson who hated radicals. Despite the extraordinary and indefensible nature of this particular punishment, Arnold wished to see flogging reduced both in the number of times it was administered and the number of strokes. Arnold was very much opposed to the existing tradition of headship that flogged miscreants for all offences for which they were presumed guilty. Nor did he feel it was an appropriate punishment for older boys. When the matter became public it was he who corrected the statement in the papers that March had received fifteen strokes to eighteen in the interests of truth.

The Marshall case

Nicholas Marshall was a Lower Fifth former. He had received permission from a praepostor to go into town but lingered with friends on the doorstep of his boarding house. There was noise, which became progressively louder until the same praepostor arrived on the scene, identified Marshall as the ringleader and ordered him inside. He replied, in front of his friends, that he would go inside when he was ready and not before. When he finally went in he was still defiant and was ordered to the Hall after dinner. When the praepostor attempted to cane him, Marshall broke the cane in two. The praepostor summoned two others to help. This was when a blackthorn stick was used, but it was broken in the struggle and Marshall's head was banged against the wall, accidentally according to the praepostors. One account suggests Marshall actually carried off part of the broken stick to display as a victory token. But the praepostors, having had their authority publicly flouted, reported the matter to Arnold. It was about 6 p.m. and dark (Friday 13 November). Marshall was immediately expelled and dispatched by chaise the 50 miles to his home in Iffley. He could not complete the journey and had to stay overnight at Banbury. Arnold had given him no opportunity to answer the accusations against him. It was for his repeated refusal to accept the authority of praepostors that

Arnold expelled the junior. Arnold held that boys should obey the law of the school, as represented by praepostors, just as people should obey the law of the land. He was less willing to accept that some adolescent infringements in behaviour are inevitable.

The matter did not end there. Marshall had a brother at the school. Marshall's father, the Reverend Edward Marshall (who had changed his name to Hacker), was deeply disturbed that Marshall had not been questioned or allowed to speak by Arnold and that he had been dispatched at night in the circumstances described. He wrote to Arnold to complain but got no satisfaction. Not surprisingly, he then removed the brother from the school. Then he journeyed to Rugby to see Arnold without an appointment. It was a disastrous meeting for both parties. Arnold had just concluded an interview with an irate parent, who was complaining about the flogging of his son by a praepostor and Arnold walked into the room unprepared to confront Hacker. Arnold absolutely refused to discuss the Marshall incident and actually 'showed Hacker the door'. Hacker had made a 100-mile round trip in vain, in pre-railway travel conditions, without even being able to present his case, even though he had been unwise to do it without any guarantee of an appointment. He decided to appeal formally to the trustees. But the trustees had already backed Arnold publicly in March in a letter whose contents were known to the older pupils (letter home from Clough, March 1836, see also p. 89) and Hacker's appeal came to their July meeting. They simply reiterated that as far as the school was concerned, the matter was closed. It was not good public relations and it was not natural justice, to sentence without even a hearing. But it was consistent, both with Arnold's utter trust in sixth formers and with his own well-aired pre-Rugby views that expelling trouble-makers was not often enough done in the public schools. Even in a climate in which the rights of pupils below the sixth form were not axiomatic as they are now, it shows a lack

18. School House Studies, Rugby, showing Arnold's study and staircase in the right-hand corner.

– *from a contemporary photograph*

of judgement on Arnold's part, or perhaps his famous temper getting the better of him once again.

Classroom teacher

Arnold taught the sixth form, in which all members followed a common curriculum, as many heads did in their schools. The classroom was the newly built library in the tower chamber above the school gate. He used to run up the corkscrew staircase and commonly remarked that 'when I find I can no longer run up the library stairs, I shall know that it is time for me to go'. When teaching, he sat on a plain kitchen chair, a wooden carver's chair as it would now be known, at a small table on a level with the tables of his pupils, not lecturing from the teacher's dais common at the time. A fireplace was on his left. As the sixth form grew, the small room would be crowded. The library books were shelved on a mezzanine level above.

Education to Arnold was fundamentally the religious and moral training of character, the cultivation of a person's mind. Every lesson he taught began with prayer, preceded by silence as Arnold glanced round to see that all were suitably serious. The daily prayer for the sixth form before the first lesson was: 'Lord, strengthen the faculties of our minds and dispose us to exert them' (Whitridge, 1928, p. 111). The full text is in the back of his 1842 teaching notebook, so as to be quickly opened and read before the commencement of class. He had a manner of 'awful reverence' when speaking of God or of the Scriptures (Stanley, 1845, p. 32) and there was a feeling that 'when his eye was upon you, he looked into your inmost heart' (ibid., p. 184).

> The depth of his tones, and the pathos of his voice [reading Wordsworth] still linger in the chambers of memory . . .
> Under his vivid teaching, the rolling eloquence and grand

146

prophetic inspiration of Deuteronomy grew into one's soul, spite of struggling through it in the crabbed [Septuaguint] Greek. (Gover, despite his lack of feeling for Arnold, see p. 132)

Arnold's 1842 day notebook serves as a mark record. The list includes Walrond, Stanley and Vaughan. He also records attendance and late work. The surviving pupil notebooks show that he checked them and made neat corrections in black ink where required. The power and presence of 'the Doctor' was awesome. Even Stanley admits a 'peculiar vehemence in language' (1845, p. 198) in speaking of contemporary events, 'an unhasting, unresting diligence' (ibid., p. 234). This no doubt was felt in his classroom persona. Fitch (1897, p. 37, 50f) suggests that Arnold put new life into received methods of teaching rather than inventing new ones, bringing to the task commitment and enthusiasm. Unusually for the time he would always admit when he did not know the answer and try to learn with his class, sometimes sending a pupil to ask another teacher for information. He was also willing to admit his own mistakes or ignorance. This same thread runs through his later lectures as Professor of Modern History (1841–2). Mere cleverness he did not admire, likening it to the cleverness of lawyers divested of moral character with conviction or acquittal, not truth, as the aim. He admired the plodder rather than the genius to whom learning came easily. Arnold also used the question technique as a teaching method far more than was then common. This meant that pupils had less chance of being passive and were also more likely to understand issues than if he had merely lectured, as teachers of older pupils tended to do at the time. The boy Stanley wrote home that Arnold would put 'queer, out-of-the-way questions' that made him think. Arnold was known to check himself on the verge of giving an answer and substitute another question which would lead the pupil to discover the answer. He was also concerned that pupils should not merely acquire facts, but also the ability to communicate them, in other words to teach and explain for others. When he did provide didactic explanations, they were brief and to the point, in language which the pupils could understand. The result was that they became more memorable for his pupils. Perhaps he was helped by the vividness with which he could 'see' some of the events he was describing. Mary Arnold records:

> He mentioned having had last night one of those curious dreams which he has had occasionally. He thought he was one of the assassins of Caesar remembered a conversation with Decimus Brutus & seemed in all the tussels [tussles? handwriting unclear] of the scene. (20.9.1825)

Arnold provided clear cues as to his feelings about a pupil answer. A pleased look and a cheerful 'Thank you' followed successful answers or translation. The 'stern elevation of the eyebrows' and a sudden 'Sit down' followed unsatisfactory answers. In extreme cases boys were sent out of the room to allow Arnold's temper time to cool. Arnold is described by Stanley as courteous and deferential to the sixth but ready instantly to check impertinence or unsuitable levity. A good lesson brought praise along the lines of what a pleasure it was to him to come into the library (his classroom). A former pupil, J. L. Hoskyns, provides a picture of Arnold in action teaching the sixth form of his golden triumvirate, Stanley, Vaughan and Lake:

> Arnold referred to them [the three] in matters of criticism or points of history. 'Stanley, what do you think about that?' . . . folding his gown and leaning upon the table, and looking towards them with such *respect* shown in the very

tone of his voice, and always getting a good answer.
(Bamford, 1960, p. 79, Hoskyn's italics)

To his critics, this smacked of favouritism. Arnold commented on what he hoped pupils would learn. The best answer is

> that which shows a boy has read and thought for himself
> . . . the next best, which shows that he has read several
> books and digested what he has read . . . the *worst*, which
> shows that he has read but one book, and followed that
> without reflection. (Stanley, 1845, p. 125, his italics)

He referred to this again in his final Oxford lecture in 1842:

> We here are not likely to run away with the foolish notion,
> that lectures can teach us a science without careful study of
> our own. They can but excite us to begin work for
> ourselves; possibly they may assist our efforts; they can in
> no way supersede them. (Lecture 8: 315)

A favourite among his pupils was his own extempore Latin and Greek translation (Susanna enjoyed his translations of Herodotus read beside her crib, see p. 34). Arnold defended this against word-for-word translation as entering much more into the spirit of the writers. He also attempted to translate into the appropriate style for the text, idiomatic or more correct. He made his pupils attempt to find the correct style for translation and not merely the correct words. It helped to give pupils the whole sense of a passage and avoid absurd translations of particular phrases. This technique was derived from his own time as a pupil of Gabell at Winchester. Once asked whether repetition of the same texts with different generations of boys did not bore him, Arnold replied absolutely not, that he always found something new in them. He did experiment with some of the texts used. Thucydides, Herodotus, Homer and Aristotle were firm favourites.

Curriculum

Many of the reforms of public school education which were later credited to Arnold, strengthening of the prefectorial system, modernizing the curriculum, developing a cult of compulsory, organized games including Rugby football (which is held to have originated in 1823), were either not original to him, or were wrongly attributed. Arnold was indifferent to compulsory, organized games. It is interesting to note that he did not play organized games himself, despite such a physically active life. 'New gymnastic affairs' were set up on the Island (letter home from Clough, 1836): 'swings, vaulting poles, and all kind of monkey-trick instruments'. In Arnold's time cricket became established from 1831 and by 1840 the school had played at Lord's, losing to the Marylebone Club. Tom Hughes, the captain, was 30 not out. But the promotion of cricket did not come from Arnold. Cross-country running was also practised. Archer (1921, p. 73) tersely notes that Arnold's entire contribution to organized games was 'that he sometimes stood on the touch line and looked pleased'. Arnold would have known that Aristotle argued that too much emphasis on sport and athletics can brutalize (*Politics*, VIII: 3–35). The boys in Arnold's time were largely free to follow their own pursuits out of school hours; even Strachey notes the irony that Arnold was wrongly remembered by 1918 as being 'the founder of the worship of athletics and the worship of good form' in public schools (Strachey, 1918, p. 239).

Arnold was also opposed to major curriculum reform. Fitch (1897) underlines this by commenting that Arnold was not 'a great reformer or revolutionist' in the sense in which Comenius,

19. Football at Rugby in 1845.

Rousseau, Locke or Pestalozzi were. Trevor (1973) is wrong to describe Rugby as 'thoroughly modernized' for a school of the 1830s; it was definitely not. Arnold accepted the traditions of English education based mainly on the study of the classics, both language and literature. Fitch rightly places Arnold in 'the pre-scientific era of educational history' (1900, p. 52). The study of the past was to him the study of culture at its height. The sixth form voices of the *Rugby Magazine* for 1835–6 eloquently defend this position; Arnold had carried at least the writers with him. But Arnold was careful to use the classics as a means to an end, not an end in themselves. That made him different in the classroom from many of his contemporaries. The classics were means of exploring history, poetry, philosophy, linguistics, ethics and aesthetics.

> Expel Greek and Latin from your schools and you confine the views of the existing generation to themselves and their

immediate predecessors, you will cut off so many centuries of the world's experience, and place us in the same state as if the human race had first come into existence in the year 1500.

But that meant a good grounding in language, Latin and Greek, and new arrivals at Rugby were placed in a form according to their ability and vocabulary in these two. Arnold gave each thirteen-year-old applicant a viva in person. Stanley was asked to read from Homer and Virgil and questioned about his Latin verses. Arnold also addressed the problem that people forgot so much of what they learned at school. His answer was that the benefit of a classical education was that it shaped and prepared the mind for further learning.

> Arnold was the first man, not only in English schools,
> but in English universities, who realised the opportunity
> which classical instruction offered as an introduction of
> the pupil to ethical, philosophical and political problems
> and who illustrated it in practice in such a way as to
> evoke imitation. (Archer, 1921, p. 36)

If the content was forgotten, the skills and aptitudes would remain. Arnold held that it makes the mind liberal in its tastes and comprehensive in its views and actions. But this only works if the teaching is intelligent and stimulating, not mechanical and sterile. The acquisition of facts is less important than the understanding of principles and forces behind them. This line of thinking was not unique to Arnold. But he was concerned to breathe new life into the teaching process. So his titles for Latin, Greek and English verse or essay composition were imaginary speeches such as a conversation between Thomas Aquinas, James Watt and Walter Scott, descriptions of historical events, philosophical issues, e.g. the ideal is superior to the real, and ethical issues. As a gifted teacher, Arnold may have got away by making a curriculum succeed which even then had ceased to be defensible for most or all pupils. He argued strongly that Plato and Aristotle are our contemporaries in terms of the problems they faced. But industrialization was already challenging that view.

The Rugby curriculum, then, was largely traditional and unexceptional for its time. French had a very subsidiary role, science, as now understood, almost none (despite Trevor, 1973, p. 27). German was introduced in 1835, but not for all pupils; the aim was to read German scholars. For Arnold, science was a way of organizing systematic knowledge, a study of insights, motives, reasons, causes, consequences, links. It was wider than a particular subject content, like biology. What was needed to back up classical languages and literature was history, divinity, geography and 'ethical and political science'. History mattered because ancient history is paralleled in modern history; in fact the terms themselves were misleading in Arnold's view. Every people has its ancient and modern history; Greek 'ancient' history with its republics and empires is more 'modern' than English 'ancient' history before the eighteenth century. Thucydides marks the transition from an age of feeling to an age of reflection and is therefore 'modern'. Roman civilization from the Gracchi period is also 'modern'. 'Mere lapse of years confers . . . no increase of knowledge.' The experience of 153 commonwealths known to Aristotle has much to offer modern times. Arnold believed that the young should start with the 'poetry of history' – pictures, key names, great events – and move to its philosophy as they grew older. He also wanted pupils to appreciate that behind actions and events lay compelling beliefs. Whether Romulus ever lived may not be known, but the belief in his life shaped the development of Rome. At the same time it was important to be able to distinguish legend from history. Such was the great relevance to Arnold of studying 'ancient' history. A person who only knows ancient history 'will be far better fitted to enter on public life than he who could tell the circumstances and the date of every battle and of every debate throughout the last century [the 18th]'. Nevertheless, modern history was taught in a weekly lesson and was much liked by boys in Arnold's own form, perhaps because it was a welcome antidote to the weighty ancient culture and language studies. Geography, which had been a personal interest of Arnold's from childhood, was an important ancillary subject to history and literature, as it helped to furnish the background. Scripture as a lesson appeared twice weekly. The Greek text was used for Old and New Testaments, although lessons included early church history and the Reformation in England. He did not enter into the current controversies of the Church of England, in which he was so busily involved outside the school. His pupils felt he had the power to make real the events in the scriptures. Maths was taught at Rugby, ranging from arithmetic to the conics, but calculus was not taught.

Science at Rugby, in common with most other public schools of the time, was under-represented for the reasons outlined above. Adam Walker, and then his son D. F. Walker, had maintained a custom of a triennial series of twelve, two-hour science lectures at the school over some 60 years. The timetable was modified to accommodate these, but under Arnold it became clear that these lectures did not enjoy the head's real support. Walker complained in 1835 that his last series had to be abandoned mid-course, as only about ten boys were being freed from their other commitments to attend. The 1837 series was worse and Walker complained to a press eager to receive anti-Arnold titbits. Walker, who must have been enthusiastic in the face of such indifference or discouragement by Arnold, arranged to hold his lectures in the half-holidays, thus making no disturbance of regular timetable at all. Arnold struck at this, however, by ruling that boys attending would either have to pay an extra fee of a guinea, or produce a written guarantee from their parents that this extra would be paid. Walker, who had chosen to lecture at the *Spread Eagle* and travelled from London and transported and assembled equipment in preparation, was again left without an audience. The emphasis in the Walker lectures seems to have been on physics and the apparatus in the father's lectures included globes, planetaria, engines, pumps, eye models and an imitation thorax. The younger Walker was said to have called the boys 'brutes' for preferring the playing field to the lecture room. But it was their half-holiday and Arnold had provided the additional barrier of high expense to discourage them. It is a cameo which is difficult to interpret (the papers claimed it was because Walker was a Tory) because Arnold had a personal interest in science, which appears in his correspondence and he set in his occasional holiday tasks for boys to bring back specimens to Rugby. Arnold knew William Buckland the geologist (his friend's brother) and on several occasions attended geological meetings of the British Association in Birmingham. Science was still the province of the clerical gifted amateur and as a profession was in its infancy. But it is still hard to account for and harder to defend Arnold's attempt to kill by neglect what was only a triennial occasion anyway.

Arnold did not merely consider the content of teaching. He also took assessment into account and held that *viva voce* examinations at school or university should never be entirely replaced by written papers. The viva has advantages: it enables fluent expression; it tests knowledge over a long thesis or syllabus; it saves time, as people can speak much more quickly than they can write; if such examinations are public, the audience can benefit; it encourages presence of mind; combined with a written paper it can be a very accurate means of assessment. If this view is no longer popular, his points are still valid.

Arnold and 'religious education' (spiritual development)

It is possible, from the sermons and the way in which Arnold structured Rugby School, to reconstruct his view of spiritual development. He called it 'religious education' and it is important not to confuse his usage with the twenty-first century name for the classroom subject, which in Arnold's time was called Scripture or Divinity.

> None can be more sensible than ourselves to the worthlessness of mere intellectual advancement, unless superintended by that Discipline which invariably combines the enlargement of the Understanding with the gradual correction and improvement of our moral nature. (unpublished essay at Laleham, 1826)

Adolescence was to Arnold a time of trial and temptation between the idyll of childhood and the maturity of adulthood. There was plenty of evidence in contemporary behaviour in public schools to illustrate this, from cases of homosexual rape – boys still slept six to a bed in some schools in the 1820s – to bullying, including roasting 'fags' (junior boys), extortion, gambling, alcohol excess, riding to hounds, poaching, attacking local residents and other illicit activities. Arnold's radical solution was to reduce adolescence to a minimum, by expecting adult behaviour and trust among adolescents, especially older ones, and by curbing excesses when they did arise by firm but fair discipline.

The question then is, really, can the change from

childhood to manhood be hastened in the case of boy and young man . . . without injury to the future excellence and full development of the man? That is, without exhausting prematurely the faculties either of body or mind. (Bamford, 1970, p. 80)

In an often quoted dictum referred to on p. 60, Arnold remarked that he wanted to produce Christian *men*, for Christian *boys* he could not hope to make. There were a few positive aspects of childhood. They included that children were very teachable and therefore needed good examples, and that the transition to adult-hood could be hastened. This phase was marked when a time of 'principle' was attained, potentially in the sixth form years. Those not entering the sixth missed the high point and climax of the whole education process. Arnold's own character was consistent with this. Whitridge (1928, p. 90) sums it up as a passionate belief in Christ; a hatred of sin; an unswerving sense of conduct; the con-viction that education could not thrive without Christianity; and that mental cultivation is properly a religious duty.

> He made us understand that the only thing for which God cares . . . is goodness, that the only thing which is supremely hateful to God is wickedness. All other things are useful, admirable, beautiful in their several ways. All forms, ordinances, means of instruction, means of amusement, have their places in our lives . . . In his view, there was no place or time from which Religion is shut out, there is no place or time where we cannot be serving God by serving our fellow-creatures. (Stanley, 1874, p. 1)

Arnold believed that reducing adolescence could be done without damage and that 'over-study' or 'a premature advance in book knowledge' was no part of the recipe, but rather a change from

157

carelessness to thoughtfulness, from ignorance to wisdom, from selfishness to unselfishness. His critics felt that he did it at the cost of not accepting the real nature of adolescence and of depriving some boys of part of their childhood by making them over-intense, a cultivation of morbidity and introspection. He maintained that 'the natural liveliness and gaiety of youth' held 'a great deal of folly' and that it could be 'riotous, insolent and annoying to others'. Arnold held that boarding establishments, by removing parental influence, could themselves harm adolescent boys. This was highly plausible in the pre-railway era of his early years at Rugby. Until railways made shorter terms practicable, the school year was divided into Long Half (21 weeks from early February to late June) and Short Half (16 weeks from late August to late December), a two-term year. Boarding school society is 'wholly composed of persons whose state, morally and intellectually, is, by reason of their age, exceedingly imperfect' (Bamford, 1970, p. 134).

For Arnold a Christian school should be a 'temple of God', although just like the Jerusalem Temple it can be corrupted and can then harm its members, e.g. by condoning drunkenness or bullying or lying. Individual members have a duty towards the school. They are not there to please themselves. In some schools, hatred of authority, general idleness and peer pressure to behave badly are the very opposite of Christian love. Set in this context, the male community of the boys' public school under Arnold became a sort of Christian monastery, with Chapel at the heart and with all its teaching religious in intention. By 1839 prayers were held daily at 7 a.m. and 7.45 p.m.; on Sundays they were held at 8.30 a.m. and 7.45 p.m. with first Chapel from 11 a.m. to 12 noon and second Chapel from 4 p.m. until approximately 5 p.m. Sundays also brought an hour's learning of a gospel passage after breakfast, and sometimes a psalm, and an hour after lunch to prepare three or four Bible chapters for the Second

Lecture held from 3 p.m. to 4 p.m. In School House, which Arnold headed, the night prayer was read by a praepostor after a reading by Arnold himself in English, translating from his Greek Testament. Arnold was very much aware of the difficulties faced by all schools.

> This common and well known Feature of a School, – its Roughness, Coarseness, Want of Feeling, to say nothing of its positive Unkindness and Spirit of Annoyance, does this bear any Resemblance to the Temper of those who are the inhabitants of the Kingdom of God? (Sermon on Psalm 94.2, 27.11.1836)

Teachers should not be in the old master–slave relationship but should be like parents. Their example can be crucial. 'Religious education' is to enable children to reach out to life eternal, 'making them know and love God, know and abhor evil . . . teaching our understandings to know the highest truth . . . the highest good' (*Sermons*, 1842, p. 88). Can teachers accomplish this great task? Is it impossible? In commercial schools the religious teaching varies probably more than anything else, according to the personal character of the instructor. It is not like teaching the Three Rs, but the catechism, the words of hymns and the 'great truths of the gospel' provide a 'map of the road' (ibid., p. 184). The curriculum has to allow proper space for this development. Physical science cannot instruct the judgement – perhaps a clue to its lowly place in the Rugby curriculum. Only moral and religious knowledge can accomplish this. Teaching history, moral and political philosophy with no reference to the Bible is not possible without giving children an anti-religious education. Arnold recognized no middle ground. Curriculum was either religious or, by the absence of religion, anti-religious. William Temple, a Rugbeian son of a Rugbeian head, was later to make the identical point in the 1943 education debate. Arnold again:

> I cannot reject from religious education whatever ministers to the perfection of our bodies and our minds, so long as both in body and our mind, in soul and spirit, we . . . may be taught to minister to the service of God. (*Sermons*, 1842a, p. 208)

But this sort of education is effected by the whole school community, not merely classroom lessons. The characteristics of childhood include experience of temptations, being 'slaves to present influences' (neither looking backwards nor forwards to interpret the present situation), and children being unfit to guide themselves (*Sermons*, 1844, p. 14). Children, after the innocence of early childhood is lost, are ignorant and selfish, living only for the present. Arnold believed that adolescence in children in attitudes and behaviour corresponded to the adolescence of the human race. Adolescents needed the claims of Christianity setting before them clearly and uncompromisingly. It was a mistake to appeal to the reason of the child in a situation where obedience should be required. Children are 'under the law' (I Timothy 1:9) and therefore require a system with rules, disciplines and, where necessary, punishments. Without that, childhood innocence could be corrupted by adolescents into hardness, coarseness, cruelty and stupidity. Corporal punishment for boys is neither degrading, nor unchristian *per se*. It must not be too excessive or too frequent, nor must it be applied to older boys. Fagging and the use of praepostors (prefects), properly controlled, regulate what would otherwise be the impossibility of equality between different year groups of children. Addressing the members of the Rugby Mechanics' Institute in 1838, Arnold urged that 'a docile and yet enquiring mind best becomes us both as men and as Christians' (*Misc. Works*, 1845, p. 424).

Chaplaincy and pastoral care

School House

Hughes, a devotee of Arnold's, put the credit side of his achievement:

> besides teaching the sixth, and governing and guiding the whole School, editing classics, and writing histories, the great Headmaster had found time in those busy years to watch over the career even of him Tom Brown, and his particular friends, – and, no doubt, of fifty other boys at the same time; and all this without taking the least credit to himself, or seeming to know, or let anyone else know, that he ever thought particularly of any boys at all. (1857, p. 298)

Arnold made himself personally available to pupils, not just the sixth form, and from 1831 his presence in his study was advertised by a flag outside, a public invitation to call. Pupils availed themselves of this. More dauntingly, individuals in his house were 'invited' periodically for what would now be called a tutorial, of about an hour, with 'the Doctor' in the evening. Boys were also invited to meals with his family and even on family holidays.

> Many is the brave heart now doing its work and bearing its load in country curacies, London chambers, under the Indian sun, and in Australian towns and clearings, which looks back with fond and grateful memory to that

School-house drawing room, and dates much of its highest and best training to the lessons learnt there. (ibid., p. 182)

Outside the classroom he proved a rumbustious older brother to many; if many held him in awe, as they undoubtedly did, it does not seem to have been a deliberate cult on his part. He called the boys 'fellows', their own name for themselves. But, in contrast to this, Stanley suggests that Arnold had a 'natural shyness' and 'an awkwardness in his address' that meant that outside the sixth and School House, he was not well known to the boys. One of his reforms at Rugby was to replace 'dames', non-teaching women who took in boarders, with housemasters, teachers who took on boarding supervision duties. This was not original. Other schools such as Westminster were doing the same thing. But it was effective. He became head of School House himself. It contained between 60 and 70 boys. The pupils' petition to ask him to carry on in this capacity when he proposed to lay it down to concentrate on other duties still survives at Rugby:

> We, the undersigned, have heard with regret your intention of giving up the School House. We venture to say that the personal regard we feel for you would make us extremely lament your leaving us; and we humbly hope that this expression of our feelings may be allowed some weight in influencing your determination.

The March and Marshall incidents (pp. 139ff and 143ff) have to be read in conjunction with this petition. In the boarding houses each boy was allocated a separate bed, by no means standard then, and no one, teachers included, was to enter a boy's study without knocking first. The process of boys having separate study-bedrooms was begun as early as the previous head but one, Ingles (head from 1794–1806). The detailed running of and discipline in the house were left to praepostors. Hughes provides a view of School House at night roll call as a young boy sees it:

> The steps of the head-porter are heard on the stairs, and a light gleams at the door. 'Hush!' from the fifth form boys who stand there, and then in strides the Doctor, cap on head, book in one hand, and gathering up his gown in the other. He walks up the middle, and takes up his post by Warner, who begins calling over the names. The Doctor takes no notice of anything, but quietly turns over his book and finds the place, and then stands, cap in hand and finger in book . . . and reads out the Psalm in that deep, ringing, searching voice of his. (1857, p. 115f)

Among Arnold's favourites were Psalms 19 and 107. The Sunday evening prayer at the School House included the searching passage:

> Thou knowest, O Lord, and our own consciences each know also, whether while we worshipped Thee in form we worshipped Thee in spirit and in truth. Thou knowest, and our own consciences know also, whether we are or are likely to be any the better for what we have heard with our outward ears this day . . . forgive us for all our carelessness, inattention and hardness of heart; forgive us for having been far from Thee in mind, when our lips and outward expressions seemed near to Thee . . . Thou knowest our particular temptations here . . . Save us from being ashamed of Thee and of our duty. Save us from the base and degrading fear of one another. Save us from idleness and thoughtlessness. Save us from the sin of falsehood and lying . . . Save us from ourselves and our own evil hearts. (in Stanley, 1845, p. 348)

Naturally, it was written by Arnold and encapsulates his view of adolescence perfectly. His opponents believed that he did not like children. It is more probable that he did not like child*hood*, in its adolescent phase. Like all boarding establishments at the time and since, it was impossible to monitor and control pupils' actions for 24 hours of the day. Arnold believed that boarding education could be a bad influence, not merely in itself, but in reducing family feelings. Certainly at Rugby activities continued that might be construed as high-spirited pranks or bullying, according to the mind-set of the victim. Studies could be turned upside down in their occupant's absence, including the table tied to the ceiling, the sofa on top of the doors, pens and pencils glued to the ceiling and an ingenious trick with a full inkwell inverted (using a paper cover which was then slid away) so that when its owner righted it, the contents were bound to spill everywhere. 'Smoking outs' could also occur as a prank in occupied studies, when red hot pokers were pushed around the study door, followed by lighted brown paper dipped in brimstone, smoke from burning hay funnelled into the room and finally water poured down the chimney. Studies were routinely nailed up by their occupants as a security precaution before departing for the school holidays. *Tom Brown* omits 'Lemon Pecking', a Shrove Tuesday custom in School House, when the doors were closed after dinner and a fight for the squeezed half-lemons used on the pancakes in the meal took place. Boys divided into two sides, pelted the other side and collected up lemons until one side had won. Perhaps it prepared them for Lent penitence.

Chapel and the chaplaincy

The Chapel was 'a scene of Arnold's triumphs' (Archer, 1921, p. 65). Even 'the very cross at the top of the building' was for him a symbol of the Christian end of education. The Chapel had been built by Wooll in the two years from 1819, requiring the felling of an ancient elm, 'Treen's Tree'. It was a plain rectangular building, with a plaster ceiling painted to look like wooden boarding. Arnold disliked the ceiling and referred to it as his 'old enemy'. He gradually replaced the plain windows with stained glass, as he could raise the money. He regarded the first stained glass window as 'strikingly relevant to a place of education': the Wise Men's Offering. He later acquired a fifteenth-century window from Aershot, near Louvain and a fourteenth-century one from Rouen. An old German window was presented in 1840 by old Rugbeians. Arnold liked these additions, as he felt that the building lacked antiquity. Arnold also caused the vaults to be opened for the burial of those who died in the school: 'May they [current pupils] be enabled to think, as they shall kneel perhaps over the bones of some of us now here assembled, that they are praying where their fathers prayed' (Founder's Day Sermon, 1833). Major alterations were to take place in the building after Arnold in 1847, and again by Butterfield in 1872.

Anstey, the chaplain on Arnold's arrival, had been appointed in 1825 at £90 per annum. When he resigned in 1831, Arnold applied to the trustees for the position of chaplain. He did not distinguish between religious and secular instruction and made it his chief task to Christianize the school, taking on himself the role of chaplain and preaching on most Sundays to the gathered boys in the two services.

> Whoever is chaplain, I must ever feel myself, as headmaster, the real and proper religious instructor of the boys. No one else can feel the same interest in them, and no one else (I am not speaking of myself personally, but merely by virtue of my situation) can speak to them with so much influence. (letter of application to the trustees, Stanley, 1845, p. 143)

Some public schools of the time had no chapel. In others the pupils attended the Sunday morning service of the local parish church. But Archer (1921, p. 65) notes that it was 'the only place where, on ordinary occasions, the headmaster was brought into direct contact with his school as a whole'. Although Arnold wished to waive the extra income from the chaplaincy, the trustees insisted he have it. Arnold used the money to improve the library. Registration after Chapel was abandoned in favour of a seemly silence as pupils left the building, filing past Arnold, who remained in his place watching them. Voluntary communion services, on four occasions per year, were routinely attended by between 70 and 100, out of about 300 pupils. On some of these occasions, Arnold was moved to tears or a trembling voice in administering the sacrament. A boy said that the 'tremble was the more striking, because you felt it was such a strong man's voice' (Goulburn, 1856, p. 56). For Bamford (1967, p. 41) this was 'a pouring out of exaggerated sentiment', like when Arnold was moved during sermons, especially in recalling Jesus' agony in Gethsemane, part of a more general sentimental Victorian trend. Confirmations were held at the school biennially. Characteristically, Arnold would append to the service an address of his own in addition to the confirmation address by the visiting bishop. He did not, however, mark Christian festivals, other than those falling on Sundays, by extra chapel services, as he thought these could be counter-productive and produce a negative reaction on the part of the pupils.

The service book (*Rugby School Psalms*, 1824) contained mainly metrical psalms with a sprinkling of hymns. The Morning Hymn had a first verse that must have appealed to Arnold:

> Awake my soul and with the sun
> Thy daily course of duty run.
> Shake off dull sloth and joyful rise
> To pay thy morning sacrifice.

He would have known that the writer, Thomas Ken (1637–1711), had been chaplain at Winchester and had added this to his *Manual of Prayers* for school use there. Read carefully it is clearly a hymn targeting the immature: 'Redeem thy misspent moments past', 'Let all thy converse be sincere', 'God's all-seeing eye surveys thy secret thoughts, thy words and ways', etc. The Evening Hymn was another by Ken, 'Glory to Thee, my God, this night', perhaps with adolescent boys clearly in view in:

> If in the night I sleepless lie
> My soul with heavenly thoughts supply;
> Let no ill dreams disturb my rest,
> No powers of darkness me molest.

Despite public reticence on the matter, there were less than heavenly thoughts and there were nocturnal molestations (see Chandos, 1984: Chapter 14 *passim*).

In worship the Nicene Creed was chanted, despite Arnold's unmusical ear (even Stanley admits him to be 'by nature wholly indifferent' to music), as he believed that the creeds should be treated as triumphant hymns of thanksgiving. A favourite verse was in the Te Deum: 'When Thou hadst overcome the sharpness of death, Thou didst open the kingdom of heaven to all believers.' But Arnold valued most of all the opportunity provided by preaching, and after taking on the chaplaincy he preached on almost every term time Sunday until his death. It was the one occasion of the week when he addressed all the boys. No sermons lasted more than twenty minutes (short by contemporary standards) and none was repeated. They were composed between the morning and afternoon services. The neatly written notebooks of them survive. Few alterations were made as Arnold prepared his sermon and the longhand mss reveal very few corrections or changes. Jane ('K') later wrote:

My Father's [sermons] were written in the midst of a busy life, almost invariably on a Sunday afternoon, in the couple of hours before he went into chapel, and are therefore no elaborate productions, but direct practical addresses to the congregation before him. (Bamford, 1970, p. 39)

Hughes provides a eulogy of what Chapel could be to Arnold admirers:

The tall gallant form, the kindling eye, the voice, now soft as the low notes of a flute, now clear and stirring as the call of a light infantry bugle, of him who stood there Sunday after Sunday, witnessing and pleading for his Lord . . . The long lines of young faces, rising tier above tier down the whole length of the chapel . . . It was a great and solemn sight . . . when the only lights in the chapel were in the pulpit and at the seats of the praepostors of the week, and the soft twilight stole over the rest of the chapel, deepening into darkness in the high gallery behind the organ. (1857, p. 125)

The tone was plain, forceful, direct, sometimes delivered with emotion, most especially earnest in its entreaty to renounce evil. It was 'almost conversational plainness' (Stanley, 1901 edition, p. 145). The early sermon themes were the sources of evils in schools and the pure moral law of Christianity.

I spoke last Sunday of the wickedness, the very great wickedness, of tempting others to do wrong, or laughing at them and abusing them for doing right . . . But in schools, as in the world at large, the very good and the very bad are both but few; it is those who are a mixture of

168

It is a remark which a thinking Boy may
often make to himself, after having heard perhaps
a great deal said to him on a Sunday about
the great importance of the Gospel and that the
Knowledge of Christ is the most valuable knowledge in the world "why then is the greatest portion of my time employed under the direction
of the very persons who say all this, upon things
that have nothing to do with the Gospel: why
am I called upon to attend to things of less
value so much more than to a thing of greater
value? and I am afraid that from seeing the
matter in this light Boys are often tempted to
doubt the sincerity of their teachers, and to
think that they cannot really believe that
the most valuable thing in the world, which they
by no means devote the largest portion of their
time to communicating to others. a doubt of their
sincerity must of course be a great hindrance
to the effect of all that they can say let them be
ever so learned or so eloquent in attempting

20. Page from one of Arnold's sermons at Rugby, *circa* 1830.

good and bad who make up the great majority.
(Sermon on Romans 1:16, 1850 edition, p. 71)

The misconduct of individuals was not mentioned. On the rare occasions when Arnold wished to refer to individuals, the sermon was held before the service and the other teachers were absent from the chapel. The tone was of entreaty, to take up arms against evil:

> Unquestionably, the time of life at which you are arrived, and more particularly the younger boys among you, is in itself, exceedingly dangerous. It is just the time, beyond all others in life, when temptation is great, and the strength of character to resist it exceedingly small. (Sermon on Galations 3:24, ibid., p. 111)

Life was presented as 'no fool's or sluggard's paradise' but rather 'a battlefield ordained from of old, where there are no spectators, but the youngest man must take his side, and the stakes are life and death' (Hughes, 1857, p. 126). Arnold could be visibly 'almost overcome' with emotion during some of these appeals (Stanley, 1901, p. 147). Faith was presented as first of all a natural attitude for humankind, e.g. faith in the advice that parents offer; then as 'the feeling of preferring the future and the unseen to the present . . . [a feeling which] would raise and improve the mind; then faith in God, the heavenly parent' then finally in God as known to Christians, 'God as the Father of our Lord Jesus Christ' (*Sermons*, 1832, 1850 edition, pp. 6ff). The sermon emphasis was on individual integrity and on personal and collective effort.

The suppression of the Rugby Lower School

The decline of the Lower School discriminated against local boys, who as foundation pupils of the original free grammar school founded by grocer Lawrence Sheriff in 1567 for boys in Rugby and nearby Brownsover, needed places there to have a chance of gaining the coveted education of the Upper School. It was only in Lower School that they could achieve sufficient classical education to prepare them for access to the Upper School. Originally there was one class and one teacher, but over time the teacher began to take in boarders to supplement his income. These boarders became more important until by 1800 the school was taking children of 'the gentry' from all over the UK and further afield. The ideal of the founder had been lost, as in the case of many other schools of this type. Between 1800 and 1829 only 86 middle-class children had been admitted and no lower-class, except as servants. A challenge in Chancery in 1808 had failed. Wratislaw, a local solicitor, himself had petitioned both Houses of Parliament before Arnold's arrival (1826) about the injustice of local boys having to pay anything at all for schooling at Rugby. The Rugby trust at that time had conceded on its residual investment income and awarded free local places – but subject to boys having a sufficient classical education before entry. This was still in breach of the original trust. An efficient Lower School, to cover the ages eight to thirteen and provide the classical, especially Latin, background was now essential.

At first under Arnold the numbers in Lower School rose (23 in 1828, 47 in 1829, 94 in 1830). Then for reasons that are unclear, Arnold allowed, even actively encouraged, the Lower School to decline. Standards of teaching were such that parents were having to engage private tutors to supplement the school work. By 1838 the first two 'prep' forms had been abandoned. Another legal challenge was mounted. This time the Chancery trial took three days and was heard by the Master of the Rolls, Lord Langdale. Wratislaw's court case was therefore potentially strong. Arnold, he claimed, had told him that boys under twelve should not be in school at all and that this remark had been witnessed by a trustee.

It was said that he had explicitly advised parents not to send their sons into Lower School. There were other disincentives: Lower School had to wait for breakfast for 45 minutes longer than Upper School. Yet the trust income at the time could have educated up to 500 boys living at home in addition to the 43 who were actual recipients from it. But Wratislaw argued that the plan to remove the Lower School went back to 1831 when a teacher (J. Sale) had been put in place for Form 1, the younger form, who had himself raised the problem with Arnold that he had no classical education at all and knew no Latin. He had been the writing master in the Upper School and had been transferred down. Moreover, since he was expected to continue with classes for writing in the Upper School, it was hard to see how he could do justice to the teaching needs of Form 1. He succeeded James Prince Lee, one of Arnold's best staff, a graduate and a future bishop. In 1835 Sale had eleven pupils in form 1; by 1836, four. In Form 2 the teacher, Louis Pons, a Swiss national, could certainly teach Latin, but the boys found his English accent so difficult that they could not comprehend his Latin pronunciation at all. He was known to have riots in his classes. Form 2 under his care fell successively (1833, 25; 1834, 18; 1835, 14; 1836, 13; 1837, 6). Killing the Lower School could not have been better planned, as the counsel for Wratislaw argued. Arnold and the trustees argued that the decline of Lower Schools was a national phenomenon. Arnold said that the two teachers were 'adequate'. He had examined the classes and had received no complaint. But how could he have examined their Latin? Did he seriously expect young pupils to dare to complain to him? Perhaps these are the 'little boys' referred to romantically by Stanley, whom Arnold would sometimes take on his knee to examine by showing them picture books of the Bible or English history, with the captions covered by his hand, and get them to talk to him about the narrative. But Sale was still on the Rugby staff at the time of the court case. He was not called by the trustees as a witness. Perhaps they decided that what he might say would not be in their interest. The case took place on 12, 14 and 15 January 1839. Judgment was given on 5 May. Langdale found against the trustees, with costs:

> the declarations imputed to Dr. Arnold . . . and not
> denied, and the masters who have been employed, it does,
> on the whole, appear to me that it has been thought
> desirable to discourage the entrance of boys under twelve
> years of age. (Bamford, 1960, 139)

In other words, Langdale found a deliberate policy to close Lower School. But he could not require the trustees to reinstate two forms with no pupils in each. The trustees intimated that they wished to comply with the judgment, although Arnold's contract of employment did not allow them to intervene in this way with the day-to-day running of the school. The school immediately admitted the children who were at the centre of the case, from the Wratislaw and Gibb families, and did nothing at all to make further restitution. Thus Arnold was the *de facto* winner.

This is a professional reflection on Arnold which cannot be accounted for or excused, like the March case, by the 'defence' of loss of temper or rashness of approach. It was a considered, calculated, apparently ruthless, decision to suppress an institution into which Arnold had personally admitted boys, yet on the surface without the courage to come into the open and declare at the outset that this was his aim and to face the wrath of local parents and perhaps the trustees. If similar things were happening in other schools, Arnold, of all people, must have recognized that this did not constitute a moral defence of his own actions. Moreover, the decision to suppress the Lower School is in contrast with Arnold's public and vociferous commitment towards the education of the poor. It does not help in assessing his actions that the motivation is a mystery. His non-systematic keeping of correspondence and records hinders an understanding of his side of this issue. Was the reason money? He claimed to receive the same *per capita* payment for pupils, whether they were foundationers or not. Was it that he wanted to put incompetent teachers where they would be least disastrous, still a problem for modern heads? The answer must certainly be negative, because Arnold could easily dismiss them instead – and in any case he had appointed Pons to Form 2, unless this too was an amazing error of judgement. Was it that he did not like small children, as some alleged? But even if this were true, it need not have prevented his recognizing his obligation to the foundation and the potential gain for the children from such an education. They were, after all, the equivalent of the boys in Buckland's house at Laleham. Arnold's supporters are almost completely silent on this case, perhaps because it is his least defensible educational decision and his surviving defensive letter to John Coleridge (8.5.1839) does not make his motives clear. But the relevant source documents are not now available and it is difficult to gain any real insight into what led him to this indefensible position.

Arnold and Charles Dickens's crusade for better schooling

Arnold thought it a waste of time to read *Nicholas Nickleby* or articles by 'Boz' (pronounced 'Bose'). Matthew Arnold as his most literary child would continue to deprecate Dickens. In contrast, Dickens was very impressed with what he knew of Arnold's work at Rugby. Arnold's antipathy to Dickens is not immediately easy to understand: Dickens appealed to the teaching and general theological framework of Christianity as a moral basis for thought and action; Arnold agreed with that as the essential basis for human advance. The dislike was partly intellectual on Arnold's part. He saw Dickens's writings as 'low brow':

> [Pickwick and Nickleby] completely satisfy all the
> intellectual appetite of a boy, which is rarely very voracious,
> and leave him totally palled, not only for his regular work
> . . . but for good literature of all sorts. (Bamford, 1970,
> p. 141)

Or, again, in a letter to Cornish:

> Childishness in boys, even of good abilities, seems to me to
> be a growing fault, and I do not know to what to ascribe
> it, except to the great number of exciting books of
> amusement, like Pickwick and Nickleby, Bentley's
> Magazine &c. &c. (6.7.1839)

But Dickens was critically aware that something was deeply wrong in the society in which he lived and his fiction has a clear political edge. He appealed to a broad spectrum of readers. Moreover, *Nickleby* contains the infamous Yorkshire school, Dotheboys Hall, with its head Wackford Squeers. Squeers seems clearly based on Greta Bridge head William Shaw, with whom he had more than coincidence in common. His professional advertising cards were worded exactly like Squeers's. Squeers and Shaw were both one-eyed men. Shaw's conduct of this academy led to pupils being blinded by malnutrition and to court cases whose evidence Dickens almost certainly drew on in the chilling scenes depicted in the book. Moreover, Dickens had briefly met Shaw. Between 1810 and 1834, 25 boys between the ages of seven and eighteen from Shaw's school were buried in the local graveyard. Shaw was fined £500 for all this and, amazingly, permitted to continue to run his establishment. Yet his school was no more than 'a cheap depository for unwanted children' (Hobsbaum, 1972, p. 50).

How could Arnold resist Dickens's reforming impulse when it exposed this level of corruption by his writing? The answer is probably simple: it is very doubtful that Arnold had ever person-ally read *Nickleby*, which appeared in magazine instalments in 1838. Moreover, the whole book is a cornucopia of melodrama, digression and caricatures alongside well-drawn characters and sheerly entertaining writing. It is not that Arnold would have wished to defend Squeers; rather, that he did not view novels as instructive and therefore worthy of study. This sounds extreme, solemn, pompous on Arnold's part and perhaps it was, but in so hectic and filled a life-style as his own, Arnold had to be selective in what he read. Not only that, but as we have seen, Arnold was under no delusions about his life expectancy in the light of his family coronary history, so that using 'the time' well was another underlying motivation. Frivolous reading did not fit into this short life expectation. Dickens was also, in Arnold's lifetime, not at the height of his most socially charged writing. He had only *Sketches by Boz*, *The Pickwick Papers* and *Oliver Twist* behind him before *Nickleby*.

Did the Rugby experiment succeed?

When Stanley spoke at Rugby, 32 years after Arnold's death, it was fitting that he quoted the passage read in Chapel on the Sunday after Arnold's death, Samuel's farewell reminder (I Samuel 12:2) that his sons were with the people. His last head boy referred to Arnold's extraordinary sense of the reality of the invisible world. Arnold could see the spiritual as well as the moral. Arnold's supporters told his critics that his system of education was not *based* on religion; it *was* religion (Wymer, 1953, p. 171). But there were two types of pupil at Rugby: those who came under Arnold's personal scrutiny and were subjects of his attention, mainly the sixth and School House boys, and those who were in neither category, leaving at the end of the fifth. Even Stanley concedes that it would often happen that 'a boy would leave Rugby without any personal communication with him at all' and that in the sixth they sometimes wished for more opportunities of asking his advice or tutorial help. Stanley attributes the latter problem as due to Arnold's insistence on not saying anything without a real occasion – he had no small talk – his natural shyness and his leaving older boys to make their own judgements about matters, including when to approach him. His spell did not fall upon all, as the buttons in the collection box testify (p. 13). Boys continued to be boys, despite Arnold's views on adolescence and the 'evil of boy-nature'. Bad behaviour in boarding house prayers was evidence of 'Satan's work in turning holy things to ridicule' and Arnold lost no opportunity to impress this on the boys concerned, but Satan proved every bit as resilient as Arnold feared. Bullying was not entirely eradicated. We may surmise from other contemporary accounts of public school life (Chandos, Chapter 14 *passim*) that there was a sexual underworld at Rugby which did not surface in *Tom Brown*. Arnold, if for no other reason than having been a pupil at Winchester, must have been aware of it. Arnold's old boys were divided into supporters and opponents, and the voices of some – March and Marshall, for instance – are silent after they left the school.

The evidences of Arnold's success are in the vast correspondence and in the visits to the school of his former pupils, in the impression Rugbeians made on the universities in attitude as well as in academic achievements. A mere sadist and flogger could not have produced this. Success also lies in the number of imitators of his headship style and the attempts to translate his system into the grammar schools. Arnold's three main aims as head of Rugby had been to inculcate, in descending order, religious and moral principles; gentlemanly conduct; and intellectual ability. To this he added massive energy devoted to work – as sixth form teacher, head, chaplain, historian, correspondent with many old boys – and as a devoted family man. The later Arnold myth in education is partly accountable for by the fact that he lived out the work and moral ethic that many later Victorians came to emulate. Moberly in a letter to Stanley, commented on Rugbeians at Oxford:

> his pupils brought a different character . . . [They were] thoughtful, manly-minded, conscious of duty and obligation . . . We cordially acknowledged the immense improvement in their characters in respect of morality and personal piety, and looked on Dr. Arnold as exercising an influence for good, which . . . had been absolutely unknown in our public schools.

Some of his leading pupils became influential heads a generation on in day and boarding schools: Benson at Wellington; Bradby at Haileybury; Cotton and Bradley at Marlborough; Gell in Van Diemen's Land (Tasmania); Hill at Warwick; Prince Lee at King Edward's, Birmingham; Phillpotts at Bedford. Charles John Vaughan, Craven scholar, senior classic, Porson prize winner, Chancellor's Medal recipient, and Fellow of Trinity Cambridge, became Head of Harrow. He raised pupil numbers from 69 to 469 and reformed a school of whose violent pupils the local inhabitants had been in considerable fear. He would have gone on beyond the fourteen years Arnold deemed appropriate for a school post had he not been blackmailed into immediate resignation by the parent of a far less than innocent pupil. The same blackmail prevented him from accepting major preferment in the Church on two occasions and is why he left express instructions that no biography of him was to be written. Thus Stanley's brother-in-law, a man whose star might easily have risen above Arnold's in the Church, was removed from post. Vaughan had been tipped as a future Archbishop of Canterbury. But some leading teachers and pupils of Arnold's did become bishops: Prince Lee at Manchester; Temple at Exeter and Canterbury; Tait; Benson; Lightfoot; Westcott. Vaughan and Bonamy Price were unsuccessful candidates for the headship of Rugby after Arnold's death, Vaughan missing the post by one vote on grounds of youth.

There was a second generation influence. Pears at Repton had been a housemaster at Harrow under Vaughan. Priestly, head at the nonconformist school at Mill Hill from 1834 to 1853, corresponded with Arnold and tried to adapt his approach. Thomas Jex-Blake is another clear example of Arnoldian influence, although he never knew Arnold personally. As a boy he was destined for Eton, but when his father read Stanley's *Life of Arnold* (1844), he was so deeply impressed and 'told me that he had no idea that any school attempted to act on the Xan [Christian] ideal' (in Simpson, 1967, p. 102). Jex-Blake was sent to Rugby instead. After a double First at Oxford and a short spell at Marlborough he taught at Rugby from 1857 to 1868, moving to the headship of Cheltenham and returning to Rugby as head from 1874 to 1887, defeating Temple's nominee, the redoubtable John Percival, who, in the event, succeeded him.

Despite Strachey and the decline of Victorian moral idealism, Arnold's legacy in English education was not finally eclipsed until the vastly changed social and religious landscape of the 1960s and the gradual disappearance of most of the grammar schools. It is hard for day or boarding pupils now even to imagine the authority that school head boys and head girls possessed even as late as the mid-1960s, let alone a century earlier. Even in the 1960s, day (i.e. non-boarding) grammar school head boys or girls might have their own office and the power to punish non-sixth form pupils. They might 'cover' for absent teachers, taking charge of classes, and like Arnold's praepostors they could refer disobedient pupils direct to the headteacher, to whom they had privileged access, sometimes greater than that of junior teaching staff. The 1960s' prefects might have a lounge or social area with tea and coffee provided, along with special privileges of school dress, and sufficient status to mean that in some schools they conducted pupil detentions after school on behalf of the staff or controlled dining rooms or school bus queues, all with an authority accepted in this capacity by younger pupils.

In many ways it can be said that in the nineteenth century, senior pupils were treated more as adults than at any time since, even in an era of FE ('further education') or tertiary education in which 'adulthood' can be reduced to sixteen- to nineteen-year-olds being allowed to smoke in designated areas, to call tutors by their forenames and to stay at home when not actually timetabled in classes. Arnold's views on the educational benefits of giving power to praepostors (prefects) vanished in the sixth forms of comprehensive schools, where a new emphasis on egalitarianism, including 'open access' sixth forms in which entrance was not dependent on academic merit, meant that either the prefectorial system was abandoned, or all sixth formers were made prefects and the status and role of the office and the quality of the holders were reduced. In any case, outside a boarding environment, the role of prefects can only be reduced. It is difficult now to appreciate that the praepostors of Arnold's time were viewed as young *men*, a tier of management between paid staff and boys, with powers and authority which modern pupils could not imagine being given to other pupils.

There are blemishes in the record such as the March and Marshall cases. The suppression of the lower school, although not an offence against a particular child like March, shows a heavy-handedness and an apparent lack of principle, coupled with disdain both for the foundation of the school and old allies like Wratislaw, that is inexcusable by the standards of the time or later. These cases do Arnold no personal credit.

It is hard to see how a modern headteacher could remain in post after mistakes of such magnitude. But then modern headship has checks and constraints and safeguard procedures built into the job, for staff and pupils, of a sort that Arnold's time could not have even imagined. The present headteacher is subject to more protective or restraining procedures, whichever way one views them, than heads of even one generation ago. They are now senior managers or chief executives or principals and many do not often meet children, let alone teach them. Arnold belongs to that tradition of headship – even helped to create it – in which the headteacher was seen as a leader of staff and pupils, the personal summation of the school's values, a force for good (not merely philosophical, but moral) and the ultimate sanction in the school. Arnold was not always a 'good' head, even by the standards of his time, but he was consistently a visionary one. Few had taken Christianity seriously enough to try to place it at the centre of a living school and make it work. He has to be given credit for trying. This was a sustained and serious educational experiment which will be appraised on pp. 255ff in summing up Arnold's significance.

The inscription for the later memorial brass in All Saints, Laleham (1898) was written by W. C. Lake, Dean of Durham (1869–90) and thought to be the senior surviving pupil of Arnold at the time:

To the memory of
Thomas Arnold, DD, Headmaster of Rugby 1828–1842,
Regius Professor of Modern History in the University of Oxford
1841–1842
Scholar, historian and theologian,
Who as the head of a great public school
Raised the character of all English education;
Powerful to rouse and train the intellect,
But desirous above all
To impress Religion and Duty
Upon the hearts of his pupils.
In this parish
Beloved by him as the home of his early labours
Is offered this grateful tribute
Of respect and admiration

Born at West Cowes June 13 1795
Died at Rugby June 12 1842

Erected March 1898

3 Arnold the Theologian and Churchman

All societies of men, whether we call them states or churches, should make their bond to consist in a common object and a common practice, rather than in a common belief; in other words, their end should be good rather than truth. (Appendix to Arnold's inaugural lecture at Oxford, 1841 [1874], p. 39)

Bamford thinks that Arnold was only 'on the borderline' of the Church of England, kept there only by his profound commitment to a properly conceived Church–State alliance, with Christianity as the core of citizenship, and English Christianity as the core of English citizenship. Otherwise Arnold's attitude to creeds, his condemnation of 'priestcraft', and his tolerance towards dissenters would have easily led him into one of the dissenting churches. The Arnold of Chandos's study was

> by temperament a crusader, puritan and autocrat; by profession an evangelist, moralist and reformer, and thus in fervent sympathy with the revivalist spirit in the low-church party in the Church of England, and even outside the Church, in Methodism. (1984, p. 248f)

Chandos, as we have seen (e.g. p. 12f), is no admirer of Arnold, and this assessment of him does not do justice to the breadth of Arnold's religious position. Arnold was utterly committed to the establishment, on his terms, of a properly constituted reformed and catholic (in the sense of broad in sympathies, wide-embracing) Church. Nor would Arnold have thrived in the narrowness of much small town dissent, for example as characterized by the later writings of Mark Rutherford (William Hale White). White was expelled from the Independent (Congregational) New College in the academic year 1851–2 for a lack of orthodoxy rather less than Arnold's and from a college in which Arnold's writing was known, but never read, as that of a 'heretic' or, in conventional nonconformist terms, someone of 'unsound' views.

For Arnold the worst apostasy was the separation of things secular from things spiritual. Such a situation would leave the temporal world to the Devil and lead the Church into a retreat into priestcraft and introspection. For Arnold, everything is secular, in the sense of taking place on earth and in time. Everything is spiritual in the sense that it can affect us morally for better or for worse 'and so tend to make our spirits fitter for the society of God or of his enemies' (*Fragment*, 1845c, p. 12). The end of the Church was 'the putting down of moral evil' and its nature was 'a living society of all Christians'. But the Anglican Church in Arnold's day fell far short of this ideal. The momentum brought by Methodism had been within living memory lost to the Church of England by its secession (1797). The commitment of the Anglican clergy at parish level was still very variable. Life as a clergyman, especially in a well-paid living (rates of pay varied from living to living), could be a safe job for the second son of a noble family, if the first son went into the army or the law, and required only the reading of the Sunday services as minimum duties – not even that if the rector or vicar wished to install and pay a curate to do the job and draw the larger income from the living *in absentia*. There was no ordination training. Bishops simply ordained candidates of whom they approved. Almost any university-educated young man with a respectable family background would be acceptable. Wealth was presupposed in university education, which was not supported by state financial aid and as 'tests' restricted admission or graduation in the two universities, Oxford and Cambridge, to Anglicans, the right church background was assured. The bishops were seen as social barons and the great wealth of some of them – their income also varied – was resented by many of the poor. The clergy contained godly and conscientious men, but there was no mechanism to filter out the more worldly. Moreover, it was beginning to be obvious that the Church of England's strength was in the country-side and that the new industrial towns were becoming, if bastions of anything, bastions of dissent. Chadwick calls the ancient parish system rigid and rustic (I, 127). It was easy to find evidences of church corruption. Reform was in the air. The rise of the middle class was also accompanied by the rise of the urban labourer, the factory 'hand'. Both were groups which Arnold wished to see legitimized. Most of the real urban working classes were outside all churches, though this was not as clear as it became later in the century and especially after the 1851 religious census.

Arnold's religious views were derived from Richard Hooker (*c.*1554–1600) and Samuel T. Coleridge (1772–1834) in the English tradition, but also Barthold Niebuhr and Christian Carl Josias 'Chevalier' von Bunsen (1791–1860) in Europe. From Hooker he took church polity; from Coleridge he took some philosophy; from Niebuhr the values of a 'scientific' approach to the study of history and a social history of people; from Bunsen a shared approach to the study of the Bible. But the relationships of Arnold to the members of this quartet were not equal. Arnold read and respected Hooker. For Hooker the Church is an organic not a static institution and therefore church government and

185

administration will change according to circumstances. Hooker was unwilling to condemn all dissent or to assert the absolute necessity of episcopal ordination, and his doctrine of the eucharist seemed less than acceptable to some Anglicans. Clear hints of all this can be seen in Arnold's position.

Arnold dipped in and out of Coleridge's ideas, which were notoriously unsystematized. Arnold was a critical admirer of Coleridge: 'with all his faults old Sam was more of a great man than anyone who has lived within the four seas in my memory' (Fallows, 1963, p. 276). 'Old Sam' would not have been very pleased with this epithet, as he much preferred to be called Samuel, but in some ways he would have owned Arnold as a disciple. With Niebuhr Arnold was in something more like a teacher–pupil relationship, with Arnold as the pupil. With Bunsen there were letters almost monthly each way, in intimate terms of friendship: they were fellow explorers of the Bible and both supporters of the project to create a joint Anglican–Lutheran bishopric in Jerusalem, which succeeded in 1841. But if Arnold was influenced by this quartet, as he undoubtedly was, he brought to their writings his own independent mind and his own commitment to social action.

The Noetics

Arnold was also a member of the 'Noetics'. This nickname, derived from the Greek *noetikos*, pertaining to the mind or intellect, was applied to the circle in the Oriel senior common room which included Coplestone, Hawkins, Whately and Hampden, who were prepared to question and criticize the Christian orthodoxy of their time. Tuckwell identifies the main Noetic characteristics (1909, p. 258f) as: politically non-party, but in practice liberal; academically in support of university reform including the use of entrance examinations; ecclesiastically in favour of the

Reformation, the royal headship of the Church, the increasing of lay influence in the Church, opposing the identification of the Church with the clergy; educationally in favour of religious teaching provided by the state on common ground to all denominations, using comprehensive and carefully devised text books; theologically in a position between the bibliolater at one extreme and the rationalist at the other, applying historical criticism to the Bible without fear and accepting the results. They were also anti-sabbatarian and anti-Tractarian. Faber criticizes the Noetics (1936, p. 117) for their lack of knowledge of European religious thinking and for an English parochialism that came from a secure established Church, 'a comfortable domestic amalgam of religion, culture and country life'. But these comments do not apply at least to Arnold, who travelled and studied European thought with care and whose Europeanism is reflected in Matthew Arnold. Faber argues that the Noetics did not realize that the implication of their thinking would destroy clericalism – but that was exactly what Arnold would have welcomed. It was a deliberate part of his programme for church reform.

The Noetics were small in number but they met frequently in the common room and had easy opportunity to exchange ideas. Francis Newman's first undergraduate contact with what its opponents dubbed the 'Oriel heresy' was to encounter their anti-sabbatarianism; one Oriel Fellow supported Sunday cricket while another preached the University sermon on the lack of biblical support for sabbatarianism. Francis Newman's next contact came via Davison's support for the idea that doctrine developed and improved over time. Doctrine was not immutable and so by implication was not directly divinely prescribed. A glance at the residence dates of the most prominent Noetics at Oriel gives some insight into this small but influential group and Arnold's position in it:

John Eveleigh, Provost 1781–1814
Edward Copleston, Fellow, 1789–1814, Provost 1814–28
Richard Whately, Fellow, 1811–31
Thomas Arnold, Fellow 1814–19
Renn Hampden, Fellow, 1814–17
Edward Hawkins, Fellow, 1813–28, Provost, 1828–74
Baden Powell, degree 1817
Blanco White, Fellow 1826

Arnold's religious outlook was still unusual for the time. He had a broad and also radical view of the Church, more radical than that of the other Noetics, a view to which he was so passionately committed that when he saw a trend arise which was in his view taking the Church backwards, namely the Oxford Movement, he enjoined in battle against it with all the force of holy war. 'I must write or die' was a remark he used on more than one occasion to sum up his commitment to speak out. It was to cost him friends, advancement in the Church and almost his job at Rugby. But there were other battles first.

Catholic emancipation, 1829

The legal disabilities to which Roman Catholics had been subject for centuries ended when the bill for emancipation was enacted unwillingly by George IV in 1829. It had been a cliff-hanger to the last minute, with the rumour that the king would refuse to sign it receiving credence until he proved otherwise. Twenty of the Church of England bishops in the House of Lords voted against the third reading, including the most senior ones, Canterbury, York, London and Durham. They did not accept that settling the grievance might protect the constitution and prevent possible violence in Ireland. There were fears that if emancipation were permitted, Ireland could elect 60 Roman Catholic MPs to

Westminster and that they would use their position to strike at the privileges of the Anglican Church as the established church. In fact the removal of the popular vote in Ireland protected the Protestant ascendancy and ensured that only eight Roman Catholic MPs were returned to Westminster in the 1830 election. There were other objections: a Roman Catholic prime minister might abuse the power, on behalf of the Crown, to appoint Anglican bishops. A number of clauses were written into the bill to protect the religious and political establishment from the arrival of Roman Catholics. No Catholic bishop or dean could use a title already in use in the Anglican Church; converts to the Society of Jesus, seen as a powerful missionary arm of the Roman Catholic Church, would be banished; not only the monarch but also the Regent, Lord Chancellor and other national figures could not be Roman Catholics; Roman Catholic MPs must take an oath not to undermine the established church. In return for all these securities, the bill was passed. The king sobbed as his gouty hand signed the enactment (Chadwick, 1971, I, p. 7).

The Church of Rome was still seen as a foreign power (the Vatican still held territories) and Roman Catholics as not fully English people. It was thought that they gave their real allegiance abroad to the Pope and not in England to the monarch, who was head of the established church. The media perpetuated this image but it was not merely a matter of tabloid ignorance. There was no love lost between the Anglican clergy and Roman Catholicism. Cartoons showed Wellington and Peel carrying rosaries and kissing the Pope's toe. Placards and pamphlets carried pictures of Bloody Mary burning Protestant heretics. Since the whole of Ireland was politically under Westminster rule, its majority of 5.5 million Catholics (to 1.5 million Protestants), contrasted with a total population in England and Wales of 14 million, which also included a Roman Catholic minority. Roman Catholics were indisputably significant in the UK. The Whigs were prepared to support emancipation; the Tories opposed it. It was finally conceded on grounds of expediency rather than principle. Arnold, who at one time considered going over to teach in Ireland to try to 'civilise and Christianize' the people and the gentry, was in a minority of Anglican clergy not only willing to support emancipation but also anxious to publicize and defend the cause.

When Arnold wrote *The Christian Duty of Granting the Claims of the Roman Catholics* he was not nationally famous. A rise in pupil admissions at Rugby followed (1828, 67; 1829, 96; 1830, 113) but although one parent wrote that it was the pamphlet that led to her placing her son at Rugby, the rise can be attributed to other factors such as the energies of a new head and good reports from parents of pupils already in the school. But the pamphlet did bring Arnold to the attention of Henry Brougham. He had founded the Society for the Diffusion of Useful Knowledge in 1826, one of many philanthropic attempts to reach the poor. Arnold had been invited to join, as his concerns for the poor were already known among his acquaintances. But Arnold wanted it to be the Society for Diffusion of *Christian* Knowledge. Brougham and his friends were more motivated by politics than by religion and were sceptical about the state of the clergy of the time. But a reforming clergyman – and Arnold's pamphlet demonstrated that he was one such cleric – did appeal to them. Brougham became Lord Chancellor in 1830.

While these events were being acted out on the national stage, Arnold did not fail to involve himself at local level in campaigning for Catholic emancipation. He wrote a pamphlet which was posted at key places in Laleham village, even though he was by then resident at Rugby. It was entitled 'To the Inhabitants of Laleham'. He had heard that they were petitioning against Catholic emancipation. He urged them 'not to lend your aid to the unchristian violence' sweeping the country. He compared the position of the Catholics to the position of minorities within the three-vestry combined parish of Staines, Laleham and Ashford in which, by unscrupulous means, a minority within the parish, such as Laleham, could in theory be deprived of the chance to partake in parish affairs by a majority decision of the Staines and Ashford groups against them.

> The case which I have supposed to be your's [*sic*] is exactly the case of the Roman Catholics of IRELAND and your petition the other day was just as if some of the people of Staines had gone to their vestry door and begged the meeting never to let the Laleham people have a vote . . . More than six hundred years ago we conquered Ireland by force, against all right, and we have ever since held it by force . . . [We] make the people pay our Ministers, whom they think false Ministers . . . We go further and say, that no Roman Catholic shall sit in Parliament, lest our Church of England should be destroyed . . . We make the Irish Catholics pay taxes and will not let them have a vote about the disposal of their own money. Is this common honesty? Much more is it fulfilling CHRIST's command 'to do unto others as we should they would do unto us' . . . We Protestants are to the Roman Catholics more than two to one. They ask for justice and fair dealing, and we say 'No, for you will make us all Papists, or else burn us!' . . . But they who talk about Bloody Mary, and the burning of Protestants, talk they know not what. In those days, all sides were bloody alike . . . So we both have a great deal to forgive, and to ask to be forgiven for. In conclusion, love our own pure religion, and do not be afraid that it will suffer by doing justice to others. Do to the Irish Catholics, as you would they should do unto you, for this is the Law of [*sic*] the Prophets.

The local situation was clearly as hot as the national scene. Arnold's pamphlet was no doubt regarded as a piece of gross interference by the vicar and the curate of the combined parish, who swiftly produced a reply (Govett and Hearn, 1829) expressing their regret that they decidedly differed from their 'amiable and excellent friend, Dr. Arnold'. They argued that peace could only be preserved by keeping inviolate 'our glorious Protestant constitution'. They challenged Arnold's analogy of the three churches in one parish as 'ingenious' but misdirected. It would be better if the link between England and Ireland could be severed. Linking Protestant England to 'Popish Ireland' would not work. Roman Catholics, if allowed into Parliament, could legislate for the Church of England. If the king or prime minister of England were be 'openly or secretly a Romanist', that could lead to the same 'fiery trial' as had happened in the past, but perhaps with worse results. In past persecutions, they claimed, Protestants were executed for religious reasons but Roman Catholics had only ever been executed for treasonable, i.e. civil, offences, for 'spreading seditious principles'. Those joining the Anglican clergy subscribe to the phrase that the Roman Church is guilty of most 'filthy and horrible idolatry'.

> We are professedly a People of God, virtually in covenant with him, as were the Israelites of old – And we are bound to make our political acts grounded on the Word of God . . . Is a close and intimate union with those whom we profess to be idolaters a measure likely to secure happiness and divine blessing now . . . Be assured . . . that in signing the petition [against emancipation] you were acting as English Protestant Christians, as lovers of your God, your King, your Country, your Bible, and your Saviour.

In Laleham can be seen all the arguments of the national debate, with Arnold energetically involved on the side of emancipation. He felt that scurrilous language should not be used against Roman Catholics, nor should the Pope be referred to as Anti-Christ. Even the errant claim to papal infallibility was not simply to be equated with 'the blasphemous fruit of ambition and avarice'. Mary Arnold recorded some of the varied response to what her husband had written in his national pamphlet. From Edwin Stanley:

> I cannot express the satisfaction with which I have read your Pamphlet . . . Were I inclined to point out faults I might mention to suggest that the style is here and there – or whether I should say the arguments – somewhat obscurely worded – a blemish however I am much more willing to lay to the account of my own obtuseness, or the superficial reading a London morning in alone afford . . .

The *Lichfield Free Mercury*:

> Our attention has been directed to a Pamphlet by Dr Arnold Head Master of Rugby Free Grammar School, unparalleled we think in the comprehensiveness of view, in purity of Christian Principle, its cogency of reasoning, or clearness of eloquence of expression. (10.4.1829)

Mary writes that *The Age* newspaper 'says in 3 lines that the Head Master of Rugby might be better employed than in appearing in Print as a Partner of the Papists. This is signed a Rugby School Trustee but I give the Trustees credit, for better taste – & better sense.'

From the *Morning Chronicle*: 'Dr. Arnold has here placed in a most forcible light the principles w^h [which] ought to govern a Christian in political matters' (16.4.1829). Arnold was becoming known.

In France in 1830 there was a revolution which ended the reign of Charles X and replaced him with Louis Philippe as a constitutional monarch and with the title 'Citizen King'. Arnold was thrilled by the events in France, describing it as 'spotless beyond all example in history . . . [it] magnificently vindicates the cause of knowledge and liberty . . . [and] lays the crimes of the last revolution just in the right place'. His friends were uneasy about his tone, which seemed to be a political espousing of the Jacobin or Radical political viewpoint within a largely Tory Church. Arnold replied that 'there is not a man in England who is less a party man than I am, for in fact no party would own me'. They would not, and for this reason alone Arnold's career would not advance in the Church. The Anglican Archbishop of Dublin died in 1831. The appointment of a successor was in the hands of the Crown but for practical purposes, Brougham's nominee would get the job. His private secretary urged on him Richard Whately, Arnold's sponsor for Rugby. Brougham thought also of Arnold himself. Finally, he took both names to the Prime Minister, Charles Grey, the 2nd Earl Grey. After some deliberation, Grey chose Whately. By coincidence, the letter of appointment arrived at Rugby, where Whately and his wife were staying on a visit to the Arnolds. In 1831 Arnold was offered a canonry at Bristol Cathedral worth £600 per annum, for which he need not be resident. It would solve his financial worries. But he refused it (see p. 82).

Church reform

In December 1829, S. T. Coleridge published his last work, a monograph *On the Constitution of Church and State*. Coleridge was by this time the respected 'sage of Highgate', north London, and his ideas were read and discussed widely. He took a Platonic view, that there was an Idea for each of these institutions, which could be distinguished from their temporal shadow appearances with all their imperfections. Progress and permanence had to be kept in balance within Church and state, so that conservative reform should take place. Writers, artists, scientists, teachers and the clergy should combine together to form 'the clerisy', an intellectual and aesthetic elite committed to education, the exchange of liberal ideas and an ongoing cultural progress or evolution. Knights (1978) argues that not only did this influence Arnold in his own view of what the clergy should be in a united national Church, but that the idea of the clerisy was partially realized in undergraduate student groups, such as Rugbeians at Oxford and also the 'Cambridge Apostles'. It lay in their seriousness, sense of mission and the influence this had on university reform. Although Arnold was committed both to church and university reform, he was also committed to reform in the state. The leader in the opening issue of *The Englishman's Register* sums up his position:

> England cannot remain what it has been; and the
> endeavour to detain a state of things which is passing away
> is, at the best, a waste of those efforts which might be better
> spent in preparing for the approaching and inevitable
> change . . . The anti-reformers have spoken as if the
> sufferings of the poor were the result of inevitable necessity
> . . . the ultra-reformers present the rich as tyrants and the
> poor as slaves, and they speak of them as the natural
> enemies of each other . . . Thus one party tries to lull the
> consciences of the rich, and encourages them in their error
> and neglect; while the other appeals to all the bad passions
> of the poor.

The *Register*, however, ran to only nine issues, between May and July 1831. Arnold believed that forces were at work to make labourers akin to the slaves of the ancient world, on whom society depended, but for whom no rebellion was possible as they had no rights and were outside society. 'The happiness of the nation was never thought to be affected because its slaves were oppressed and miserable.' The degraded poor of his day, Arnold argued, were not true members of society and hence seen as no danger to the state. This was an unchristian state of affairs. He wrote in the *Courant* under the pen name 'A':

> Society . . . should put the poor man, being a free man, into a situation where he may live as a freeman ought to live . . . either by home colonies or by emigration. [In ancient times large captive populations] were provided for by being settled on the unappropriated lands of the state . . . And this was the only way of avoiding one of two evils . . . the existence on the one hand of a free population in beggary; and on the other a total overthrow of society.

But he recognized that 'the masses' were becoming so brutalized that they might not see that property was a solution to their plight:

> Having no property of their own, they hate property – having no means of intellectual enjoyment, they are driven to seek the pleasures which we have in common with brutes – having never been made Christians, their undisciplined natures are incapable of valuing Christianity, and their evil passions teach them to hate it. (Bamford, 1960, p. 42f)

He felt he could not argue for social equality, however, but for social justice:

The Aristocrat aims to reduce all ranks but his own, the Jacobin to reduce all ranks to the lowest level . . . our business is to raise all and lower none. Equality is the dream of the madman or the passion of a fiend. Extreme inequality . . . is no less a folly and a sin. But an inequality where some have all the enjoyments of civilised life, and none are without its comforts – where some have all the treasures of knowledge and none are sunk in ignorance, that is a social system in harmony with God's creation in the natural world. (Bamford, 1960, p. 45)

While the March case was raging locally (see pp. 139ff), Arnold published his 88-page pamphlet, *Principles of Church Reform* (1833). It passed through four editions in six months and brought Arnold to national prominence in the sphere of Church reform. For so radical a set of proposals, *The* [Tory] *Times* surprisingly reviewed them with cautious favour (25 and 26 January 1833). They were seen as able, intelligent, 'good sense', 'liberal and charitable' in spirit but also fraught with extreme difficulties such that they are unlikely to gain 'a single influential proselyte'. The *Northampton Herald*, which had run out of steam on the March affair, could now attack Arnold as a dangerous heretic, who wanted to undermine the 39 Articles and swamp the established Church with nonconformists. It saw in Arnold's proposal to increase the number of bishops a piece of self-seeking, and warned 'the country will not tolerate his elevation to any higher ecclesiastical dignity till he has completely exculpated himself from the charges now brought against him'. Was such a person a suitable influence for the minds of the impressionable young? He was bringing them up on politics and revolution. Bamford (1960) argues that Bonamy Price carried Arnold's ideas to Oxford from Laleham and that Arnold had discussed the Church reform pamphlet with Stanley, Clough and other older boys.

Bamford asserted that his radical sermons to the boys were toned down or even in some cases not used in the published collections. Arnold was more fearless about likely controversy and later wrote: 'what many men call "caution" . . . is too often merely a selfish fear of getting oneself into trouble or ill-will' (letter to J. Hearn, 25.1.1841). Whatever his failings, Arnold could never be accused of caution. But what had he actually said in the 88 pages? Arnold's view can be summarized along the following lines. First he identified himself clearly within the Church. The call for reform from some outsiders was really a call for the destruction of the Church and the appropriation of its endowments. Such people were really 'Church Destroyers' (*Principles*, 1833, p. 4) and their motivation was church robbery not reform. The life and example of Christ were the essence of Christianity. Christ is to be identified with goodness, wisdom and holiness. Christ is, so to speak, the un-negotiable goodness and presence of God. Anything that obscures this centrality of Christ, even the Church itself if it does this, is bad. What has arisen in post-apostolic Christianity is interpretation, even opinion, emphasis on the periphery rather than the centre. This may or may not be helpful, but it must certainly be subject to scrutiny and question. Extraneous beliefs must be stripped away.

Many Anglicans would have been happy to go along with this, as they would have understood the idea of extraneous and wrong beliefs to be one of the typical Anglican criticisms of the Roman Catholic Church at that time, but Arnold did not restrict his principle to that. He intended it to be a reforming principle in the Anglican Church and beyond. The purpose of the Gospel is 'righteousness', actual and operative. It is the 'restoration of our moral nature from its state of corrupt principles and practice, and the raising it into a capacity of enjoying everlasting communion with God'. Presenting Christianity as an 'awful mystery' separates it from real issues. The appendix to the later inaugural lecture (1841, p. 40) put it like this:

> Whoever was willing to receive Christ as his master, to join his people, and to walk according to their rules . . . was admitted to the Christian society. We know that in the earliest church there existed the strangest varieties of belief, some Christians not even believing that there would be a resurrection of the dead. Of course it was not intended that such varieties should be perpetual; a closer union of belief was gradually effected: but the point to observe is that the union of belief grew out of the union of action: it was a result of belonging to the society rather than a previous condition required for belonging to it.

As it grew, Christianity produced wide divergence in views. This was not surprising as 'it is false that there exists in any church any power or office endowed with the gift of infallible wisdom; and therefore it is impossible to prevent differences of opinion' (*Principles*, 1833, p. 18). Creeds and prescribed ceremonies were 'a mistaken way' to provide unity; they lacked infallibility and they produced 'outsiders'. In that sense the Church was responsible for creating dissent. Some dissent, as represented in some nonconformist churches, was based on

> a coarse-minded ignorance that sought to isolate itself from all the noble recollections of past times . . . under the opprobrious names of superstition and idolatry, that captious superstition which quarrels with the form of a minister's cap, or the colour of his dress. (ibid., p. 21)

But Arnold recognized that dissenting ministers were more free than Anglican clergy to work 'in a mine or by a canal side, or at

199

the doors of a manufactory' (ibid., p. 24), that their more flexible liturgy could be more easily adapted to such situations and that some of the ministers could be drawn from working-class people and speak with more authority to them. The very existence of dissent promoted sectarianism, however. 'The minister at the meeting house rejoiced to thin the Church' and the parson rejoiced to empty the meeting house. While such sectarian rivalry was ongoing, an unchurched population had arisen. Arnold feared that the 'unchristianising of the nation' might happen if this process continued unchecked and that would lead to 'sure moral and intellectual degradation' (*Principles*, 1833, p. 84). Only a united church could prevent this. Patchwork reform of the Church will not be enough. Arnold could write apocalyptic-ally that if the changes he was proposing seemed too great, 'the danger threatening us is enormous'. The main danger in this context was an 'unchristianised' society. Another danger to which Arnold returns again and again was priestcraft.

In a posthumously published *Fragment on the Church*, Arnold distinguished 'the Christian religion'

> knowledge of God and Christ, and that communion of the Holy Spirit, by which an individual is led through life, in all holiness and dies with the confident hope of rising again with Christ at the last day

from 'the Church': 'that provision for the communicating main-taining and enforcing of this knowledge by which it was to be made influential, not on individuals but on masses of men' (*Fragment* 1845c, p. 3). Christianity contains 'a divine phil-osophy, which we may call its religion, and a divine polity, which is its Church' (ibid., p. 5). The early Christians were working for and with one another, with and to Christ and God, co-operating for moral improvement, bringing Christ into their everyday human communion. A good example is found in the Christians of Bithynia, *c.*100 CE, who met before daylight, sang a hymn to Christ, bound themselves to one another by oath, shared communion and went to work. On their return they shared a meal, with communion and prayers and hymns. As it grew, Christianity spawned social structures, in parallel to the political and social hierarchies of kings and barons. The structures derived from Christianity included archbishops, cardinals and popes and tended to make the pronouncements of those holding these high offices authoritative. Pronouncements from the very highest officials in these church structures were held to carry a sense of holiness. This was to Arnold one aspect of 'priestcraft' as it obscured the essential centre of Christianity, its only priest and intercessor, Christ himself. 'How can [a Christian] obey the rightful authorities of the Christian church and the usurped authority of priestcraft?' (letter to Bunsen, 27.1.1838). Priestcraft could reduce Christ to the status of a founder, or a symbol instead of the presence of the Living God. Moreover, priests could reduce the status of the laity by purporting to be mediators between the people and God. Such mediation displaces Christ, the true mediator, and downgrades the notion of equality among Christians. It destroys the spirit of the apostles' principles, crushing the Church with its tyranny while also distracting it with its anarchy and paralysing the free action of the Church: 'This mingled usurpation and rebellion, – this root of anarchy, fraud and idolatry, – is the very main principle of all popery, whether Romish or Oxonian [i.e. the Oxford Movement] ... of Pusey and Newman' (letter to Bunsen, 27.1.1838).

The Church is injured by 'the extreme predominance of the activity of some members [priests], by which the others are rendered less active [laity]' (*Fragment*, 1845c, p. 14). But what constitutes a 'priest'? A priest to Arnold is a person made necessary to our intercourse with God without being necessary or beneficial to us morally. His interference makes the worshipper neither a wiser man nor holier than he would have been without it [his purported mediation between humankind and God] and yet it is held to be indispensable. This unreasonable, unmoral [*sic*], unspiritual necessity is the idea of priesthood. (*Fragment*, 1845c, p. 15)

Priesthood to Arnold is seen most clearly in the claim to administer the Lord's Supper. 'In the New Testament it is declared "as plainly as words can speak" that all Christians are equal before God' (ibid., p. 32). Baptism and the Lord's Supper, often referred to as sacred mysteries, are not mysteries at all in the biblical sense of hidden truths. They are made plain for all. By the end of the New Testament period there is no evidence of a doctrine of sacraments requiring priestly mediators, nor can Arnold find it in 'the earliest uncanonical Christians' (*Fragment*, 1845c, p. 122). He discusses in detail Barnabas, Clement, Ignatius, Polycarp and Irenæus:

My quarrel with Newman and the Romanists [Roman Catholics], and with the dominant party in the Church up to Cyprian [except Ignatius] . . . is, that they have put a false Church in place of the true, and through their counterfeit have destroyed the reality, as paper money drives away gold. And this false Church is the Priesthood, to which are ascribed all the powers really belonging to the true Church, with others which do not and cannot belong to any human power. (letter to Hawkins, 4.12.1840)

Arnold did not, like later Christian house churches and some other denominations, seek to abolish the idea of a full-time professional clergy in the Church. Preferring the word minister (a word common in nonconformity then and now, but also prominent in the Anglican Book of Common Prayer), Arnold saw a minister as one who serves, spreads their knowledge freely; whereas priests are associated with secrets, mysteries, religious truths within an inner circle, the power of one group of believers over another. The role of the minister is to live out Christianity in an exemplary way; to provide a focus for the Church more important than its building; to act as an expert consultant for the whole Christian community. A resident clergyman in a parish should be available to all its people. For this reason, on one occasion Arnold refused to contribute towards a new church building but offered to make a donation towards the stipend for a clergyman (letter 22.12.1839). Such a person should be 'a man of education, relieved from the necessity of following any trade or ordinary profession', placed there to do good both physically and morally. Arnold conceded that ministers were too often from the landed gentry. Their language and whole way of life were different from that of most of their flock. Ministers must be recruited from the lower classes as well. Arnold was ready to concede that in his time, the most socially comprehensive church in England was the Roman Catholic. The minister should be elected by vote among the congregation, as was the system with some dissenting churches. Graduate status for ministers (then expensive to acquire and therefore, in practice, socially selective) should no longer be compulsory. A system of discipline to ensure the removal of idle, ineffective and 'hunting' clergy should be introduced. Non-residence in a parish from which a clergyman drew an income would be prohibited, as would the holding of more than one church living. The pay of clergy would be equalized so that some livings would no longer be paid excessively well and others badly. The Church should not be viewed as synonymous with the clergy, as in the phrase 'X is going into the Church', i.e.

becoming a member of the clergy. Reviewing the parish offices of parish clerk, church wardens, overseers of the poor, beadle and constable, Arnold can only scoff: 'What an organisation for a religious society!' (*Principles*, 1833, p. 47). A revival of the old order of deacon, 'an office extinct in all but name', is one way forward here. Even the eucharist could be celebrated without a priest:

> as long as the true view of Communion was retained,
> namely, that it was a commemoration of Christ's sacrifice,
> in which every man offered himself also as a living and
> spiritual sacrifice to God, so long would the pretended
> necessity of a priestly mediation be false and profane. But
> when the Communion was represented, not as a
> commemoration of Christ's sacrifice, but as a repetition of
> it . . . it followed naturally enough that a sacrifice *required*
> a priest. (Bamford, 1960, my italics)

The same held true for baptism in Arnold's view. Any believing, sincere Christian could conduct it. His opponents were quick to point out that Arnold's butler could presumably celebrate communion as validly as the rector of Rugby.

The national Church

Arnold believed that although the Anglican Church was the national Church by law established, it could only become a true national Church by taking into itself the separated churches. Arnold also argued for the principle of an established church.

> Civil society aims at the highest happiness of man
> according to the measure of its knowledge. Religious
> society aims at it truly and really, because it has obtained a

complete knowledge of it. Impart then to civil society the knowledge of religious society, and the objects of both will be not only in intention but in fact the same. In other words, religious society is only civil society fully enlightened; the State in its highest perfection becomes the Church.

Since Christianity is belief and morality based on Jesus Christ, it follows that such faith transcends nation and race. But the scriptures, though providing the sole authority for Christian truth, offer no blueprint for church organization:

> The peculiar form of these Scriptures, which in the New Testament is rather that of a commentary than a text; – the critical difficulties attending their interpretation, and the still greater difficulties attending as to their application . . . all these things prevent the Scriptures from being decisive on controverted points. (*Principles*, 1833, p. 16)

A national Church must be active not passive:

> I cannot understand what is the good of a national church if it be not to Christianize the nation, and to introduce the principles of Christianity into men's social and civil relations, and to expose the wickedness of that spirit which maintains the game laws, and in agriculture and trade seems to think that there is no such sin as covetousness, and that if a man is not dishonest, he has nothing to do but make all the profits of his capital that he can. (in Willey, 1949, p. 63, and Stanley's 1898 *Life*, p. 243)

A national Church could only be real, as opposed to nominal or pretentious, if it could be reconciled with dissenting groups. To extinguish dissent by persecution was 'wicked and impossible': it must be dealt with by comprehension. 'Different tribes should act together as it were in one army and under one command'. Anglican Article XVII offered a conciliatory way forward. Every attempt at co-operation with other denominations should be encouraged. 'Not all who pray to Christ are required to entertain exactly the same ideas of his nature' (*Principles*, 1833, p. 37). Calling Jesus 'Lord' and 'God' is the language of prayer and praise; people should not be expected to explain what they mean by it. Arnold held, unusually for his time, that what united Christians was far greater than which divided them. Union could be considered under the headings of doctrine, church government and liturgy. There was little of real significance to separate the established Church from Baptists, Independents (Congregationalists), Methodists of all the various Methodist denominations (Wesleyan, Primitive, New Connexion, Bible Christian, Calvinistic, etc.), Moravians and Presbyterians. The universities should immediately admit nonconformists as students with full studying and graduation rights. Three groups constituted a problem. First, the Quakers, by virtue of their radically different worship based on silent waiting on the Inward Light and abandonment of outward sacraments (Arnold held that the Articles on war and swearing could easily be removed to conciliate Quaker scruples). Arnold admired Quakers, for characteristically Arnoldian reasons, namely their emphasis on living Christianity rather than doctrines:

> I have always thought that the Quakers stand nobly
> distinguished from the multitude of fanatics, by seizing the
> true point of Christian advancement, – the development
> of the principles of the Gospel in the moral improvement
> of mankind.

The second problem group were the Roman Catholics, by virtue of their claims to be the one true church. The most difficult problem to Arnold of all were the Unitarians, for whom Christ might not be divine. In the final analysis these latter to Arnold could not constitute Christians. Even so, he distinguished two types of Unitarians: those who could not subscribe to the Athanasian Creed, who might participate in a united church, and others who preferred the label 'Unitarian' for respectability but were really 'unbelievers', i.e. agnostics. These could not be accepted into a united church. It was in the interests of the established church to accommodate these groups because 'dissent . . . when it becomes general, makes the Establishment cease to be national'. A united church would have implications for credal statements. Here Arnold's old personal difficulties with doctrine influenced his thinking:

> a whole Church never can be expected to agree in the absolute truth of such a number of propositions as are contained in the Articles and Liturgy . . . For otherwise the Church could by necessity receive into the ministry only men of dull minds or dull consciences; of dull, nay, almost dishonest minds, if they can persuade themselves that they actually agree in every minute particular with any great number of *human* propositions. (letter to A. P. Stanley, 20.12.1839, my italics)

Variance in views on God's metaphysical nature among Christians are 'wholly unimportant' as they are often 'wholly inoperative on our spiritual state; they neither advance us in goodness; nor obstruct our progress in it', thus, 'a command given to one man, or to one generation of men, is and can be, binding upon other men and other generations, only so far forth, as the circumstances in which both are placed are similar' (*Sermons*, Vol. II,

207

1832, p. 431). Or again: 'Two individuals might agree three hundred articles [of belief] but as they add to their own numbers they must diminish that of their articles' (*Principles*, 1833, p. 39).

Early Anglicanism was characterized by its freedom from the 'irksome control' of the Roman Catholic system (Lecture 5, p. 204), which interferes considerably with freedom of thought and action, notably by requiring confession, and inflicts too much in the way of ritual and ceremonial ordinances. 'Let any man read Shakespeare and the other great dramatists of the period, and he will observe nothing more remarkable in them than their extreme freedom.' Anglicanism must maintain this. Arnold stressed that in his plan for a united church, no one was being asked to give up their beliefs or their preferred way of worship, but only to allow the addition of others.

Arnold's united church would unite the ministers and could offer different types of worship during most of Sunday and part of every weekday, using the old parish church building as the normal base. It has 'a sacredness . . . in its antiquity'. This would be far better than its present use, perhaps only once a week for 'one uniform service, never to be added to, never to be varied' (*Principles*, 1833, p. 48). The current Anglican Liturgy, although fine, should not be the only one. Services should vary, not only to embrace the denominations uniting into the one church, but also the varying moods of individuals, who sometimes need 'a freer and more social service' and at others need 'the deep solemnity of the Liturgy' (ibid., p. 67). Matters which were then controversial in some dissenting churches, such as the use of organs (they were not biblical instruments and were therefore forbidden in some churches) would cease to matter, as some services would use organ music while others need not. Several ministers might lead different services. It would be better to hold these different services in the same building at different times than to hold competing services at the same time in various buildings. As people shared the same building, barriers would fall away. This would prevent the 'melancholy sight' of buildings being used only once a week and would make available 'some of the most perfect specimens of architecture in existence' for use in worship by all, thus ridding English Christianity of the 'utter coarseness and deformity' exhibited in 'the great proportion of the Dissenting chapels throughout England'. Religious orders should become more open to all by not requiring life vows but rather renewable ones for fixed periods.

Every large town would constitute a diocese and the Church must cultivate episcopacy without prelacy. Dioceses should be similarly in size and based on population numbers, not medieval cities, some of which were now reduced to villages, while great industrial towns had no bishop. The notion of the 'divine right of Episcopacy' has greatly damaged the Church. Bishops should be guided by committees of lay people and clergy, partly elected from the parishes. Bishop and council should decide about who should be appointed to particular livings, but this patronage should be advisory, not mandatory. Bishops should continue to sit in the House of Lords, however, as eminent representatives of their profession and the potential for 'a great national good'. For those likely to be shocked by Arnold's reduction of the power and perhaps status of bishops he had an answer: the present office of bishop was so different to that in the early church that the principle of change and development according to the Church's needs was well established. Arnold held that re-drawing the role of bishops in this way and circumscribing their power would remove the objections that dissenters had to them. The clergy should not rule the Church alone. There is always the danger of their becoming a caste and dominating the Church. Bishops needed checks and restraints to prevent than becoming diocesan tyrants. Parishes should be made manageable units, small enough to promote and reflect community spirit. Current deaneries

could become new dioceses. The order of deacon as practised in
the ancient church should be revived, as an end in itself, not as
merely a prelude to a second more important ordination, to
priesthood:

> In large towns many worthy men might be found able and
> willing to undertake the office out of pure love, if it were
> understood to be not necessarily a step to the Presbyterial
> order, nor at all incompatible with lay callings. You would
> get an immense gain . . . by softening down that pestilent
> distinction between clergy and laity. (letter to Stanley,
> 27.2.1839)

The benefits of this would be reflected in every Christian congregation; even the Newmanites could not oppose the measure and
it might be 'the small end of the wedge, by which Antichrist [the
secular–spiritual distinction] might be burst asunder like the
Dragon of Bel's temple'. It was to be more than a century before
the institution of NSMs (non-stipendiary ministers) in the
Church of England implemented a revised version of Arnold's
thinking on this.

But Arnold believed strongly that to achieve a single Christian
society the established church would have to stop treating nonconformists as rebels and schismatics. It had to acknowledge its
own historical guilt in the factors that had led to the breaking
away of dissenting groups. It had to stop resting in complacent
satisfaction and recognize that it had never had the allegiance of
working-class people; that this was required; that the dissenters
had made more headway in this regard. It was 'the natural binding force between prince and pauper'. The two main problems
faced by the established church were its hierarchical structure,
which hindered it and the total lack of appreciation it had of the
reality of Britain in the industrializing 1830s. But the royal

supremacy is defended on the grounds that it prevents the Church from being controlled by priests. *The Times* review argued that denominations were used to seeing themselves as innocent victims in historical disputes with others, or defenders of 'pure' Christianity against the corruption of the originating denomination. Such traditions in their self-perception would be hard to overcome.

Arnold also entered into comment on the colonial mission church issue. He believed that in British colonies, it was not appropriate for the English national church to expect to be supreme. Scotland had a different (Presbyterian) national church with 'equal rights' (his phrase):

> I would have the two churches stand side by side, each free, and each sovereign over its own people; but I do not approve of such a fusion of the one into the other as would produce a third substance, unlike either of them. (letter to J. Franklin, 16.3.1841)

He did not address the issue of the relevance of British denominations to a colonial context, but that was not anticipated until by implication the work of Bishop Colenso in Natal more than twenty years later.

But Arnold did engage in active support for the proposals for a Prusso-Anglican bishop in Jerusalem. Bunsen was also inspired by this project and when in 1840 Frederick William IV came to the Prussian throne, Bunsen, whose diplomatic experience of handling Prussian relations with the papacy from 1823 to 1839 was widely recognized, was able to press the case forward. The aim was to serve the Anglicans and Protestants of Syria, Chaldea, Egypt and Abyssinia. The bishop was to be alternately nominated by England and Prussia. The whole project was opposed by the Tractarians, for whom an alliance with a Protestant church was seen as undermining the tradition and order of the undivided Catholic Church going back to apostolic times. The first appointee, Michael Solomon Alexander (1799–1845) had an excellent supporting curriculum vitae. He was a converted Jew, who had grown up in Germany, where he had taught German and the Talmud, moving to England in 1820. He was baptized in 1825, ordained in 1827, joined the London Society for Promoting Christianity among the Jews and becoming Professor of Hebrew at King's College in 1832, where he translated the Book of Common Prayer into Hebrew. He was ordained bishop at Lambeth in 1841. Arnold was delighted as it represented exactly the sort of Christian co-operation for which he was campaigning, and the see linked 'persons using different Liturgies, and subscribing different Articles of faith; it will sanction these differences, and hold both parties to be equally its Members' (letter to T. S. Pasley, 23.9.1841). It was *Church Reform* starting to come true.

The Church should seek to integrate into the life of the people, not into traditions of the past. The people should be made to feel that the Church is theirs, reflecting their commitment and understandings. Arnold's church would be

> thoroughly national, thoroughly united, thoroughly
> Christian, which should allow great varieties of opinion,
> and of ceremonies, and forms of worship, according to the
> various knowledge, and habits, and tempers of its
> members, while it truly held one common faith, and
> trusted in one common Saviour and worshipped one
> common God. (*Principles*, 1833, p. 28)

Arnold's views were contentious. J. H. Newman, in a letter to Hurrell Froude, said that 'Mohammedans' [*sic*] and Jews could also easily be accommodated in Arnold's church, on Fridays and

Saturdays. Moreover Newman saw no point in getting under one roof people who disagreed about their beliefs. A Unitarian minister, Carpenter, praised Arnold's 'wise and liberal views . . . which suit so well the spirit of the times' (1833, p. 19). J. H. Newman would have shuddered both at liberalism and the goal of accommodating the spirit of the times but Carpenter urged that Unitarians were Christian by 'sentiment' and should be included in Arnold's church. They appeal to 'myriads' in the UK and the USA and they can claim to love Christ, praying to God through him (ibid., p.10f). William Palmer (1811–79), an anti-Roman, anti-Dissent Tractarian found Arnold's *Principles* 'extraordinary' (1833, p. 6). Difference of opinion in the Church is the essence of the battle between orthodoxy and heresy, not a matter for toleration; possessing no source of infallibility means no instrument for deciding between truth and error. Arnold has surrendered Christian doctrine itself: 'There is no limit to Dr Arnold's benevolence' (ibid., p. 11) and his principles will lead in the end to Deism. All this sets the scene for Arnold's violent attack on the Oxford Movement, which he saw as taking the Church in the exact opposite direction to where it should be going.

The Oxford Movement: Apostles or Malignants?

John Keble's Assize Sermon (14.7.1833) at Oxford is the generally recognized beginning of the Oxford Movement. The sermon's subject was National Apostasy and its theme was to attack the interference by the state in church affairs, namely in the suppression of ten bishoprics in the Church in Ireland as part of a process of church reform. The fear was that the Church was becoming a pawn in politics and that even within the Church itself there were people willing to challenge basic doctrines (Arnold's *Church Reform* had appeared in January of the same year). Keble was the godfather of Matthew Arnold. In opinions Keble could be as unbending as Arnold. In the same year (3.10.1833) Froude preached that the sort of vision of a united church in which different sects would come together implied that 'no one of these communities has any claim to preference above the others', that such plans were 'a demoralising influence', and 'sure to perplex the mass of Christians'. Keble, Hurrell Foude, John Henry Newman, William Palmer, Arthur Perceval and others decided to produce a series of tracts, at the time a common vehicle for provoking educated religious debate, aimed at awakening the clergy to the dangers faced by the Church from outside and within and recalling them to the divine spirit of the Church and its continuing structure, organizationally and doctrinally, from apostolic times. Reference was made to

> the sedulous attempts made in various quarters to reconcile members of the Church to alterations in its Doctrines and Discipline. Projects of change, which include the annihilation of our Creeds and the removal of doctrinal statements incidentally contained in our worship, have been boldly and assiduously put forth. (i.e. by Arnold and others, Bamford, 1960, p. 94)

Arnold was quick to reply that the Church's salvation could not be found in its past and that

> if the gifts of the apostles had been transmissable, the succession would have been a valid reality; but their gifts were inherited by no-one . . . The clergy, in the second generation after the apostles, had no essential superiority over other men.

Arnold and Newman had met briefly, in 1828, when they had

dined together after formal disputation for their BD degrees and they did not meet again until a College Gaudy in 1842. The 1828 meeting at the Oriel high table seems to have been remembered by neither of them. Pusey publicly joined the Tractarians in 1834 with Tract 18, 'Thoughts on the Benefits of the System of Fasting, enjoined by our Church'. This gave the movement a major boost within Oxford just when it seemed to be waning. J. H. Newman, Keble, Pusey and Froude were all at Oriel. The time of the Noetics seemed over. Newman held the living of St Mary's Oxford and his sermons from this influential pulpit were crowd draws; his preaching had a magic quite different from Arnold's spell. The tide seemed to be rising in favour of the Oxford Movement. Although Richard Bagot, the Bishop of Oxford and coincidentally a Rugbeian, did not support them, Hawkins and Hampden at Oriel might well have thought that the tide was turning against liberalism: J. H. Newman later wrote that it was the success of the liberal cause that fretted him.

The Hampden affair

In January 1836, Edward Burton, the Regius Professor of Divinity at Oxford, died. His thoughts about church reform had been no more radical than the discouraging but not actually prohibiting of livings held in plurality. He had even defended the ordination of candidates by bishops after only short notice and without training on the grounds that if they were candidates at all, it was proof of their being serious and honest. Lord William Melbourne, the Whig Prime Minister and an admirer of Arnold, had already decided against making him a bishop on grounds of prudence. Archbishop William Howley, last of the prince-archbishops, an unreformed extreme Tory and high churchman and opponent of Catholic emancipation, sent a list of five candidates for the vacant Chair, with Pusey as the first name, Newman fourth and Keble fifth. Whately and Copleston lobbied for Renn Dickson Hampden (1793–1868). They had been fellow Noetics in the Oriel common room with Arnold (see pp. 186ff). Hampden had been a private pupil in the house of the vicar of Warminster and was resident in Warminster at the same time as the boy Arnold. Hampden was a moderate broad churchman. In February Melbourne offered Hampden the job. He accepted by return. The King, who had to confirm the appointment (it was a Regius Chair), and had never heard of Hampden, confirmed by return. Although the offer to Hampden was rumoured throughout Oxford, no public announcement was made. Hampden himself would not comment. The *Standard* attacked Hampden and Melbourne wavered, writing to him that it might be better if he did not succeed Burton after all, even though he (Melbourne) held the King's letter of approval.

Newman, Pusey, Keble and Golightly opposed Hampden on grounds of heresy. Chairs of Divinity could be subject to such challenges. He already held the Chair of Moral Philosophy and was Principal of St Mary's Hall, but was suspect to Oxford Movement supporters for having welcomed the relaxing of university regulations against dissenters in 1834–5. This was hardly heresy. More evidence had to be found and so Hampden's Bampton Lectures of 1832 were scrutinized. His Bamptons had attacked, in a dull and sober manner, the accretions on the original and simpler gospel of early Christianity from Greek philosophy and later medieval scholasticism. It was an established but not universal eighteenth-century view within Anglicanism, in which opponents could rightly detect a reduction of the doctrinal elements of Christianity. The real issue was whether these doctrinal elements thus reduced were accretions or essentials. To the Oxford Movement they were essentials.

Petitions were raised against Hampden and J. H. Newman stayed up all night to write a pamphlet in attack. For some Tories it was a good excuse to embarrass a Whig government. A petition went to Howley, who lost no time in communicating with the Prime Minister. Their relationship was always wary. But Melbourne decided that the appointment must stand. It was still not publicly known that the King had already approved it. The King, aware by now of problems, told Melbourne to consult Howley. Melbourne replied in writing that the King had already approved the appointment; that the honour of Melbourne and the government, and also Hampden, were at stake. Melbourne went to see Howley and then went to Brighton to see the King. Finally, the appointment was gazetted (20.2.1836).

Although it was now public, the opposition continued unabated. Pusey accused Hampden of rationalism, an accusation he (Pusey) had just scraped clear of as recently as 1828. Hampden's mild inaugural lecture, in which he referred obliquely to 'a season of peculiar perplexity and apprehension of danger to the Church', failed to quell the storm. An attempt was made to deprive Hampden of his place on the university committee for choosing select preachers. At last Arnold pitched in with 'the Oxford Malignants', a blistering attack on all the 'Newmanites'. He already knew that in a private conversation with a third party, J. H. Newman had asked whether Arnold was a Christian. This conversation became one of the open secrets of Oxford. There was no love lost between them. Newman's Oxford tutor, Thomas Short, had been a Rugby pupil and teacher under John Wooll and an unsuccessful applicant for the headship when Arnold was appointed. Even Stanley admits a 'peculiar vehemence' of language used by Arnold, which Stanley attributes to Arnold's eagerness to speak out and his very clear sense of evil. In a long passage, he illuminates Arnold's violent denunciations further:

> He had a tendency to judge individuals with whom he had no personal acquaintance, from his conception of the

party to which they belonged, and to look at both through the medium of that strong power of association, which influenced materially his judgment, not only of events, but of men, and even of places. Living individuals, therefore, and existing principles, became lost to his view in the long line of images, past and future, in which they only formed one link. Every political or ecclesiastical movement suggested to him the recollection of its historical representative in past times – and yet more, as by an instinct, half religious and half historical, the thought of what he conceived to be the prototypes of the various forms of error and wickedness denounced by the Prophets in the Old Testament, or by Our Lord and his Apostles in the New. (Stanley, 1845, p. 171)

Hampden was restricted by 474 votes to 94 from the preachers' selection committee on the grounds that his theology did not possess the confidence of the university but he was not removed from his post. Hawkins pitched in with a reasoned essay on the duty of private judgement (1838): reason can and should scrutinize faith and can be the agency that removes superstition, a clearly liberal dig at the Tractarian position based on authority and tradition. Arnold wrote that he 'entirely agreed' with him and that he personally had endured too quietly 'a suspicion of heterodoxy such as was raised against Hampden'. Arnold went on to say that this was 'ridiculous' as the Newmanites themselves were further from the articles, liturgy and constitution of the Church of England than any clergy within his memory (letter: 12.1.1839). A rumour swept Oxford, said to originate among the teaching staff at Rugby, that Melbourne had written to Arnold to explain with regret that he could not now expect to become a bishop. It is unlikely that such a letter would have been sent and no documentary evidence for it exists, but it is certain that from this point onwards, Hampden's hopes of advance under Melbourne ended. His *Lecture on Tradition* (1839) was a carefully argued unemotional reply to the Oxford Movement and Arnold would have agreed with much of it: there is no divine authority in church traditions of doctrine, interpretations or rites. Tradition has strength only as it is 'shone upon by Scripture'. One 'energy which is most busily working among us [the Anglican Church] is to represent the Church in its points of resemblance to Roman-catholicism [*sic*], and throw it into a strong contrast with the spirit of Protestantism'. Scripture is easier to verify than tradition, which must be 'evidenced, corrected, purified, determined by Scripture' (*Lecture*, 1839, 4, 7). Hampden became Bishop of Hereford under Lord John Russell in 1847, not without strong opposition again. Arnold acquired neither a chair in divinity nor a bishopric. He was only granted the Chair of Modern History (1841) in the final week of the Melbourne government, perhaps because Melbourne felt safe from possible political repercussions. Melbourne had had his fingers badly burned by the Hampden affair. Whately and Copleston found that their advice was no longer welcome.

Edward Stanley, a Whig, was promoted by Melbourne to the see of Norwich when Bishop Bathurst died in his 94th year (1837). He was seen as an Arnoldite and had favoured Catholic emancipation. But he had been admired as a pastor at Alderley, if a little eccentric, and William IV was known to like the idea of promoting exemplary parish clergy provided they were suitably educated and well-bred, like Stanley. It was not entirely the safe promotion for which Melbourne hoped. Stanley immediately invited Arnold to preach the consecration sermon. Arnold warned that this might give offence, but the matter was dealt with when Howley intervened to prevent Arnold preaching. Stanley would not choose anyone else, so the choice was made by Howley. Stanley's own address at the event declared that conscientious dissent was neither sinful nor schismatic and affirmed the importance of education, both of which were famous Arnold themes. At the formal dinner afterwards the proposer of the toast to the new bishop deliberately omitted to ask him to publish his sermon. It was a calculated snub. The omission received public comment; the press got the story (it was of the recurring genre 'heretical sermon of new bishop') and Melbourne got more brickbats. But the young Queen Victoria read the eventually printed text and thought it evinced the sentiments that all good Christians should have. It was to be some time before she would meet Arnold.

Oxford Malignants article

The Oxford Movement saw itself as a rediscovery of the basic nature of the Church as a conciliar body from apostolic times, independent of civil governments and their 'interference', with a structure and sacraments ordained by Christ himself, gathering people into the sacrificial feast of the New Kingdom. Priesthood was a necessary and proper function within this community. It viewed the Reformation with distaste, as an agent that had lost to the Church its sense of Catholicity and reduced it to national sectarian status. To Arnold the Oxford Movement was an anti-reform group promoting priestcraft. Christianity had succeeded as a religion but failed as a church – so to Arnold the question was why were the Oxford Movement commending the Church rather than the religion?

> The Newmanites would not . . . yet dare to admit that
> their religion was different from that of the New
> Testament; but I am perfectly satisfied that it is so, and that
> what they call ecclesiastical tradition, contains things
> wholly inconsistent with the doctrines of Our Lord, of St

Paul, of St Peter, and of St John. (letter to Clough
28.2.1838)

Arnold's church was a social organization motivated by differing
beliefs about Christ and uniting on an ethic rather than a
sacrament:

> Christians at their very social meal could enter into the
> highest spiritual communion; it taught them that in all
> matters of life, even when separated from one another
> bodily, that same communion should be preserved inviolate;
> that in all things they were working for and with one
> another, with and to Christ and God. (Trevor, 1973, p. 40)

But this was for sacramentalists in the Oxford Movement a
reductionalist view of the eucharist. Arnold found authority for
this in the person and teaching of Christ, but was not radical
enough in biblical scholarship to admit that these, too, had been
conditioned by church tradition before they were gathered into
the New Testament. In terms of Christian beliefs and practice,
Arnold held that there were three periods of Christian history. In
the first, the forms for these practices were subservient to the
spirit. There was thus variety in beliefs, liturgy and church organization. In the second phase, careful attention had to be given to
forms in order to preserve the spirit – this was the era of church
councils and creeds. Then comes the third and dangerous phase
where forms which should have been abandoned or modified as
the spirit of Christianity is now self-evident, have been retained.
These forms are being mistaken and defended as the very essence
of Christianity by the Tractarians. Arnold's private correspondence revealed that the strong language of the *Edinburgh Review*
was not a mere debating flourish. It revealed his real hatred, dread
and condemnation of all it stood for. But in the earlier days,

221

pre-Hampden, he could be more mild and could write of people 'full of all kindly feelings, whose intense love for the forms of the church . . . has engrossed their whole nature' so that they see no defects, nor are they concerned about those excluded from the Church, i.e. dissenters (*Principles*, p. 83). This was perhaps an allusion to his friend Keble. But as the movement grew, so did Arnold's alarm. He had clashed with Pusey over his Tract on Fasting. Newman's Tract 90 was 'a very serious moral delin-quency' not from 'a fair enemy', i.e. a Roman Catholic, but from 'a treacherous one', i.e. one posing as an Anglican. 'The one is a Frenchman in his own uniform . . . the other is the Frenchman disguised in a red coat . . . I should honour the first and hang the second.' The Newmanites were worse than Roman Catholics because they were within the Church of England: 'Roman Catholics at Oxford instead of Oscott – Roman Catholics signing the Articles of a Protestant Church and holding offices in its ministry' (Trevor, 1973, p. 42). To Stanley he confided:

> I could not go to a place [Oxford] where I once lived so happily and so peacefully, and gained so much – to feel either constant and active enmity to the prevailing party in it [the Oxford Movement] – or else, by use and personal humanities, to become first tolerant of such monstrous evil, and then perhaps to learn to sympathize with it. (letter, 8.3.1841)

By 1841 Arnold could write to J. P. Gell that:

> the clergy are becoming more and more Newmanite – Evangelicalism being swallowed up more and more by the stronger spell, as all the minor diseases merged in the plague in the pestilential time of the second year of the Peloponnesian war. (letter, 3.3.1841)

The Tractarians received much opposition, but Arnold was seen as too radical in his views to emerge as a recognized leader for the opposing forces. His strain of thought continued with some moderation in William Arnold, whose *Oakfield* describes the 'surplice and white-tie fiddle faddle' of the Newmanites, but concedes that some of them have 'a deep sense of the living truth under this panoply of external frippery' (1853, p. 27f). To R. W. Church and G. Faber, the 'Oxford Malignants' was a turning point like the Assize Sermon. It symbolized the turning of the tide against the Oxford Movement.

The Bible and the 'broad church'

A broad churchman in the tradition of S. T. Coleridge, whose own *Confessions of an Enquiring Spirit* had to be published posthumously, Arnold was within a clear minority in the Church in his life time. They shared a mutual friend in William Wordsworth, although Coleridge's relationship with the Wordsworths was far more tempestuous than Arnold's. Arnold's approach to the Bible was in part inspired by his sense of history:

> There are two states of the human race which we want to understand thoroughly; the state when the New Testament was written, and our own state. As our own state is so connected with, and dependent on, the past, that in order to understand it thoroughly we must go backwards into past ages . . . till we connect our own time with the first century. (letter to J. L. Hoskyns, 22.9.1839)

If clergy are ministering in a cholera-ridden parish they should preach the scriptures simply, but when not under that pressure of immediacy, proper reading should be undertaken. To understand the New Testament a knowledge of philology, antiquities and ancient history and a critical sense of what is 'good' history are required. Arnold did not cease to be a classical scholar in his approach to the Bible. In his Thucydides he had emphasized the importance of learning other languages of the same family as Greek in order to acquire a better background understanding of the meaning of words, especially less common ones (*Thucydides III*, 1835, p. iv). But clergy should preserve the 'proportions' of their reading; Bible and Prayer Book alone are too narrow. Christian literature over centuries should be studied; even these are not broad enough.

> Keep your view of men and things extensive, and depend upon it that a mixed knowledge is not a superficial one . . . but he who reads deeply in one class of writers only gets views which are almost sure to be perverted. (letter to J. L. Hoskyns, 22.9.1839)

Scripture is 'wholly relative and practical', not 'as declaring some positive truth in the nature of things'. Thus the slaughter of the Amalekites is shocking and appalling but in its time was viewed as acceptable, even mandatory. The original meaning of passages must be distinguished from their use as types in the later interpretation of Christian truth. The true basis of religion lies in its moral and spiritual heart, therefore historical, critical and scientific 'objections' to the Bible do not damage its real centre. Even if the verbal inspiration of the biblical record is abandoned, the truths at its heart are not touched. Indeed, they may be emphasized when the inessentials are stripped away. Mary Arnold records a table-talk picture of the threat of evil and the need to be ready to relinquish the inessential in faith:

> Some reservations I had been making led him to say – It is a queer state of things that we live in at present in this

country. I asked him what he meant & he said that
together with the increase of knowledge there was a
prodigious increase of evil & that he was convinced that
the Devil was making great gain in the world. I said that I
hoped the knowledge of good was making its way also of
increasing – He acknowledged it might – I hoped it was,
but said he thought some great changes were working and
that he might live to see it . . . He said that he supposed 50
years ago, such men as he had before with great disgust
mentioned . . . did not exist; with their tastes they would
then have been mere sensualists whereas now, from the
spread of knowledge they valued themselves on their
intellect & talent & on serving the Devil heartily. It was
impossible on looking at the histories of modern times – at
its novels, poems, or plays not to be struck by the want of
Christian sentiment throughout them. Not intentional
perhaps in the writers . . . but now when he saw as he did
in the reading with his pupils that the books in general use
– where they taught any principles at all – taught so
generally what was good and bad he was quite staggered.
He could not but think that a greater contest between good
and evil was approaching than we had yet seen & it was
fearful to think of the consequences – the thing which
might well happen in the strife would be said [to] be the
greatest trial to the faith of good men that could be
imagined if the greatest talent and ability were on the side
of their adversaries & they would have nothing but faith
and holiness to oppose to it . . . He had often thought that
some trial of this kind might be the meaning or part of the
meaning of the apostles' word that by signs & wonders
they should deceive the elect. What he should be afraid of
in such a case would be that many good and sincere men –
taking alarm at the prevailing spirit would be afraid to hold

225

excess points they could not maintain instead of wisely giving them up & sticking on where they could keep their hold. – In talking of unbelief he said it was nothing but a love of wickedness beginning in indifference – to the Bible and of course leading directly to a hatred to [*sic*] it & a wish to prove it untrue – as interfering with the practice of evil. (8.9.1825)

Arnold held that neglect of Hebrew in England forced scholars into dependence on over-critical German works on the Bible. What is 'revealed' in the Bible is the will of God and the duty of humankind. If history and science appear to conflict with the Bible, it must be that the readers have failed to grasp the deeper meaning of God's message. Arnold had a passionate feeling towards Christ as a living friend and mentor and he found the gospel picture of Jesus exciting. Intellectually, he argued, the problems of faith are no greater than those of atheism. Morally, faith is superior to atheism because it is essential to the health of the soul. The unbeliever

> makes the greatest moral sacrifice to obtain partial
> satisfaction to his intellect: a believer insures [*sic*] the
> greatest moral perfection, with partial satisfaction to his
> intellect also; entire satisfaction to the intellect is, and can
> be, attained by neither (Willey, 1956, p. 77)

William Arnold, as the child said by the family to be nearest to Arnold in attitude, sums up the isolated position of the broad church view in his novel *Oakfield*:

> [I admire] the excellence of many individuals calling
> themselves evangelicals, but I do think that their party
> bitterness and ignorant self-satisfied narrow-mindedness,

has done more harm to the cause of good than the great Popery lie itself. [Evangelicals injure truth] with their unlearned semi-magical prophecy disquisitions, and wretched belabouring of that poor dead giant Popery, as the other people ['Newmania'] with surplice follies, &c . . . (1853, p. 28)

Challenged to answer whether there are any Christians who are not partisans, 'Edward Oakfield' replies that there are a few individuals, alone, isolated, misunderstood, under threat of losing their faith, on the one hand, through the repellent pressures of sectarian Christianity or, on the other, the confusions of doubt, but that there are not parties or societies of such people. It sums up the broad church mood and dilemma well.

Arnold's biblical exegesis in practice

Among the artefacts in the Rugby School archive are the two sixth form Divinity notebooks of Arthur Hugh Clough, covering Arnold's classroom work from 1835 to 1837. It appears from them that Arnold might be dictating notes to the whole class, although, equally likely, Clough, as a star pupil and admirer of Arnold, 'almost an honorary tenth Arnold child' (Hamilton, 1998, p. 34), was writing much of what Arnold said verbatim rather than as a specific dictation task. They offer a window into Arnold's exegesis in his maturity and the extent to which he was sharing his own biblical position with the young men at the head of the school. These students were advantaged beyond many biblical students now, in possessing a fluency in classical Greek that meant that they could readily handle New Testament Greek and the Septuaguint. Clough's notes contain properly accented Greek words and phrases, presumably fairly effortlessly recorded – although he was a star pupil. Of course, Arnold expected biblical

21. A page from a Divinity notebook of 1836.

exegesis to be both scholarly and instructive. His comment on the Sermon on the Mount is vintage Arnold. Jesus' intention was to put it plainly: 'You are not to conceive that I am in any way lowering the standards of duty.' Quite so. On Matthew 7:22f, Arnold comments:

> These words are indeed very awful. A man may use the
> language of Christians and do great good to others, for this
> is the daimonia ekballein [to cast out demons] of our days
> and yet himself be a castaway.

Nor must people underestimate the fallen-ness of humankind:

> The period of man's innocence before the fall – not the
> patriarchal times, which some suppose to have been purer
> than those of the Law; – this is a pure fiction however and I
> suppose ever since the fall men have been gradually rising.
> When you get to the time before the fall, of course, you
> have a pure standard. It is of the last importance to
> remember this.

Clough carefully cross-referenced his notes with sermons
preached on the same books by Arnold in Chapel. During the
academic year 1835–6 Arnold took the Johannine corpus for
sixth form study. The following extracts show the range of his
commentary:

> The Gospel of John is notwithstanding its supplementary
> character the only one in which the order of time is
> preserved. This is one of its peculiarities. Another is that
> the scene in it is almost wholly laid in Judaea, not Galilee.
> Compare also the opening of this with those of the other
> Gospels. In the others it is concerning his human birth and
> parentage, here he is shown tous [*sic*, i.e. to us] as 'God in
> the flesh': this was the point required when he wrote;
> for compare his description of the then existing form of
> Anti-Christ.

Arnold then outlined and discussed the concept of the Logos
from Philo and the idea of Wisdom as not unlike the Sophia of
Proverbs: 'A fitter form could not have been chosen to express
God in communication with his creatures – the Wisdom of God
revealed.' Arnold continues that the Gospel of John was written
to 'supply the deficiencies' of the others. He notes that John was

229

not yet in prison and he deals with the discontinuity with the Synoptic gospels, noting links with the epistles and taking into account Origen's comments and corrections to the text. Apostolic authorship is accepted, but on the basis of argument, not on an *a priori* basis. He corrects the Greek in Stephen's speech in Acts 7; 'It would seem that this was a previous translation of Stephen's speech, inserted by Luke and not his own composition. Luke uses de and kai 'rightly' the speech does not.' In a later history lecture (1842) Arnold considers that the miracles of the gospels cannot simply be dismissed on *a priori* grounds. The reality is that they took place within a sceptical Roman culture and not a credulous medieval culture (*Lecture 2*, 1842b, p. 104). Arnold faces problems: Why did John translate from Hebrew to Greek, Messiah to Christ, Cephas to Peter, and his use of the word rabbi is a puzzle. He deals with language issues:

> 'The Gospel' – I always dread to hear this Word. It is so often used vaguely. It is properly 'the Good Tidings' – viz 'the message of Salvation' 'Christ died and is risen' – Hence it is applied to all concerning all Christ's life – his miracles, parables and discourses of all kinds – his whole ministry on Earth.

How can we be sure about the meaning of words in the New Testament? Arnold appeals first to consistency of use by the same writer, then by comparing it to how other writers use the word, then by examining the Septuaguint. Study of the Gospel of John also provided opportunity for both philosophical and moral discussion. This example is from its concern with 'Moral' and 'Physical' certainty.

> It is morally not physically certain that a man who has had life so clearly set before him so clearly in Christianity will

when he has once seen it, go on. (V24) Physical certainty
we have from external nature but 'moral certainty is that
drawn from the nature and character of men.' . . . But we
know that the same motives do not always bring the same
effects – that perhaps [caprices? handwriting unclear]
interfere – so that the laws of human action, &
consequently moral certainty are not without exceptions.

Arnold refers regularly to scholarly commentary on the texts, and
to manuscript variants. He refers to Lachmann's and Grisbach's
editions and the superiority of the 'Vatican', i.e. Vaticanus
and Alexandrian manuscripts. Early church writings are also
considered as evidence. Here is Arnold on John 21:

> The vividness and life of this narrative, the way in which all
> the particulars seem to have been so perfectly retained in
> the mind of the writer and the manner in which they are all
> so minutely related give it an exceedingly striking [missing
> word in Clough's notes?] and I almost seem to see the
> whole Gospel in it.

Arnold is aware that John 21 might be 'as supplement to the
Gospel added . . . after John's death by the Church of Ephesus
but more probably by John himself at a very late period of his
life'. He still concedes that 21:24 might be an addition by the
Church. In I John there is internal evidence for a late date, 'the
failings which he writes against here, namely the want of practical
holiness is [*sic*] not likely to spring up at once in a new religion.
We hear nothing of this in the early Epistles of St Paul.' I John is
written after the Gospel, as the first part of letter presumes knowledge of the Gospel: 'The much stronger testimony of the
internal evidence [for John as the writer of I John] is in this case
more decided than in any other of the sacred writings . . . Some

have supposed it a supplement.' But in the case of II and III John, Arnold is more sceptical, noting that Eusebius doubted their authenticity. Arnold reviews other external evidence and examines internal language, especially the use of *presbyteros.* Revelation could be by another John but Arnold opts for the John of Gospel and Epistle. He refers to J. G. Eichhorn (1752–1827) in this discussion.

Arnold also attended to doctrinal issues. Good examples appear in his classroom study of Matthew's Gospel, which occupied him from December 1836 to February 1837. Matthew is 'that which of them all has fewest tokens of an individual writer':

> In Unitarian writings the translation of aion as 'the world' is condemned: but though not exactly 'the world' this word is the best we can use for the common people. The Latin translation saeculum is very good . . . [it refers to] man's natural life . . . There might have been many aions before those with which man is concerned. (on Matthew 13:49)

> [This] has been urged by Protestants against Romanists, and Puritans against Protestants . . . the language of our 34th Article which was so opposed by the Puritans and had to be defended against them, seems true v. right, & sensible doctrine. We must suppose that this was a piece of inadvertence on the part of the disciples, that they did not intend it; then Christ took the opportunity, as soon as they were found fault with, to set forth a doctrine much wanted at all times, because the natural tendency of man is to make much of such things: and at the same time to neglect what is really moral law, this almost invariably follows it; and accordingly Christ took an example of this

neglect of God's law united with the observance of paradosis. (on Matthew 15:1–20)

paradosis – St Paul calls his own instruction by this word, so that it does not always relate necessarily to time. But I do not know whether the Instruction of the Holy Ghost could be called paradosis, being immediate and virginal. – It seems to be always derived instruction.

Arnold makes observations on Matthew 15 and 16:

Here we have a very good example of the difference in his [Jesus'] language to the Pharisees, and of that he used to the multitudes and still more to his own disciples. He merely answers the Pharisees by an argument ad hominem, without saying anything about the real reason. The real reason is very important: striking at once at the root of all the superstitions concerning the Lord's Supper, Transubstantiation etc. . . . as to belief that matter can affect spirit either for good or for evil: the opposite follows on the assertion of the one. At the very same time we see that all those who touched the hem of his garment were cured of their bodily ailments. For the Laws by which the cure of our bodily diseases are regulated we do not know – and in many instances can see no connection between the external act and its effect: – matter may act on matter . . . It is important to remember this; as the distinction is very often lost sight of and the two things confused together . . . [25f]. I have always regretted the change in the translation of psyche – it was done to make it clearer, but I should not think anyone could mistake the reuse of it; and the word 'soul' being introduced changes the character of the language Our Lord uses.

233

22. Arthur Hugh Clough by S. W. Rowse, 1860.

Clough's notes suggest that Arnold's study of the Old Testament was much less intensive, sometimes only a few lines per chapter. He uses the Septuaguint for Joshua, Judges and Ruth. Clough's entire notes on the Book of Ruth follow:

> This book stands very much by itself in the Bible and I do not know what the Jews could have made of it, before our Saviour came. Here we have the affections made to triumph over national feelings and the Law . . . Such wickedness and such exceeding purity and simplicity existing together. We may be the same in our time and country also – taking those parts where society is the

purest, as compared with the worst parts of London. It is very remarkable that the only story which could be found remaining concerning the ancestry of David (under whom or his sons this was doubtless brought to notice) and of our Lord, should be of this sort. No great warriors or men distinguished for strength and bravery and great deliverances but merely this story of Ruth.

Linguistically and in terms of philology, Arnold's sixth form teaching of divinity was at a level that would elude most twenty-first-century sixth form students of Advanced Level Religious Studies, and many theology undergraduates. His approach, in terms of criticism, was entirely 'modern'. If the intensive classical education of his pupils is no longer accepted now as justifiable in terms of the percentage of their education programme it occupied, it prepared them extremely well to study the New Testament. If Arnold's conclusions, for instance in favour of the apostolic authorship of the Gospel of John, seem too conservative now, he did defend them on intellectual grounds and did not merely assume them from an *a priori* doctrine of biblical inerrancy which he did not hold. The Bible is treated like literature: he asks whether passages 'seem' like eye-witness writing. On what basis? This notoriously subjective yardstick was in Arnold's time something of a corrective to the view that repressed the human elements in the writing of the Bible and reduced it to a book of revealed doctrine. It might be argued that this literature approach has again been lost in some contemporary New Testament scholarship. But it opened the way for classical students to see the Bible as a potentially inspiring ancient text, alongside others they had studied. Of course, Arnold would have seen it as more than literature, but his entering into debate with the text opened a door for students to follow. Arnold also referred to historical commentaries. He was not content that the interaction with the text should be merely personal or uninformed. He never merely treated the Bible like a classical text and stopped there – it was examined and debated for doctrine and for that Arnold favourite, Christian moral teaching. Arnold was teaching theology in his 'Divinity' lessons and he was 'theologizing' aloud for the benefit of his students.

Collision with William G. Ward (1812–82)

Ward, who had a liberal and utilitarian background unlike many Oxford Movement members, had been an admirer of Arnold's ethical views and Whately's logic. Like Arnold he had doubts about the 39 Articles and ordination and like Arnold eventually went ahead. Chadwick describes Ward as having 'the ablest mind' of all J. H. Newman's converts, despite his distinct lack of motor co-ordination in his body and startling but perhaps intentional lack of dress sense. Ward held a Fellowship at Balliol from 1834 to 1845. He was a logician who revelled in conversational paradox and shock and gave his opponents 'the feeling of being a bit of paper blown up a chimney' (Chadwick, I, 1971, p. 200). He became a 'Newmanite' but unlike other Tractarians, he was sufficiently liberal to believe in advancing truth by argument and not merely assertion. Clough, who saw himself as having disastrously failed Arnold's high expectations when he did not get a First, came under Ward's brilliant but unsettling influence at Oxford. Clough was in some ways crunched between the two men and the damage caused contributed towards his own later agnosticism. Ward 'battered Clough out of allegiance to Arnold, but could not quite drive him into Catholicism' (ibid., p. 538). To the unhappy chaos of Clough's mind, Arnold, Ward, Carlyle and Strauss brought neither victory nor vision (ibid., p. 539). Within seven years of Arnold's death Clough could write:

Eat, drink and die, for we are souls bereaved,
Of all the creatures under this broad sky
We are the most hopeless, that had hoped most high,
And most beliefless, that had most believed.

(*Easter Day* 1849)

On one occasion (1839) Ward re-preached a printed sermon of Arnold's, but greatly altered and (as it would have seemed to Arnold) subverted it, at the parish church at Littlemore. Ward attacked Arnold's moderate biblical criticism on the grounds that it was an inevitable road to atheism via the German radical criticism of Strauss and others whom Arnold purported to attack. Ward was to maintain this fiercely anti-liberal stance into his Roman Catholic days, in common with other Ultramontanes. Ward's case was that once the door of criticism was opened, it could not be shut and that Arnold was holding an untenable position. Any critical position places the critic on a downward slope to agnosticism. Strachey refers to a cameo appearance of Ward, without appointment, on Arnold's doorstep at Rugby, to remonstrate with Arnold about his religious position. But Arnold was occupied in teaching and therefore Ward had to wait, all afternoon, in the drawing room of the head's house. It was not until late in the evening that Arnold returned from School House, exhausted from the day's work, to face a long and sometimes heated verbal duel with Ward about the Bible. The contest was inconclusive. It lasted well into the night. Ward returned to Oxford and threw himself into the Oxford Movement. Arnold threw himself into bed (another Strachey comparison for purposes of wit or ridicule) 'worried, perplexed and exhausted' and according to Strachey's unsubstantiated account remained there for 36 hours. Eventually, Ward became a convert to Rome and was stripped of his degree for heresy (1845) by 569 votes to 511, although *The Ideal of a Christian Church* (1844), pro-Roman as it was, still contained a few Arnoldian contaminant echoes, that the Church of England was not doing its pastoral duty, that it should cease to be dominated by rank and become the church of the poor.

Dialogue with Francis W. Newman (1805–97)

Frank was the younger brother of John Henry Newman and they shared a common evangelical upbringing. To Frank, John's spiritual journey was 'the embodiment of blind reaction' (Willey, 1956, p. 15); to John, Frank's different journey was the essence of that destructive liberalism against which he had devoted his life-work. But Frank arrived at Oxford as an evangelical enthusiast and purist. He took a double first at Balliol (1826) and subscribed to the Articles, with many misgivings, in order to do so. He disliked the worldliness of the bishops and as an avid student of history applying his skills to the Bible, started to be disturbed by 'dislocations', discrepancies in the biblical record. Shut out from the Church of England ministry by doubt, finding Dissent pretentious and Quaker dispensation with the two sacraments 'false', he was left in a quandary. However, these doubts were suspended in a rush of evangelical activity that took him in 1830 with some Irish friends on a two-year trip to Baghdad with the intention of converting people in one of the great strongholds of Islam. Their journey was a mixture of adventure, comedy, privation and suffering. All the women in the party died. The mission was a spectacular failure. But it confronted Frank with the reality of religions other than Christianity and the problems they raise for Christian truth claims. After a period as classical tutor at Bristol College and a short time as a Baptist, Frank moved to the staff of Unitarian New College, Manchester, again as a classics tutor. He could by now no longer accept most creeds and Christian dogma, and found the notion of the infallibility of the Bible untenable.

At some point between 1834 and 1841 Frank had two short conversations with 'the late excellent Dr Arnold' (1850, p. 67), as a great 'liberal' authority, about the many doubts which confronted him. Like Arnold, he was convinced that 'the modern churches . . . by no means hold the truth as conceived of by the apostles' (ibid., p. 29). Like Arnold, he had an antipathy towards the Athanasian creed. Like Arnold he condemned people 'in high ecclesiastical places' who 'eagerly promote sacerdotal inanities' (1849, p. 160, no doubt written with his brother in view). Arnold and Frank also shared a common interest in history which for Arnold was in the end to underwrite Christianity, for Frank Newman to drag it down. Like Blanco White (see p. 260f), for a time Frank took refuge in a devotional rather than intellectual conception that Jesus is God, but he was aware that in church historical terms this was the Sabellian heresy. At one of their meetings, much to Newman's surprise, Arnold treated all the questions that were troubling Frank Newman – the fossil evidence, how the human race could have descended from Adam in 6000 years, the impossible geography of the rivers in Paradise, the 'capricious' curse on the serpent, a poor harmless 'brute' abused by the Devil as his instrument, the longevity of the Patriarchs, the geological difficulties in the Mosaic cosmogony, etc. – with complete indifference and for good measure conceded that the Flood was 'evidently mythical' and the Joseph narrative 'a beautiful poem'. 'I was staggered at this,' Newman wrote later. It was not only healthy to raise these questions, but necessary, Arnold assured him.

> I was unable to admit Dr Arnold's views; but to see a vigorous mind, deeply imbued with Christian devoutness, so convinced, both reassured me that I need not fear moral mischiefs [*sic*] from free inquiry and indeed laid that inquiry on me as a duty. (1850, p. 68)

There were more questions Frank raised as 'a fresh strain' on scriptural infallibility: the descent of the human race from two parents, the Bible's teaching on the origin of death, the morality of the murder of Sisera; the intended killing of Isaac making Abraham 'no less guilty than those who sacrifice their children to Molech'; the treatment of the Canaanites; the cursing of the fig tree; the coin in the fish's mouth; the whole question of demonic possession; misquoted Old Testament passages found in the New Testament. Arnold's answer was that Christianity must rest mainly on the Gospel of John. Its narrative was simple, vivid, deep and undeformed by credulous legend. Newman was unconvinced: 'My study of John's gospel has not enabled me to sustain Dr. Arnold's view, that it was an impregnable fortress of Christianity' (ibid., p. 115). The Fourth Gospel writer makes Jesus and John the Baptist speak like the writer does in both the Gospel and the first Letter – in other words, the speeches are not historical record. The writer has 'put into the mouth of Jesus the doctrines of half a century later, which he desired to recommend'. To Arnold – in Newman's account – the public and stupendous raising of Lazarus and the cross-examination of the man born blind are 'grand and unassailable bulwarks of Christianity'. This answer appealed at first to Newman; the Jerusalem authorities could not deny these events as history and instead could only plot to kill Lazarus and cross-examine the formerly blind man. But Newman was undermined by the thought that the earlier gospels omit both narratives. Why? Either they did not know these stories (highly unlikely in his view) or they did not believe them. Thus, John's evidence was unlikely to be correct and his account may mistake 'a reverie, a meditation, a day-dream, for a resuscitation of his memory by the Spirit' or Comforter of which he writes. Newman sides with Strauss here, whom he had read, in downgrading all that was supernatural in the gospel narratives. If Arnold's criticism was sometimes naïve and to later times over-conservative, Newman's scepticism was based on a simple assumption of the reliability of early gospels over late ones, which discounts the possibility that late gospels might contain earlier source material. Newman also shared with Strauss the *a priori* assumption that what is supernatural does not happen now and therefore could never have happened.

Frank Newman continued his historical studies of the Bible, including the sources behind the Pentateuch, going further than Arnold thought necessary down the critical line so as in the end to reach the radical conclusion that Christianity could not be a historical religion, and that Protestant bigotry and bibliolatry, 'the English idolatry' (1849, p. 40ff) were driving some people to Rome and others to atheism. For Frank the 'Christian Evidences' are 'unmanageable' (ibid., p. 39) because the modern missionary, unlike the first apostles, is committed to promoting an infallible book. Even Christian claims to be more moral than some other religions are undermined for Newman by its party spirit and exaggerated claims to have raised the status of women (ibid., p. 102ff). The spiritual energy of Christianity has been 'lamed' by its mixture with history (ibid., p. 155). Real religion in contrast is 'created by the inward instincts of the soul'. It is a 'state of sentiment'. Frank Newman was left with a belief in God, with an unwillingness to say too much about the nature of the deity (he likened the attempt to describe God as like that of a dog to know the mind of its owner), and a commitment to uphold 'the sacred moralities of Jew and Christian' wholeheartedly. Although an eccentric man, portrayed by his enemies unfairly as an agnostic, Newman made a spiritual journey in common with others in mid- and late Victorian times. To his opponents it illustrated all the dangers inherent in the Arnoldian position, taken to its logical conclusion. Not surprisingly Frank Newman befriended Arthur Clough. They had much in common.

Willey (1956) argues that the highly controversial *Essays and*

Reviews collection on biblical criticism (1860), nearly twenty years after Arnold's death, 'may be taken to represent the delayed action upon Oxford of Thomas Arnold, or the revival of the liberal spirit after its long eclipse by Newmanism [J. H. Newman in this case]' (ibid., p. 139). Willey is right. Baden Powell, a Noetic, was one of the essayists, writing 'On the Study of the Evidences of Christianity'. But the very first essay, 'The Education of the World', was by Frederick Temple, then head of Rugby and modelling his work as closely on Arnold's model as he could. That essay was to haunt Temple when he became Bishop of Exeter.

Christian social concern

Arnold's concern for the poor was born partly out of his high feeling towards the notion of the free person in the ancient world. When Arnold saw the condition of the poor he was clear that 'there was work for the Church of Christ to do, that none else could do it, and that with the blessing of her Almighty Head she could' (*Sermons* IV, p. lii). He also felt that imitating Christ, which Christians were called to do, meant mixing with other people, not merely for business or pleasure, but 'from a desire to do good to the bodies or souls of others' (*Sermon* on I Peter 5:6 and 7.) Jesus was not otherworldly in the sense of uninvolved in the plight of humanity. Moreover, he held that if people were alerted to 'the fearful state' of their times, remedy might be found and applied. But it is not usual to define Arnold as a Christian socialist, as the group usually identified with the first phase of Christian socialism is Charles Kingsley, J. F. D. Maurice, J. M. F. Ludlow and Thomas Hughes. But this was the same Hughes of *Tom Brown* (1822–96) and as has been demonstrated, he was deeply influenced by Arnold. Hughes, who was born at Uffington, Berkshire, went on from Rugby to Oriel, served as a barrister, county court judge and Liberal MP (1865–74), and helped to form the Working Men's College of which he was principal from 1872 to 1883. He also helped to establish a model settlement in the USA, in Rugby, Tennessee.

Arnold's Christian social concern was very clear in the *Englishman's Register* and the *Courant*. It had some roots in S. T. Coleridge, who in March 1817 had published his second *Lay Sermon*. In this he argued that the Christian governing classes had a duty towards the welfare of the governed. Economic selfishness and *laissez-faire* were tearing Britain apart. Landlords and manufacturers were coming to regard society as a wealth-creating machine; they were 'Christian Mammonists' hardened by the 'spirit of Trade' (in Holmes, 1998, II, p. 447). In a free trading country it is said when businesses crash all things find their level, but people are not things. 'Neither in Body nor in Soul does the Man find his level.' Child workers were exploited: ill-fed, badly paid, ill-clothed. Manufacturers must consent to regulations. Clients and dependent workers should be educated. It was revolutionary in its time, a time of great social unrest, of 'Luddite' attacks on factories, of the Pentrich rebellion. Bamford's Arnold

> as a supreme rebel himself [was he really?– TC] . . . was sympathetic to lower class objectives, but also frightened of their ignorance, their power and sheer destructiveness when led by mob orators. It kept him literally awake at nights. (Bamford, 1967, p. 40)

Stanley unwittingly accounts for why 'Christian socialism' did not begin with Arnold rather than Kingsley, Maurice, Ludlow and Hughes. Noting Arnold's consistent interest in the social state of the country, he notes that in Arnold's later years his writing in the area was 'considerably abated' by Arnold's own awareness of his ignorance of the subject. This is quite credible, taking into account all Arnold's other activities. But he regarded the Corn Laws as a great evil, along with the national debt: 'Woe to that generation which is living in England when the coal mines are exhausted and the national debt not paid off' (Oxford lecture, 1842, in Stanley, 1845, p. 174).

Arnold's view of history and citizenship

For Arnold it is easy to under-rate what is required of the student and the writer of history. Memory and accurate recording seem to produce the record of facts which is history. But this is too simplistic: imagination; judgement; reasoning; all have their place. History is more than the biography of a society, yet the life of every society belongs to history. History is to be seen as the life of the highest and most sovereign society, a state or nation, the biography of a political society or commonwealth (inaugural, lecture, pp. 2ff). A nation's highest and purest happiness should be the setting forth of God's glory by the means of doing God's work. But nations are members of a greater body, the body of organized states throughout the world and also of the universal family of humankind – both these memberships are according to the will of God (ibid., p. 13f). In order to perfect its inner and outer life, a nation needs political institutions and laws. These are invested with one of God's own attributes, especially judgement, which entails having to determine between truth and falsehood.

The state must inculcate certain principles in its members: these take the form of education, and education is to be conceived as religious in intention. In Christian countries religion inculcates truths and forms habits. All societies of people should make their common bond in a common object and a common practice rather than a common belief. Dogma is divisive. Union in action may in the end lead to union in belief, but this can never be guaranteed. A state may declare that a religion is the basis of its law: Does this mean, Arnold asks, that the religion is therefore imposed on the people? But the people and the state are not separate, except in corrupt states which act against their people. A nation acting through its government may choose a law for itself that it deems most for its good. How should it then treat dissenters? It must not overstrain the consciences of individuals on the terms of citizenship. It must not attempt to compel belief, although obedience to law is of course required. Christian law must provide for education and must try to 'realize' (i.e. make real) Christianity to its people (ibid., pp. 45–7). To begin with a strict creed is a sure way to hypocrisy and unbelief. Vigorous Christian institutions matter more. State and Church are not divorced: they have common ground in the promotion of moral values. The Christian monarch or parliament excludes the interference of a priesthood; the Church, without a priesthood (see p. 187) needs a Christian ruler or parliament.

But a state is also concerned with material matters such as the possession and right use of property. This is the base for economics. So history is also, in part, economic history: 'geology and physiology are closely connected with history' (ibid., p. 126), the existence of coal in England and the tea plant in China have influenced the development of both countries and the economic divisions between the northern and southern states in the USA is causing conflict. Wars have ongoing economic consequences: the English national debt stands at £700 million, 'more than half our yearly revenue' (ibid., p. 149), mainly as a result of the Napoleonic wars. War is a very great evil and 'though I believe that theoretically the Quakers are wrong in pronouncing all wars to be unjustifiable, yet I confess that historically the exceptions to their doctrine have been comparatively few' (ibid., p. 175).

The great constituent elements of nationality are race, language, institutions and religion. But these are complex constituents. No nation is a single race. The English nation's identity is complex and mixed, including Saxon, Briton and

Roman elements. The intermixture of Celtic and Roman changed the face of Europe. Colonization is re-shaping the world both racially and culturally. It is caused by want of subsistence in the home country; by expulsion of minority groups; by the wish to increase national wealth and by desire to extend civilization and 'true Religion' (1815, p. 2). The theory of deporting convicts is good: it removes a source of evil in the state and it gives wrong-doers a fresh start in a new setting, but the practice is bad as it brings 'a mass of evil together in a situation where it will be free from control'. Yet colonies themselves, like children, can be the heirs to ageing countries and cultures. With Britain fresh from victory over Napoleon, Arnold's prize essay ended:

> There yet lives within us that mighty spirit by which we have delivered Europe. Surely it will not be less powerful to create than to destroy; and in the room of that vast fabric of evil which it has overthown, to build up a more noble and lasting temple of God. (ibid., p. 31)

It some ways it represents a youthful statement of what was to be his life's mission. Similar sentiments have been expressed at the end of other victories, such as 1945, with perhaps similar lack of effect. Political science is therefore an important study and it has its truths (1838, p. xi). These are not like moral truths, those which receive the universal assent of good people, but are more open to question. They are not 'absolutely certain'. The historian has to tease them out.

> I have tried to be strictly impartial in my judgments of men and parties, without being indifferent to those principles which were involved more or less purely in their defeat or triumph. I have desired neither to be so possessed with the mixed character of all things human, as to doubt the

existence of abstract truth; nor so to dote on any abstract truth as to think that its presence in the human mind is incompatible with any evil, its absence incompatible with any good (ibid., p. xii)

It is now assumed that being born of free parents within the territory of a particular state and paying taxes to the government 'conveys a natural claim to the right of citizenship' (1835, p. xi). In the ancient world, citizenship, by contrast, unless specially conferred, depended solely on race and could be denied to migrants and their descendants, although 'distinctions of race were not of that odious and fantastic character which they have borne in modern times' (ibid., p. xi). Race in the ancient world was linked to specific morals and religions. Particular races worshipped particular gods and subscribed to particular moral codes with differing values, e.g. about polygamy or infanticide. In ancient multi-racial societies there could be confusion: so wide a tolerance being required that it led to 'a general carelessness and scepticism, and encouraged the notion that right and wrong have no real existence, but are the mere creatures of human opinion (ibid., p. xii). When civilization went in hand with conquest and commerce, and people were regarded 'solely in the relation of buyers and sellers' the desire to win customers would lead to a dilution of religious or moral institutions and to the 'demoralization' of a society. But despite this 'the mixture of races is essential to the improvement of mankind' and 'an exclusive attachment to national customs is incompatible with true liberality'.

How, then, can a multi-racial society be developed which avoids 'moral degeneracy' within a vortex of relativism, 'Epicurean indifference' or at the other extreme 'narrow-minded bigotry'? Arnold's answer is that Christianity makes religious and moral agreement independent of race or national customs. It is international and multi-racial in its nature. It distinguishes the essential and eternal from the temporal and local and requires toleration of local variations. It requires that reverence be given not to custom or national prejudice or human authority but to the truth of God. The potential binding force for citizenship is now Christianity, in which all races and nations can potentially become fellow citizens. Those without this bond, who merely pay taxes in the same country, are fellow sojourners not fellow-citizens.

Modern history treats of national life still in existence, but the major elements of modern history are derived from the ancient world: Graeco-Roman culture, philosophy and the Christian religion. Thucydides can claim to be modern history, because he demonstrates some of the methods of enquiry and reflection which are the tools of the modern historian, and because he deals with Greece, a nation made independent again in 1830. Thucydides (*c.*460–400 BCE) had written an eight-volume history of the Peloponnesian War. He had unsuccessfully commanded a squadron of ships at the battle of Thasos (424 BCE), failing to relieve Amphipolis. Condemned as a traitor for this, he retired in exile to his Thracian estate, where he owned gold mines, and wrote his history. His style is difficult and his research is partly based on the speeches of politicians but analysed by an attempt at rational principles of historical criticism and intended impartiality, and subjected to revisions which Thucydides did not live to complete. Arnold supplies the Greek text, with a full apparatus criticus, commentary and notes on the geography of the battles, within the context that

> History is to be studied as a whole, and according to its
> philosophical divisions, not such as are merely
> geographical and chronological . . . The history of Greece
> and Rome is not an idle inquiry about remote ages and
> forgotten institutions, but a living picture of things

248

present, fitted not so much for the curiosity of the scholar, as for the instruction of the statesman and the citizen. (1835, III, p. xvi)

Arnold returned to this theme in 1838 asserting that the history of Rome bears 'a nearer resemblance to our own [times] than many imagine' (*History of Rome*, p. x). The territory of modern history is therefore so large that no one can have a knowledge which is wide and also deep. Generalization, if undertaken at all, should be undertaken cautiously. The trustworthy historian needs an active impatience of error (Arnold surely had this) and desire of truth: these qualities are intellectual and moral and are as 'incompatible with great feebleness of mind as they are with dishonesty' (*Lecture 8*, 1842b, p. 297). Does history give us only 'a powerless knowledge, seeing an evil from which we cannot escape'? Arnold faces the issue of determinism (ibid., p. 308) and rejects it in characteristic manner:

> I do not suppose that any state of things can be conceived so bad as that the efforts of good men, working in the faith of God, can do nothing to amend it; yet on the other hand the evil may be far too deeply rooted to be altogether removed; nor would it be possible for the greatest individual efforts to undo the effect of past errors or crimes . . . What, or what amount of evil is incurable, or how widely or deeply individual good may become a blessing amidst prevailing evil, we are not allowed to determine or to know. God's national judgments are spoken of in Scripture both as reversible and irreversible . . . Surely it is enough to know that our sin now may render unavailing the greatest goodness of our posterity; our efforts for good may be permitted to remove, or at any rate to mitigate, the curse of our fathers' sin. (ibid., p. 311)

23. Arnold's hand-drawn diagrams: the genealogy of good and evil.

The genealogy of good and the genealogy of evil

The table-talk recorded by Mary Arnold includes two hand-drawn diagrams from Arnold that give an insight into his moral theology. He notes that these two diagrams 'have often been in my thoughts' and that he thinks that there is 'a great deal of truth' in them.

The eclipse of Arnold's theology

Arnold's immediate legacy after his death was perceived to be to education, in which he had by then become a respected national figure (see p. 96f). He had succeeded in education in a recognized and well-paid 'top job'. In the Church he was neither a recognized national leader, nor in a top job. This meant that his views on religion, which were always minority views, tended to fade away more quickly than their argument merited. Arnold's influence in the changing attitudes to study of the Bible, to Christian toleration, to one of the most comprehensive views of the Church before or since and to a radical approach to the nature of the Church, has been under-stated in subsequent writing on Victorian religion and beyond. Posterity does not look to Arnold as a theologian. This is in part Arnold's fault. He could engage in controversy with such vehemence that not all the people on his 'side' would wish to own him as a leader. But it is his success in education that perhaps led to his demise in these more controversial areas. Yet in many ways, Arnold's theology has outlived his views on education, and raises issues that still deserve to be addressed.

4 The Arnold Legacy for the Twenty-first Century: Does Arnold Deserve his Place in the Hall of Fame?

Stanley's achievement was to project Arnold from Rugby into the consciousness of the educational world at a time when it was suffering from a guilt complex and was peculiarly ready to receive him. (Bamford, 1960, p. 186)

The greatest single contributing factor to the fame of Rugby School was not Arnold but football, in Bamford's view. But Rugby football dated from 1823 and the time of Arnold's predecessor, John Wooll. Bamford's Arnold did not bring about a moral revolution and never claimed to have done (Bamford, 1967, p. 53). Rugby School was simply a centre for religion of a political, socio-liberal type, with a ready appeal to a particular class of parent, including a higher than usual proportion of clergy parents (15–20 per cent of the school's population came from clerical homes). Bamford points out that the peak in religious intensity at Rugby under Arnold was never reached again. This trend, which was early and mid-Victorian and not unique to Rugby, started not long after Arnold. By 1893, in contrast, Rugby had 24 lay teachers, compared with only six ordained, seven including the head. By then fewer of its pupils were going on to ordination. In present day Rugby, even the staff in classics, a subject nowadays thought of as struggling for survival when it is taught on a linguistic basis (i.e. involving Latin and/or Greek),

252

24. Freddie Bartholomew (Tom Brown) and Cedric Hardwicke (Dr Arnold) in the 1939 film adaptation of *Tom Brown's School Days*.

outnumber the divinity (i.e. religious studies) staff. Arnold's classroom window facing the town of Rugby looks out not merely at a different town, but onto an almost completely different society. Although Rugby was more susceptible to religious influence than any other school of its time, this does not prove to Bamford's satisfaction that any educational revolution occurred there.

But is it that simple? Did Stanley and Hughes create an idealized Arnold and hand him down to Victorian posterity as a giant he never was? Was Arnold really as unexceptional as Bamford would have us believe? It is certain that the Stanley–Hughes portrait of Arnold was extremely influential. It was aided by two of Arnold's immediate successors at Rugby, Archibald Tait and Frederick Temple, both becoming Archbishops of Canterbury, continuing to provide the school with a high public profile.

> Watch ye stand fast in the faith. Quit you like men. Be strong. (Inscription at the base of the statue of Thomas Hughes at Barby Road, Rugby)

The Hughes statue at Rugby was unveiled by Temple. Temple had quite openly sought to re-Arnoldize Rugby, even to shinning up the elms in the Close himself, like 'the Doctor' did. Arnold was without question an exciting and memorable classroom teacher and pulpit preacher. The Arnold experiment continued under Temple, whose school sermons resemble Arnold's in style, although an assessment of Temple's achievements at Rugby falls outside our task.

This influence continued to Temple's son William, also a Rugbeian and later head of Repton School. Part of William Temple's vision as Archbishop of Canterbury that fed into the landmark 1944 Education Act was that all true education is religious in nature and intention. It was pure Arnold, a third generation on.

Arnold provided a model for schooling that later Victorian educators were happy to espouse, the school as a Christian community in the making, with education as a civilizing Christian mission. 'Manliness' was presented as the conquest of moral weakness. Arnold endorsed it as a personal role model. We should have to rehabilitate 'Christian manliness' into 'Christian adulthood', which would free us to address some of the issues Arnold addressed. Whatever Arnold's faults, especially his irascibility, one that does not spring readily to mind is weakness – in the sense of inadequacy – although he was indecisive at the start of his career. Tuckwell refers to Arnold's 'crusading, contagious vehemence' (1909, p. 162). It was not weakness but overbearing strength that was detected as a failing by some of his opponents. But like 'obstinacy' (see p. xi), powerfulness and energy had their good side:

> O strong soul, by what shore
> Tarriest thou now? For that force,
> Surely, has not been left vain!
> Somewhere, surely, afar,
> In the sounding labour-house vast
> Of being, is practised that strength,
> Zealous, beneficent, firm!
> Yes, in some far-shining sphere
> Conscious or not of the past,
> Still thou performest the word
> Of the Spirit in whom thou dost live –
> Prompt, unwearied, as here!
> Still thou upraisest with zeal
> The humble good from the ground,
> Sternly repressest the bad!

Still, like a trumpet, dost rouse
Those who with half-open eyes
Tread the border-land dim
'Twixt vice and virtue; reviv'st,
Succourest! – this was thy work,
This was thy life upon earth.

(From 'Rugby Chapel' by Matthew Arnold)

These are images of strength, just as in *Sohrab and Rustum* (1853) the strength and experience of the warrior father kills the champion son, of whose real identity he is completely unaware.

. . . Sohrab [the son] heard his voice,
The mighty voice of Rustum, and he saw
His giant figure planted on the sand,
Sole, like some single tower, which a chief
Hath builded on the waste in former years
Against the robbers . . .

'Black Tom': a picture from an 'unknown' Rugbeian, Frederick Mather

Rugby School archive contains a five-page (A5 approximately) anonymous document in an elderly hand, which has just possibly a sixth page missing. The pages are small and the writing large, only nine lines per page. Associated documents and a covering letter suggest that it was written by Frederick Vaughan Mather in 1904, 62 years after Arnold's death. It is a reminder of how long authentic oral tradition can be preserved, even within one generation. Mather was born in 1824 and was a pupil at Rugby with Thomas Hughes, who was senior to him. Mather entered the school in August 1839, aged fifteen, old enough to remember accurately. Mather family tradition had it that Mather was one of the two boys, 'the light clean-made fellow who seemed to run on springs', who went to meet the coach bringing 'Tom Brown' to the school. The accompanying letter says that the statement was written when he was 80 and losing his sight, which would account for the size of the writing. It is reproduced in full below.

Dr. Arnold
Stanley must not be taken as giving a faithful picture of Arnold as a schoolmaster. For Stanley never was a schoolboy. He did not understand boys, never played games, and did not understand their feelings [*sic*]. He was a young man, not a boy. He gives us a true picture of Arnold as he knew him after he had left school. Again, he had not Arnold's sense of reverence. And interest in Arnold's visions. Made them often suit his own. I think any one reading Stanley would gather that the boys at Rugby were ruled by love. This was not so – They were ruled by high respect and by fear and by fear [*sic*]. Arnold was to them Black Tom, as he was called. We shivered when he took the form. Hoping for 'Thank you' and dreading his 'Sit down.' He succeeded in making the boys study for themselves, reading books on the subject of their lessons. Leaving them free to make their own choice. His strong Radicalism made us Tories. His violence in controversy descended in at least equal measure on Stan[ley]. We were proud of him and were certainly very interested in his sermons. One peculiarity with him was his power of making us conscious of our ignorance the depth of which he was fond of saying he never could solve [crossed out] probe. He certainly introduced the plan of trusting boys, and that with admirable affect [*sic*]. His strong personality con[stantly?]

pervaded the whole place and when he died the void was irreparable.

This is a fascinating text, even allowing for the lapse of time between the writer's school days and his reminiscences in old age. It is clearly not sycophantic and yet a vivid picture emerges of Arnold, not entirely attractive, which also accounts for his influence and describes his charisma. If only for the vigour with which he conducted the Christian experiment at Rugby, Arnold deserves a place in both the history of education and in church history. If Stanley and Hughes had never written, Arnold's imprint on some of his former pupils who went on to leadership roles in education and the Church would still be clearly identifiable. Stanley and Hughes admit us to the circle of admirers and offer an insider view, but he never depended on them for fame. They did not provide his audience with Queen Victoria (see p. 99). The Stanley–Hughes influence can be interpreted another way:

> It is always easy to show that a great man was the product of his time, but this does not prove he was *merely* its product . . . He could not have succeeded had the times not been ripe . . . But when it is urged that his reputation is due only to the lucky accident of his possessing two such biographers as Dean Stanley and Thomas Hughes, we have to ask whether it was not precisely this power of influencing pupils so unlike as Arthur Stanley and Tom Hughes which was the secret of his greatness. (Archer, 1921, p. 77f, his italics)

Arnold's eminence in education was deserved, but that does not excuse some of the very serious errors he made at Rugby, sometimes as a result of temper blinding judgement, as in the March case, sometimes from unclear but indefensible reasoning, like the suppression of the Lower School. A person as deeply involved in as many tasks as Arnold on a daily basis is almost bound to complete some of them superficially and to make errors based on hasty judgement. One suspects that even on the 'pony walks' with Mary, the pony might have had to work hard to keep up with him. But Arnold was bound to be in a hurry, for he was conscious from his childhood and the medical development of his family history, as well as his reading of the New Testament, that 'the time' was short. His haste was not that of the megalo-maniac but born of due regard for the life expectancy evidence in his own family. In this he was proved right.

Arnoldian confidence in a questioning faith

Where other Victorians seemed to question a confident faith, Arnold appears to have been confident in a questioning faith. It was not always evident to later Victorian critics of Arnold that he stood within an unbroken family tradition of Christianity and a pastorally supportive tradition of enquiry among the Noetics in the Oriel common room which made it easier to develop a con-fident liberal position in theology and to channel some of this into his own special project of christianizing a school. As we have seen, Arnold had doubts about orthodoxy at least from his early adulthood and as a pupil at Winchester had been prepared to adopt positions that were shocking to some of his contemporar-ies. But his doubts were more about the Church and the creeds than the basic truth of Christianity. From the confidence of his basic Christian position he could take 'pot shots' at opposing views and at what were to him inessentials of Christianity. On the theological scene he was to many, not merely to Oxford Move-ment supporters, something of a *bête noire*. This vein of unorthodoxy was to continue in the family. His children, Jane,

Tom and Matt, endured an increasingly typical later Victorian reformulating of faith in a climate in which, increasingly, people had to find a faith for themselves; William alone seems to have retained the old Arnoldian certainty, although he died too young for posterity to see whether he might have moved away from it.

It would be armchair psychology to suggest that it was merely the overwhelming presence and then the traumatic disappearance through death of 'the Doctor' that created his children's deeper or more wounding religious uncertainties, although supporting texts can be found:

> *Sohrab, the mighty Rustum's son, lies there,*
> *Whom his great father did in ignorance kill!*
> (Matthew Arnold, *Sohrab and Rustum*, 1853,
> his italics for a tomb inscription in the poem)

These uncertainties were part of the climate among their contemporaries and can be seen in the lives of many of the literate (and literary) middle classes: Charles Dodgson (Lewis Carroll), Mary Ann Evans (George Eliot), George MacDonald, Edmund Gosse, Alfred Tennyson, William Hale White (Mark Rutherford), Mary Arnold (not Thomas's wife but his son Tom Arnold's daughter, known after her marriage as Mrs Humphry Ward), to name but a few. Such people had existed in Arnold's lifetime – Emily Brontë and Blanco White, for example. Joseph Blanco White (1775–1841) had been born in Seville of an Irish Roman Catholic family. He was ordained to the Roman priesthood in 1800 and later became an Anglican, moving to Oriel in 1826 (after Arnold had left), where he became a friend of Whately and eventually his resident chaplain at Dublin. Later, under James Martineau's influence, White became a Unitarian. He disliked the term Unitarian and continued to emphasize that 'God to me is Jesus and Jesus is God', but he stressed that he did not mean this in the sense meant by dogma and creeds; he would have been one of the Unitarians Arnold could envisage in his united church.

So Arnold was not alone among his own contemporaries in his doubts about orthodoxy. Orthodoxy itself was constantly and slowly shifting throughout the Victorian period: a penal substitutionary atonement (in which Christ is offered by his Father as a ransom to placate the Devil); a hard-line view of predestination; a literal six-day creation, physical torments in Hell; all these were all sliding out of the orthodox frame and being softened, modified or abandoned entirely during Victoria's long reign (1837–1901). In an age which at first did not notice the rise of humanistic and scientific dogma, the supernatural and religious dogma were slipping out of fashion:

> Was Christ a man like us? Ah! Let us try
> If we then, too, can be such men as he!
> (Matt Arnold, in 'The Better Part')

William Arnold (1828–59), the child most like his father

William's wife Fanny's view, and that of the Arnold family, was that William was in temperament the most like Thomas of all the Arnold children. William was fourteen when his father died. He finished his last four Rugby years under Tait and after less than a year dropped out of Christchurch and joined the Bengal Native Infantry as an ensign. After a brief period as a schoolteacher at Mussoorie and further military service, he became assistant-commissioner at Amritsar. He returned to England on sick leave with his novel *Oakfield* in his baggage in 1853, but having found no satisfactory employment in England, he accepted a post in 1855 as director of public instruction in a newly founded department in the Punjab. He accepted this out of a sense of duty, despite legitimate fears about his health. It involved long working hours and much travel. He agonized over the question of compulsory Bible instruction for the Hindu natives and is said to have frequently asked 'What would Papa have done?' While convinced that Christianity was truth, William was also aware that all truth is not Christianity. His own estimate of the four major influences on his life, after the Bible, were 'Papa', Carlyle, S. T. Coleridge and Wordsworth. His analysis was that 'Papa' represented the Christian truth; Carlyle the human truth on all the social questions; Coleridge was a help towards wisdom in all subjects and Wordsworth blended 'the various hues' of Christianity, humanity, love and wisdom.

In the Punjab, William had a reputation for energy, fair dealing and administrative talent. But Mary Arnold, his mother, compared his 'great hastiness of temper' and impetuousness with that of her husband, speaking of William less defensively than she would have done in public about Thomas. 'K' called William 'vehement, passionate, upright' in a memoir later composed for his orphaned children, whom she had adopted. William was noted for shrewdness and fondness for plain speaking. He was also earnest. 'Earnestness' is a recurring theme throughout *Oakfield*, which is clearly an autobiographical novel with 'such variations as the form of fiction rendered necessary' (Jane 'K' Arnold). Allott sees it as a spiritual diary (W. D. Arnold, 1973, p. 26) in which invention sometimes takes over from memory. It is a window into how Thomas Arnold's ideas could be transposed a generation down. The Preface speaks, with reference to Anglo-Indian society, of 'a want of earnestness, a want of moral tone . . . much superficial scepticism that would pass for freedom of thought, a want of liberality, greater than [that] at home' (*Oakfield*, 1853, p. viii). Edward Oakfield, the earnest hero, attacks 'Sunday Christianity', 'that most portentous of all lies, a world-wide-professing, Sunday-church-preaching, week-day-Mammon-practising Christianity' (ibid., p. 119):

a man who tries seriously, on Monday morning, to follow
out the maxim [that the love of money is the root of all
evil], and lives as though he believed the Sunday discourse,
is obliged either to leave society for a dreary . . . hermit's
life, or to be regarded as a hypocrite or a fanatic. (ibid.,
p. 43)

'K' also noted in William a dimension of 'melancholy' not
present in 'Papa'. Matthew's poetry also has a deep vein of melancholy running through, 'the eternal note of sadness' ('Dover
Beach'). Edward Oakfield is a tragic hero with 'a sadness which
never . . . quite deserted him' (ibid., p. 291). Perhaps this was in
part due to what Kenneth Allott calls 'the now hardly com-
prehensible unhappiness and bewilderment of a sincere liberal
Christian trying to translate his beliefs into action in a nominally
Christian but really unbelieving world' (*Oakfield*, 1973, preface,
p. 39).

I will never go to a church where God is not worshipped,
nor mix in a society where only the animal life is
acknowledged, never even speak with respect of what does
not approve itself to me as good, be it priest, or altar, or
sacrament, or whatever man calls most sacred; but I will
worship God under the stars, and call good good, and evil
evil, the liberal liberal, and the churl churl, the wise man
wise, and the fool foolish. (ibid., p. 106f)

That language and thought could both be Thomas's as much as
William's. But father and son operated in different contexts.
Thomas had to some extent been able to create and dominate his
own worlds at Laleham and then Rugby. The army and India did
not allow William that freedom and he found in the language
and preoccupations of the officers' mess a continuation of much

that was ungodly in the unregenerate schoolboy and unreformed undergraduate, 'something so revolting as to be almost strange to me, though a public school and university life are sure to remove all prudishness'. Like Thomas Arnold, he felt that in more civilized countries, a 'recognised idea of the higher and spiritual ends in [i.e. will lead to expression in] government' (ibid., p. 222, see p. 204f). William, like his father before him and like his novel's hero, Edward Oakfield, exhausted himself and broke his health. He died at Gibraltar while returning invalided to the UK in 1859, on the day after his 31st birthday. Walter had just missed him at Cairo, travelling out to help him home. His wife Fanny had predeceased him at Kangra. Matt Arnold's tribute to him is the poem 'A Southern Night' and part of 'Stanzas from Carnac'.

The Arnold children

The Arnold children were to have their own collectively considerable impact on education: Jane on her husband, W. E. Forster and his 1870 Education Act, Matt as a school inspector, Tom in his brief work in Van Diemen's Land (Tasmania) and William, as has been seen, in the Punjab. Edward Arnold went to Balliol, became a Fellow of All Souls and subsequently a school inspector in the south-west of England. Mary, 'Bacco', did not go into education but became a dedicated Christian socialist, developing another strand of Arnoldian concern. She married a physician, William Twining, who died within a year. Walter joined the navy at thirteen, perhaps turning his back on the powerfully successful products of education among his siblings, or picking up the old sea interests of the Isle of Wight days of his father and grandfather. In all these doings of his children we might detect Arnold's influence continuing and being adapted into a generation below him. Walter, 'Quid', was perhaps, as the youngest, the most distant from the influence of his father although when Arnold died he was near to Arnold's age at the death of his own father.

Arnold's protégé, Clough, the honorary son whose loneliness in School House as 'Tom Yankee' (his peers' nickname) was first spotted by Mary Arnold, also ended up in education. He held a post as an examiner in the Education Office after private tutoring work in the USA. 'Thyrsis', an ambivalent elegiac poem by Matt on Clough's death in his 43rd year, returns wistfully to reminiscences of Greek and Roman pastoral tradition that echoed the old certainties of Rugby. But Clough lost all the old Arnoldian certainties and ended in a position akin to Deism:

> It is impossible for any scholar to have read, and studied, and reflected without forming a strong impression of the entire uncertainty of history in general, and of the history of Christianity in particular . . . Manuscripts are doubtful, records may be inauthentic, criticism is feeble, historical facts must be left uncertain. (*Notes on the Religious Tradition*, in *Prose Remains* 415, undated but *c.* 1860)

For Clough our views are conditioned by 'climate, parentage and other circumstances'. No-one can hold 'the complete truth'. But we have still to be guided by science, by history and by 'the pulsations of the spiritual instinct'. We need 'to widen and not narrow and individualise our creeds'. This is no longer Arnold's sycophant writing, but there are still traces of Arnold in the last sentiment.

The development of the Arnold myth

Arnold's three main aims as head of Rugby had been to inculcate, in descending order, religious and moral principles; gentlemanly conduct; and intellectual ability. To this he added massive energy devoted to work – as sixth form teacher, headteacher, chaplain, historian, correspondent with many old boys – and as a devoted family man. The later Arnold myth is partly accountable for by the fact that he lived out the work and moral ethic that many later Victorians came to emulate. He endured a noble, exemplary death, full of faith, of the sort that some later Victorians wished to emulate. In a society where death was common and was commonly witnessed by family and friends, the desire for a 'good death' was strong and understandable rather than morbid. Arnold's imprint was clear, as we have seen, upon his children. There was a second type of Arnold child, not the biological children of his marriage, whose educational influence was considerable, but his pupils at Rugby. Some of his leading pupils became influential headteachers a generation on. The second generation influence has already been noted (see p. 179). Arnold's influence on Victorian society is clear, if, in the view of his critics, somewhat undeserved.

Archer criticizes Strachey for his cleverness in regrouping truth so that he 'could make St Francis appear as a super-tramp and Caesar as an arch gambler who won the world by going "double or quits" over his gaming debts' (Archer, 1921, p. 78). For Archer, Arnold did not do all the things that a 'modern' reforming head (by 1921 standards) would do: try to civilize pupils by inviting them to his wife's drawing room, introduce them to modern literature, art and music; make them realize what mattered to people. Nor would the bullies of *Tom Brown* have welcomed such a civilizing programme. But 'if anyone underestimates Arnold because he did not anticipate the devil's moves a hundred years ahead, that man does not know the devil' (ibid., p. 81). Of course, the Arnolds *did* welcome pupils to their drawing room and many seem to have appreciated that, but Archer's contention that he would not have been seen as a reforming head in twentieth-century terms is fair.

Bowen criticized Arnold (1902, pp. 371ff) for an over-serious, over-dignified approach to the classroom; for not venturing jokes in class; for expecting stiff attitudes on the part of pupils as a condition of good discipline; for excessive use of emulation and a semi-conscious belief that work which is beneficial cannot be enjoyable; and that a teacher with so many outside interests as he had could not really be devoted to the school. Rugbeians at Oxford could be held to be sometimes too self-conscious and to hold in scorn 'what satisfies commonplace people' (Fitch, 1897, p. 107), i.e. they could be snobs, but with an assumed superiority on the basis of a lofty moral position or outlook rather than advantage in money or social class. In *Oakfield*, the hero, Edward Oakfield, is labelled a snob by one of his enemies (1853, p. 109). The term was being applied then and is likely to have been used of William. Thomas Arnold called wisdom that which was 'knowledge rich and varied, digested and combined, and pervaded through and through by the light of the spirit of God' but that could easily transpose into an excessive high-mindedness of mental outlook. Righteousness can easily spill over into, or be mistaken for, self-righteousness. However, it is never fair to judge people by their disciples if this becomes a substitute for judging them on their own record.

Was Tom Brown *romantic fiction or autobiography?*

Bamford argues that Rugby School was in part 'made' on the 'phenomenal' success of *Tom Brown*:

> It was built on actual experience, with all the thrills of fighting, of football and bullying, ending with virtue fully triumphant, leaning on the arm of Dr. Arnold. His reputation spread to a wider public, and somehow people forgot in the wisdom of the Headmaster the general picture

of a turbulent school typical of the time. (Bamford, 1960, p. 187)

Chandos points out the irony that Arnold, who wished to reduce boyhood and introduce earlier maturity and young manhood, was preserved in *Tom Brown*, which did exactly the opposite: it romanticized boyhood and was part of a process that retarded the development of adult maturity in public school males.

Thomas Hughes was enrolled at Rugby in 1834. Although he claimed that the character of Arnold in *Tom Brown* was the only one of its characters drawn to life, it is possible either that he did not wish to embarrass various people still living, or that various of his characters were composites, drawn from several people in the school. Fanny Hughes, his wife, was adamant that the Arthur in *Tom Brown* could not be Arthur Stanley, as Stanley and Hughes did not know one another until after *Tom Brown* was written. Hughes was enrolled, aged 11, in 1834; Stanley had been enrolled, aged 13, in 1829. Self consulted Fanny Hughes and Jane Arnold, 'K', about the characters in *Tom Brown*. He also drew on the theories of others. J. G. Holloway alleged that the bully Flashman was known to be a particular individual but that 'no one boy sat exclusively for any of his [Hughes's] characters' (Self, 1909, p. 5). Theodore Walrond, Augustus Orlebar and W. P. Adam may have contributed to Arthur. The real Stanley might be the fictional Gray in Chapter 7. The two Brookes are thought to be George and Tom Hughes, and Henry and Theodore Walrond (ibid., p. 8). The original incident for the 'sorrowful wolf' (see p. 122f) which looks highly credible as an Arnold incident, as it is so in keeping with what is known of Arnold's temper and the description is graphic, could not be traced by Self's inquiries (ibid., p. 15). Boughton-Leigh owned Brownsover Hall (he had changed his name from Ward). He was a Rugbeian. Harry 'Scud' East may have been drawn from William Patrick Adam. He was enrolled in

TO

MRS. ARNOLD,

OF FOX HOWE,

THIS BOOK IS (WITHOUT HER PERMISSION)

Dedicated

BY THE AUTHOR,

WHO OWES MORE THAN HE CAN EVER ACKNOWLEDGE OR FORGET

TO HER AND HERS.

25. Thomas Hughes's dedication to Mrs Arnold of the first edition of *Tom Brown's School Days* (1857).

School House in 1835 and was nicknamed 'Scud' for his prowess in running. He was also a personal friend of Thomas Hughes, going on to Trinity, Cambridge, and the bar, then as secretary to Lord Elphinstone in India, and later Liberal MP for Clackmannon and Ross and eventually Governor of Madras. But Tom Arnold (junior) believed that East was based on John Sayer, a Rugbeian who became a friend of Hughes after their Rugby days. Matt Arnold might well be Crab Jones, 'the coolest fish in Rugby', which would fit his languid public persona as well as the Arnold family nickname for him. Cotton may be the anonymous 'young master'. There are too many coincidences.

But was Hughes himself Tom Brown? They both came from the Vale of the White Horse. They both entered Rugby in 1833. They were both in School House. Both were not in the fast track academically, but both were good at games, especially cricket. Queen Adelaide's football match; a fight behind the Chapel and the Rugby MCC match of 1841 are part of both boys' experiences. Both were 'Tom'. The evidence is finally inconclusive. Perhaps Tom Brown had aspects of Thomas Hughes in him. But it was written at some distance from his own school days. *Tom Brown* is of course a novel and never claimed to be anything else, but it reflects the genuine experience at Rugby of one pupil, romanticized in later life as part of a passion for an England that, if it had ever really existed, could no longer be seen clearly in an increasingly uncertain and rapidly industrializing society. Arnold, in contrast, was a creature of history, not fiction, a high-profile figure who could be seen very clearly by friend and foe alike. What *Tom Brown* did for him was to extend the circle of his posthumous admirers and help to keep his reputation alive; what it did *to* him was to mummify him at his schoolteacher's table and help to eclipse his at least equally significant contribution to Victorian religious thinking.

The decline of 'earnestness' in a later culture of cynicism

Hamilton, in a biography of Matthew Arnold, writes of Rugby that the place 'crackled with moral fervour' (1998, p. 2). He adds:

> Arnold's little Rugbeians had it drilled into them, day after day, that they were on the brink of an all-determining life choice: they could seek promotion to the Arnold-controlled upper realm of 'moral thoughtfulness' or they could linger in the mire, as 'beasts or devils'. (ibid., p. 3)

It might have seemed like that to some of the boys and, no doubt exhibiting the eternal characteristics of adolescence which Arnold wished so fervently to dissolve, some would pretend to go along with Arnold's view of things and others would very carefully ignore his programme in quiet pursuit of their own alternative. The record of expulsions in Arnold's time suggest that some would continue to defy Arnold in a more open way, although some expulsions were clearly based on another recurring characteristic of adolescence, not so much deliberate defiance as the inability to see the consequences of an ill-considered set of actions, sometimes with alcohol in the equation. Arnold's critics must be right when they claim that he failed to change the human nature of the child, but then psychology and the study of child development were little understood in the 1830s. Yet by trying to produce a climate in which children were trusted and in which the older were given responsibility and care for the younger, Arnold's brave experiment had major impact and some success. The hard-boiled teacher then and now tends to mistrust the words of children on principle, particularly when a misdemeanour is under investigation. Arnold took the reverse view and the savagery of his punishments for those who added the

271

attempt at deceit to the original offence can be understood, if not always condoned. If Arnold was more fearsome than the teachers of the twenty-first century, he was also more trusting.

Enculturing children through the education process

A dimension not apparent in the nineteenth and twentieth centuries which supports in principle, though not in practice, Arnold's attempt to change adolescent nature is that it is only beginning to be realized that children are encultured into certain behaviour patterns at school. That is to say, in the UK they are encultured to 'try it on' in the classroom, especially with new or inexperienced teachers. This sort of behaviour pattern has been transmitted for two centuries at least. Arnold was quite clear that schools can spoil, damage, even ruin children and he would have been horrified to see the present UK climate in which individual children are sometimes allowed to project their disturbance onto the rest of the class with extremes of conduct disorder in a climate of sheer and regular rudeness, dispossessing the teacher and the other children of their rights to teach and be taught in the process. In other cultures – Africa, or China, or parts of the former communist bloc – pupil behaviour is encultured differently; teachers are respected figures and education is seen as a privilege. A culture which in its schools tends to placate conduct disorder and to coax may eventually unwillingly learn some things from Arnold's willingness to challenge and confront. This is not in any way a hidden plea to restore flogging or to expel difficult children on impulse. Rather, it is an argument for twenty-first-century western society to start to define a view about what its expensive mass education enterprise is for. What are its eleven years of compulsory schooling intended to achieve? What values is it transmitting, including by the behaviour it will or will not tolerate from its young people? The nineteenth century had different schools, but some common values, often based on the Christian ethic. Is the twenty-first century any better?

The twenty-first-century West has not merely different types of school, but many different schools in atmosphere and style within a single type. The wider culture embraces the presence of various religions alongside socially respectable and intellectually defensible agnosticism and atheism. The curious result appears to be that in many schools in the UK and the USA, children are being encultured via a secular curriculum into a secular world view. Current debates about indoctrination via religious teaching or religious schools often mask an almost total lack of debate about secular indoctrination via non-religious teaching in non-religious schools. In the UK many members of the secularist lobby are not even aware that they are programmed in a secular manner; they see themselves as religion-free or value-neutral or 'balanced'. In this society a common view of family life appears to have collapsed and the values transmitted via fashion, the world of pop music and the media might be as important as the influence of some parents who are absent by virtue of long working hours or divorce from the lives of their children. In some families where parents and children are physically domiciled together, family life is still non-existent; no family outings or common activities occur and even meals are taken from the fridge or freezer and consumed on an individual cafeteria basis, sometimes in an atmosphere of silence, not the silence of the Benedictine refectory meal with its ordered reading, but of the dominating power of the TV set. With such diverse backgrounds among present-day school pupils, the question of values in schools has too often been ducked as potentially divisive. The introduction of 'citizenship' into the UK National Curriculum from 2002 was done without any discussion of the 'city' and its values. Is the 'city' for which we are busily preparing 'citizens' England? Britain? Europe? The world? Instead a rag-bag of political education, secularly based moral education and human rights studies was thrown together as politicians looked to 'citizenship' to dissolve low voter turnout at elections and reduce unwanted teenage pregnancies.

Arnold had very clear values and an educational experiment to test them. At the same time he was a successful 'career teacher', even in our terms. His certainties and single-mindedness distance him from our uncertainties and pluralism. What makes him credible is that he tried to implement in practice what he believed in theory. His was not a remote theory of education, like that of Rousseau, who had a case study based on one imaginary child, Émile. Arnold's aims were long term: to produce Christians and gentlemen. Our aims are shorter term, to produce literate and numerate young people who can jump through the hoops or levels of attainment tasks, GCSE, AS and A levels or GNVQs and go on to degree courses or further vocational training. Those of our children who are compliant enter an educational hurdle course in which the height of the fences is always increasing but the goal is never defined.

The modern headteacher or high school principal has a full-time job implementing the National Curriculum and RE, taking responsibility for the management of school staff and finances, being answerable to governors and inspectors and sometimes the press. The modern state school, just as much as the modern private school, needs its sales pitch, website, glossy brochures and public relations management. The task is so consuming that in large schools the head*teacher* may no longer teach at all. This may be inevitable, but any classroom teacher in such a school, primary or secondary, can testify how that disadvantages heads in their management function from a real perception of what it is like at the 'chalk face', and it removes the pupils from the head's direct influence. In some schools the lengths to which headteachers will go to avoid taking lessons, even to cover the occasional absence of colleagues, has become a standing joke in the staffroom. Arnold would never have understood the idea of leading from behind, nor would he have accepted the concept of a 'non-teaching headteacher'. Arnold personally taught the sixth form and examined the other forms, reading the reports on all pupils. Most modern heads are too busy. It was easier for him in a school of 300 and even then he did not eradicate all misbehaviour and bullying. Boys continued to be boys. In our society, modifying the behaviour of disturbed children has become an extremely difficult task because of the sheer number of such pupils. We cannot, like Arnold, simply keep on expelling, because the expelled pupils do not disappear but transfer their disaffection elsewhere, into other schools or onto the streets. Nor can we afford to keep throwing increasing numbers of 'learning support assistants' into the fray: it would be economically cheaper and educationally simpler to have a zero tolerance of bad behaviour in the classroom. But changing hearts and minds is even more difficult than modifying behaviour. The latter can more easily be assessed. Arnold was quite clear that he aimed to do both.

The question must arise, if modern schools sometimes appear merely to produce young people disaffected or bored by the whole education process, did Arnold merely produce high-sounding prigs? Sanders (2000, p. 446) sees Arnold as:

> the godfather of Victorian earnestness . . . fostering in his pupils an awareness of mutual obligations and the promptings of hyperactive consciences . . . His system produced a generation of restless, socially conscious boys forced into adult decision-making before their proper time and often exhausted by the process.

But Sanders's judgement is based heavily on the cases of Matthew Arnold and A. H. Clough. Earnestness was in the air. Thomas

Arnold did not invent it, although Tuckwell (1909, p. 102) reports an oral tradition that it used to be said 'laughingly' that he did. Earnestness was at least as old as evangelicalism, and if evangelicalism within Anglicanism was being challenged by the Oxford Movement, it still had plenty of strength left in Arnold's time, including the strength to promote sabbatarianism successfully by legislation, to which Arnold was personally opposed. Tokenism in religious belief and practice was being seen as the outdated eighteenth-century legacy of what was, in practice, for many, deism posing as Christianity. The opposite of tokenism has to include some element of earnestness. Arnold was part of a wider pendulum swing in promoting moral earnestness. What was again distinctive to him is that he wished to apply it to schooling. Sanders (2000, p. 458) points out that Carlyle published *Past and Present* in 1843, the year after Arnold's death, quoting Schiller with approval: 'Ernst ist das Leben' (Life is earnest). *David Copperfield* (1850) says that there is no substitute for thorough-going, ardent and sincere earnestness. In the USA Henry Thoreau could write about the lack of valuable 'or even earnest' advice from his seniors (1854). Earnestness was in vogue, not just in the UK. But by the late 1880s and 90s the climate was changing. Earnestness was acquiring connotations of homosexuality. George and Weedon Grossmith's *Diary of a Nobody* (1892) mocks asexual seriousness reduced to trivial domestic proportions in the suburban Pooter household. In 1895 earnestness could be lampooned in a 'trivial comedy for serious people', *The Importance of Being Earnest*, by Oscar Wilde. By 2001 it has become difficult to treat seriousness seriously. Lady Bracknell says in Wilde's Act 1:

> Ignorance is like a delicate exotic fruit; touch it and the bloom is gone. The whole theory of modern education is radically unsound. Fortunately, in England at any rate, education produces no effect whatsoever.

Arnold, in contrast, desperately wanted education to be effective and beneficial. But if we translate earnestness into more modern terms, such as sincerity, commitment to the task and integrity, are Arnold's principles so worthy of derision?

When the Firth Park Secondary School (actually a grammar school) opened in Sheffield in 1920, it had a motto, 'Each for All, All for Each', and a school song written in Latin by the headteacher, Dr Lloyd Storr-Best, commencing 'Ludus est nobis'. One of the last new grammar schools in England to open, in 1957, the Ecclesbourne Grammar School in Duffield, Derbyshire, took as its school motto, 'Integrity, Tenacity, Service'. It had a school song in English by its first headteacher Donald Redfern, 'A school stands here in Duffield, by Ecclesbourne's fair bank ...'. The song was abandoned as an embarrassment in 1976 but the motto continued to appear on school blazers and letterheads. Arnold would have approved of the Ecclesbourne motto. Songs, mottoes, the use of what now seems pretentious Latin, show how the grammar schools copied not Arnold *per se*, but the leading independent schools as the acme of excellence. The comprehensive schools deliberately distanced themselves from what was seen as privileged and outmoded. What would a school newly opening in the twenty-first century choose as a motto, or would it view the whole idea of a motto encapsulating ideals as archaic? Or are ideals themselves archaic in a post-modern world?

The end of the line for Arnold in twentieth-century UK education

Arnold survived into the twentieth century, especially for his elevation of the role of praepostors, which was copied in a necessarily diluted way by the grammar schools. But the loss of a Christian vision for education after 1944 and the disappearance of most grammar schools in the 1970s, coupled with an egalitarian and anti-authoritarian emphasis that did not want to put a small pupil elite in charge of other pupils, led to his eclipse even as a secular educational role model. By the end of the twentieth century, few teachers outside the public school sector had even heard of Arnold. Those who had heard of him might have seen him as relevant to the history of education, not to its present. If there is a 'real' Arnold, does he speak to the twenty-first century, or is he part of the showcase of English history? Matthew Arnold saw his father as a quintessential European and wrote of

> papa's immense superiority to all the set, mainly because, owing to his historic sense, he was so wonderfully, for his nation, time, and profession, European, and thus so got himself out of the narrow medium in which, after all, his friends lived. (*Letters* II, 1869, 1996 edition, p. 5)

UK education seems to be stuck in such a narrow medium, tightly under the control of politicians vying with each other to 'raise standards' and inflict more paperwork on already overburdened teachers. Perhaps Arnold's *range* can offer more vision for education now than his detail and that is the legacy worth resurrecting, along with his challenge first to define and then to implement the values underpinning education in the day-to-day running of schools.

Arnold's religious legacy

The intellectually and morally flabby hero of Samuel Butler's *The Way of All Flesh* (1903) is Ernest Pontifex – the surname is due to dogmatism in laying down the law. Pontifex is a failed clergyman in a book which 'damns the thwarting power of an inherited Victorian ideology which confuses theology with righteousness' (ibid., p. 461). Did Arnold confuse theology with righteousness?

While his image within Rugby School may have been one of vehement righteousness, he must be credited as one of the founders of a tradition of liberal Anglicanism, the 'broad church', that was to help in creating the defining identity of world Anglicanism into this century, of a world communion of churches containing evangelical and liberal and eventually Anglo-Catholic elements, each to some degree accepting the existence of the others, not always without friction, as authentic members in a common church. The broad church was never a party, in the sense of an organized group of people with an agreed set of principles and aims. It was more a mood towards the study of theology, that the Church must enter into dialogue with modern thinking, that it must be prepared to shed bibliolatry, that it must not preach a faith which requires the crucifixion of the intellect and blind obedience to a set of unchallengeable doctrines. Some broad church people would, by virtue of this open approach that allowed considerable individual freedom, take it further than others and slide out of mainstream Christianity, either into agnosticism (or in late Victorian times Unitarianism, which was by then a convenient half-way house between orthodoxy and agnosticism) or into more shocking forms of expression within their own church, as in the case of Bishop Colenso in Natal. This happened also outside Anglicanism, for example in the preaching of such people as Reginald Campbell at the City Temple, London, a prestigious Independent (Congregational) church. It is significant that Campbell wrote a biography of Arnold, whom he admired and Campbell produced the 'New Theology', which was attacked by Anglo-Catholic Charles Gore. It was in some ways a replay of Arnold versus Newman, a theological generation on, although Arnold is unlikely to have endorsed Campbell's 'new' theology.

Stanley's deanship at Westminster Abbey (1864–81) was controversially Arnoldian in its desire to make the Abbey a national

shrine, rather than a merely Anglican one, to receive Darwin's
body for burial despite his known loss of faith, to admit trans-
lators of the Revised Version (1881) among whom was a Unitarian, to communion at the Abbey, to oppose the prosecution of
Bishop Colenso. Like Arnold before him, Stanley was too shocking to become a bishop. In the twenty-first century Don Cupitt is
the inheritor of some of this tradition within Anglicanism,
although by the late twentieth century, English Anglicanism at
least had produced a plural church in which these elements were
more inter-mixed than in 1900, i.e. by 2000 there were Anglicans
who combined the evangelicals' sense of mission, the broad
church's critical approach to the Bible and the Anglo-Catholics'
sense of the sacraments.

Arnold was one of the Oriel Noetics (see p. 186f) and together
with them was anxious to bring Anglican Christianity into the
nineteenth century. Their contribution in context was also a
hedge against a possible swamping of the Church of England by
the Oxford Movement, although this was also opposed strongly
by those evangelical Anglicans conscious of their Protestant identity and seeing themselves as being carried Romeward by Newman and his friends. Arnold opposed tractarianism because to
him it was bad Christianity rather than a Romeward version as
such. It contained the essence of his old enemy, priestcraft,
although Arnold's views on priesthood and church unity were
too radical for most Anglicans of his time – and since.

It has already been suggested that Arnold's religious legacy was
eclipsed by his educational rise which continued posthumously.
Now that his educational supremacy has ended he is left with
neither. But perhaps that clears the scene for attention to be
returned to Arnold's religious vision, which originally led to his
educational experiment. Twentieth-century UK largely failed in
its attempts at organizational Christian unity, except for the
Methodist churches (1932) and the United Reformed Church

(1972), both of which continued to haemorrhage members on a massive scale and to close churches unabated. Denominational conversations at national level and increasing co-operation at local church level kept ecumenical dialogue alive and the relentless pressure of secularization forced many local mergers of churches to take place as buildings were no longer economically viable and worshippers too few to finance them. Many churches closed suddenly with the arrival of one roof repair estimate too far. A similar fate befell many church schools after the 1944 Education Act, when the founding bodies could no longer finance them. The late Victorian question whether Christianity was believable was replaced in the Second Elizabethan era by the question whether it was affordable, in a tide of secularization in which few critical questions were being asked about secular beliefs.

But Arnold's vision of a non-threatening form of church unity in which separate liturgies and spiritualities could be preserved was never seriously considered, perhaps because it threatened everyone who was wedded to a less wide view of the Church than his, and everyone who viewed doctrine in a less casual way than Arnold did. Earnestness in Christianity was reflected in the twentieth-century tone of the conversations between churches about doctrine and church order and the weighty reports that were produced. This was not Arnoldian earnestness; he would have had no patience with attempts to reconcile doctrines that were to him of secondary importance and bound to lead to divergence and disharmony. The blossoming of twentieth-century Christian house churches was perhaps offset by their adherence to fairly rigid doctrines, even though these were seen too simply as 'biblical' and not as derived from the denominationalism these house churches and groups prided themselves on having abandoned. They had in common with Arnold a desire to return to simple and what was perceived as undoctrinal

Christianity. They were more reluctant than he to acknowledge the role of the Church and Christian tradition in shaping the writing and defining of the Bible itself. They do not always share his willingness to subject the Bible to intellectual and literary criticism, as this is sometimes seen as subversive to faith.

Arnold offers a model of how a committed and believing Christian thinker can tackle the Bible and emerge with faith unscathed, even strengthened. But his pupils did not always find this process to be so for them, despite his attempts at Rugby to promote a supportive Christian environment in which this study could take place. For some of his pupils, critical approaches could become a Trojan horse in the citadel of faith. Of course, the story of such people might suggest that they would have drifted out of Christianity anyway; biblical criticism merely acted as a catalyst to a process that was already started within them. This may be so, although it is inevitably conjecture based on the proverbial 'ifs' of history. It was not academic biblical criticism by others that moved Francis Newman out of mainstream Christianity, but his own unstoppable questions. Did Arnold unwittingly help to dissolve Christianity for some? Or did he strengthen it for others by helping to provide an intellectual framework that would help secure its survival in an increasingly scientific, technological and deterministic view of the world? So 'unsettling' a religious teacher as Arnold was never owned and transmitted by Christian orthodoxy, hence many Christians in the late twentieth century were more ignorant of biblical culture, background and criticism than his sixth form pupils had been in 1841. That cannot have helped Christianity in a time of apparently indomitable secularization. Arnold was a potential champion and a proven gladiator who was sidelined by his own success in education and by his well deserved reputation as an *enfant terrible* in the Church. In this latter capacity he resembled David Jenkins in the twentieth century, although Jenkins went on to become Bishop of Durham, a traditional top job for a scholar bishop; an unemotive study of Jenkins's writings reveals no lack of orthodoxy. There is no evidence that had Arnold lived, he would ever have become a bishop and his views on the Church would still shock many Christians today.

Conclusion

Towards the end of his life, as we have seen, Arnold became not only a national celebrity but also an establishment figure in education, elevated to a pedestal on which he was to remain, not without serious assaults, for some 120 years. In the study of history he made a steady and cumulative contribution, reaching an unexciting but justifiably deserved climax in his Oxford Chair. Few schoolteachers today can also teach and research at university level simultaneously, and understandably Arnold felt rather precarious in the world of university scholarship competing among full-time academics. His work as a historian became dated, a piece in the history of history so to speak. As the dominating interests in historical scholarship moved away from the ancient world and into the medieval, modern and beyond, Arnold's contribution was used only by the diminishing number of students who had the classical language background to benefit from it. Now he would be consulted as a historian only by cultural historians of the nineteenth century.

In theology and the Church he was a national figure quite early in life, although never an establishment one. Arnold was to remain something of an *enfant terrible* in the Church of England and in this sphere he never received promotion. This was where 'the savage mangling of opponents' (Tuckwell, 1909, p. 101),[01] something he could do swiftly and well, is not to his credit. Whately is said to have told him that he had three faults, 'rashness, rashness, rashness' (ibid., p. 119). Posthumously, as we have seen, his educational persona and its aura eclipsed his religious one. This would have grieved him, as he would have seen his educational persona as entirely derivative from the religious one. Education was to him Christian in intention and he had a theology of childhood which he attempted with some success to use as the basis for running a major school.

T. W. Jex-Blake never met Arnold and the circumstances of his being sent to Rugby are described on p. 179. He went on to become head of the school and in his own assessment of Arnold provides a reminder that if we assess Arnold in compartments: as a headteacher; as a historian; as a theologian, we miss the unifying and remarkable whole in the person and short life of one man. Judgement on everything he did has to be balanced against everything else that he was doing at the same time.

> I have often thought of the quantity, as well of the quality, of Arnold's work, though he died so young; and I have felt that almost any other man of genius would have been killed by the strain of it earlier.

Arnold's is a simply amazing life for the sheer amount that he packed into such a short span. Energy seems entirely inadequate as a word to describe his daily round. His always latent and occasional blazing temper – perhaps overwork contributed – can be contrasted with the capacity to inspire warm and enduring affection among some with whom he had contact and many with whom he had no personal contact. His stone in the pond produced ripples for a very long time, in his family and their work, among former pupils and their work, among those who read him and read about him. Now those ripples have almost ceased. In terms of sharpness of thinking on Christian education, on the relevance of Christianity to a continuing industrializing society, a vision for a world Church, a radical sense of priesthood, a capacity to arouse theological debate, a sense of the excitement of history, especially as found in the New Testament, a call to act *now*, institutional Christianity seems to be left with a more fetid pond, 'the green of the stagnant pool, which no life freshens' (image from Arnold's letter to Hearn, 25.1.1841). Academic theology still has intellectual analysis as great as Arnold's and greater, but it does not come from the pen or word processor of one engaged in all the daily tasks of full-time teaching, administration, personnel management, correspondence, sermon writing and pastoral care. Yet, to press the 'stone' metaphor a little further, stones can also be dangerous. They have the capacity to create ripples but also to injure. Arnold certainly injured some and his unnecessarily gladiatorial approach made enemies. His passions were deep and his feelings were strong. He saw things too clearly. His empathy for what people like John Keble and J. H. Newman were trying to do was correspondingly weak.

But massive misjudgments such as the March case, vituperative writing like 'Oxford Malignants', wrong-minded dealing like the suppression of the Rugby Lower School, a strident and sometimes exaggerated and almost messianic confidence in his own rightness – these cannot eclipse the achievements of this irascible adventurer in theology and education. His energies were outstanding and his legacy wide and immense. His challenge to Christians for a vision for the Church and for Christian education and a Christian critique of secular education remains a gauntlet to be picked up again. His challenge to theology to become *praxis*, action, not merely *theoria*, contemplation, also remains. In some ways Arnold at his best is like Mr Valiant-for-Truth, a pilgrim described by Bunyan (1626–88), to whom Christiana entrusted her children when she died ('if at any time you see them faint, speak comfortably to them'). Bunyan sees Valiant-for-Truth as a role model:

Who would true valour see,
Let him come hither;
One here will constant be,
Come wind, come weather;
There's no discouragement
Shall make him once relent
His first avowed intent
To be a pilgrim.

Whoso beset him round
With dismal stories
Do but themselves confound;
His strength the more is.
No lion can him fright,
He'll with a giant fight,
But he will have a right
To be a pilgrim.

Hobgoblin nor foul fiend
Can daunt his spirit;
He knows he at the end
Shall life inherit.
Then fancies fly away;
He'll fear not what men say;
He'll labour night and day
To be a pilgrim.

These words were not sung in Arnold's Rugby, for the simple reason that the music was written by Ralph Vaughan Williams, based on a Sussex folk song, for a hymnbook published only in 1906. The 'hymn' was to enjoy a long period of extensive use in school worship and the words encapsulate much of what Victorians called 'Christian manhood'. But the comparison between Arnold and Mr Valiant-for-Truth can be over-done, for although

Arnold is undoubtedly like Valiant-for-Truth at times, at others he is more like Wild-head who with his friends Inconsiderate and Pragmatic attacked Valiant-for-Truth in a battle which raged for more than three hours. Arnold could inspire the sort of divisiveness that forces people to take sides as if for battle. Arnold might not have recognized the metaphor of a bull in a china shop, although it was in use by 1841; he might well have known its idiomatic predecessor, 'a cow in a cage' and he would certainly have known 'the roar of the bulls of Bashan' (Amos 4.1, Psalm 22:12f), a loud, excessive roar. But his heart, which finally failed him, was in the proverbial right place. He desperately wanted, like Abraham of old, to 'charge his children and his household after him to keep the way of the Lord by doing righteousness and justice' (Genesis 18:19). And if the apocalyptic struggle described in Ephesians against the 'cosmic powers of this present darkness, against the spiritual forces of evil in the heavenly places' (6:12) has had resonance at various times in subsequent Christian experience, we can see Arnold among those Christians who have tried to put on 'the whole armour of God' and take up 'the sword of the Spirit' (6:13).

In imagination we can perhaps take our leave of Arnold with a post-breakfast scene from about 1840. Having said goodbye to 'K' and Mary, donning his black gown and mortar board, he rapidly strides the short distance from the head's house across the yard, then through the small door and runs up the corkscrew staircase to the library for the first lesson of the morning, entering the small gatehouse classroom quickly, slightly breathless but entirely dignified. He strides the short length of the room from the door to his table as the boys – really young men – stand behind their desks, having quickly abandoned any pranks and chat when they heard his rapid footsteps on the stairs. The door is kept ajar so they are sure to hear him coming. He turns to the class, pauses, looking round as a preliminary check that all are present, to expel any levity or unreadiness by a glance, and taking up his small teaching notebook opens the back page to read the pre-lesson prayer. That over, he motions the class to sit and, seating himself at the small kitchen table, takes up the Greek text of the New Testament and prepares to expound some of the latest scholarship on the Gospel of John. 'The Doctor' is about to expound his favourite biblical text to his most trusted and esteemed students. We could call it the gospel of Thomas (John 20:24–9). We tiptoe out so as not to arouse 'the Doctor's' wrath by interrupting the lesson when it is in full swing and leave the sixth form to their treat.

Select Bibliography

Adamson, O. R., *Our Dear Laleham* (Shepperton, Ian Allan, 1989).

Archer, R. L., *Secondary Education in the Nineteenth Century* (Cambridge, Cambridge University Press, 1921).

Arnold, M., *Letters* (ed. Lang, C.P.) (Charlottesville, University Press of Virginia, 1996, 2 vols).

Arnold, T., *The Effects of Distant Colonisation on the Parent State* (prize essay) (Oxford: printed by S. Collingwood, 1815).

Arnold, T., 'Thoughts on the advancement of academical education in England' (unpublished essay in Rugby School Archive, Laleham, 1826).

Arnold, T., *The Christian Duty of Granting the Claims of the Roman Catholics* (pamplet) (Rugby, 1828).

Arnold, T., *To the Inhabitants of Laleham* (pamphlet) (self-published, Rugby, March 1829).

Arnold, T., *Principles of Church Reform* (Oxford, Fellowes, 1833).

Arnold, T., *The History of the Peloponnesian War by Thucydides*, (3 vols.) (London, Parker & Co., 1835 [8th edition, 1882]).

Arnold, T., *History of Rome* (London, Fellowes, 1838).

Arnold, T., *Sermons: Christian Life, its Hopes, Fears and Close* (London, Fellowes, 1842a).

Arnold, T., *Introductory Lectures on Modern History* (London, Longmans, Green & Co., 1842b).

Arnold, T., *Sermons: Christian Life, its Course* (London, Fellowes, 1844).

Arnold, T., *The Interpretation of Scripture* (London, Fellowes, 1845a).

Arnold, T., *Miscellaneous Works* (London, Fellowes, 1845b).

Arnold, T., *A Fragment on the Church* (written 1839–41, ed. Mary Arnold and A. P. Stanley, London, Fellowes, 1845c).

Arnold, T., *Sermons Preached in the Chapel of Rugby School* (London, Fellowes, 1850 edition of 1832 original).

Arnold, W. D., *Oakfield or Fellowship in the East* (London, Longman, Brown, Green & Longmans, 1853 in facsimile edition with introduction by Allott, K., Leicester, Leicester University Press, 1973).

Baldwin, A. B., *The Penroses of Fledborough Parsonage* (London, Brown & Sons, 1933).

Bamford, T. W., *Thomas Arnold* (London, The Cresset Press, 1960).

Bamford, T. W., *The Rise of the Public Schools* (London, Nelson 1967).

Bamford, T. W. (ed.), *Thomas Arnold on Education* (Cambridge, Cambridge University Press, 1970).

Biswas, R. K., *Arthur Hugh Clough* (Oxford, Oxford University Press, 1972).

Bloxam, M. H., *Rugby: The School and Neighbourhood* (London, Whittaker & Co., 1889).

Bold, A. and Giddings, R., *Who was Really Who in Fiction* (Harlow, Longman, 1987).

Bolitho, H., *A Victorian Dean* (London, Chatto & Windus, 1930).

Bowen, W. E., *Edward Bowen, a Memoir* (1902).

Bradby, E. H., *A New Boy's Letter's from Rugby in 1839* (Rugby, G. E. Over, 1898).

Burton, E., *Thoughts upon the Demand for Church Reform* (Oxford, Baxter, 1831).

Butler, S., *Ernest Pontifex or The Way of All Flesh* (1903) (London Methuen, 1965).

Byrne, L. S. R. and Churchill, E. L., *Changing Eton* (London, Jonathan Cape, 1937).

Campbell, R. J., *Thomas Arnold* (London, Macmillan, 1927).

Carpenter, L., *Brief Notes on the Rev. Dr. Arnold's Principles of Church Reform* (London, Hunter, 1833).

Chadwick, O., *The Victorian Church* (London, SCM Press, 3rd edition 1971).

Chandos, J., *Boys Together: English Public Schools 1800–1864* (London, Hutchinson, 1984).

Church, R. W., *The Oxford Movement, 1833–45* (London, Macmillan, 1891).

Clough, A. H., *Divinity, Rugby, 1836* (MS notebook).

Clough, B., *Prose Remains of A. H. Clough* (London, Macmillan, 1888).

Faber, G., *Oxford Apostles* (London, Faber & Faber, 2nd edition, 1936).

Fallows, W. G., 'Thomas Arnold – a prophet for today', *The Modern Churchman* 6,4, 1963.

Fitch, J. G., *Thomas and Matthew Arnold and their Influence on English Education* (London, Heinemann, 1897).

Fitch, J. G., *Educational Aims and Methods* (Cambridge, Cambridge University Press, 1900).

Froude, R. H., *National Education* ([printed sermon], Totnes, 1833).

Goulburn, E. M., *The Book of Rugby School* (Rugby, Rugby School, 1856).

Govett, R., and Hearn, J. *To the Inhabitants of Laleham* (pamphlet) (Staines, 1829).

Hamilton, I., *A Gift Imprisoned: the Poetic Life of Matthew Arnold* (London, Bloomsbury, 1998).

Hampden, R. D., *Inaugural Lecture* (London, Fellowes, 1836).

Hampden, R. D., *A Lecture on Tradition* (London, Fellowes, 1839).

Hastings, A., *The Construction of Nationhood* (Cambridge, Cambridge University Press, 1997).

Hawkins, E., *The Duty of Private Judgment* (London, Fellowes, 1838).

Hobsbaum, P., *A Reader's Guide to Charles Dickens* (London, Thames & Hudson, 1972).

Holmes, R., *Coleridge: Early Visions* (London, HarperCollins, 1989 (I)).

Holmes, R., *Coleridge: Darker Reflections* (London, Harper-Collins, 1998 (II)).

Hopkinson, D., *Edward Penrose Arnold* (Alison Hodge, Penzance, 1981).

How, F. D., *Six Great Schoolmasters* (London, Methuen, 1904).

Hughes, T., *Tom Brown's School Days* (London, Penguin, 1994 edition of 1857 original).

Hughes, T., *The Scouring of the White Horse* (Cambridge, Macmillan, 1859).

Hughes, T., *Tom Brown at Oxford* (1910 edition of 1861 original, London, Macmillan).

Knights, B., *The Idea of the Clerisy in the Nineteenth Century* (Cambridge, Cambridge University Press, 1978).

Lilley, A. L., *An Account of Sir Joshua Fitch and his Work* (London, Arnold, 1906).

Little, J. E., *Thomas Hughes* [monograph] (Uffington, self-published, 1972).

McCrum, M., *Thomas Arnold, Headmaster* (Oxford, Oxford University Press, 1989).

Midwinter, E., *State Educator: W. E. Forster* (Coventry, Community Education Development Centre, 1995).

Murray, N., *A Life of Matthew Arnold* (London, Hodder & Stoughton, 1996).

Newman, F. W., *The Soul* (London, Chapman, 1849)

Newman, F. W., *Phases of Faith* (London, Chapman, 1850).

Norris, J., 'Recollections of Thomas Arnold and family' (unpublished memoir in Rugby School Archive, *c.*1842).

Norwood, C., *The English Tradition of Education* (London, Murray, 1929).

Palmer, W., *Remarks on the Rev'd Dr. Arnold's Principles of Church Reform* (London, Boake & Varty, 1833).

Pevsner, N., *The Buildings of England: Warwickshire* (London, Penguin, 1966).

Reid, T. W., *Life of the Rt. Hon. W. E. Forster* (London, Chapman & Hall, 1888).

Rhoades, H. T., *Rugby School Chapel* (Rugby, G. E. Over, 1905, 3rd edn 1913).

Rouse, W. H. D., *A History of Rugby School* (London, Duckworth & Co., 1898, 1909 edition).

Rugby Magazine, The, Vol. I, (London, W. Pickering, n.d.).

Rugby School Psalms, Anthems & Hymns for Use in Chapel (Rugby, Rowell & Sons, 1824).

Rugby School Register 1675–1867 (Rugby, W. Billington, 1867).

Sanders, A., *The Short Oxford Dictionary of English Literature*, 2nd edition (Oxford, Oxford University Press, 2000).

Sandford, E. G., *Memoirs of Archbishop Temple by Seven Friends* (London, Macmillan,).

Self, S., *Notes on the Characters and Incidents Depicted by the Master Hand of Tom Hughes in 'Tom Brown's Schooldays'* (Rugby, A. J. Lawrence, 1909).

Selwyn, E. G., '*Dr Arnold as a Winchester Boy* (Winchester, Wells, 1932).

Simpson, J. B. H., *Rugby since Arnold* (London, Macmillan, 1967).

Stanley, A. P., *The Life and Correspondence of Thomas Arnold, DD* (London, Fellowes, 1845 edition of 1844 original; also abridged edition, 1901).

Stanley, A. P., *Arnold and Rugby* (published MS of address delivered at Rugby, 1874, in Rugby School Archive).

Strachey, G. L., *Eminent Victorians* (London, 1918, HBJ edition, New York, n.d.).

Trevor, M., *The Arnolds* (London, The Bodley Head, 1973).

Tuckwell, W., *Pre-Tractarian Oxford* (London, Smith Elder, 1909).

Whitridge, A., *Dr Arnold of Rugby* (London, Constable, 1928).

Willey, B., *Nineteenth Century Studies* (London, Chatto & Windus, 1949).

Willey, B., *More Nineteenth Century Studies* (London, Chatto & Windus, 1956).

Worboise, E., *A Life of Dr Arnold of Rugby* (London, Isbister, 1885).

Wymer, N., *Dr Arnold of Rugby* (London, Robert Hale, 1953).

Index